Hot Off the Grill

The

Healthy

Exchanges®

Electric Grilling

Cookbook

Hot Off the Grill

The

Healthy

Exchanges®

Electric Grilling

Cookbook

JoAnna M. Lund

A Perigee Book

A Perigee Book
Published by The Berkley Publishing Group
A division of Penguin Group (USA) Inc.
375 Hudson Street
New York, New York 10014

For more information about Healthy Exchanges products, contact:
Healthy Exchanges, Inc.
P.O. Box 80
DeWitt, Iowa 52742-0080
(563) 659-8324
Fax: (563) 659-2126
www.HealthyExchanges.com
HealthyJo@aol.com

First Perigee edition: April 2004

Visit our website at www.penguin.com

Library of Congress Cataloging-in-Publication Data

Lund, JoAnna M.
    Hot off the grill : the Healthy Exchanges electric grilling cookbook / JoAnna M. Lund.—1st Perigee ed.
        p. cm.
    Includes index.
    ISBN 0-399-52914-4
    1. Barbecue cookery. 2. Electric cookery. I. Title.

TX840.B3.L86 2004
641.7'6—dc22

2003063269

Printed in the United States of America

10   9   8   7   6   5   4   3   2

This book is dedicated in loving memory to my parents, Jerome and Agnes McAndrews. While double-sided electric contact grills weren't even thought of in their day, I'm sure both Mom and Daddy would be the first to "sing their praises"! After all, it would be one more venue for Mom's cooking creativity, and Daddy would have been more than pleased with how practical and cost-efficient these grills are.

Mom wrote poems her entire adult lifetime. Her subjects were as varied as my many cookbooks are! So it should come as no surprise that I always seem to find just the right poem of hers to match each of my cookbooks. While cooking with an electric grill can speed up our time in the kitchen, I hope that you remember Mom's words from this poem the next time you're upset when someone or something isn't going as fast as you'd like.

Hurry Hurry Hurry

Dear Lord, help me to have patience
* with those who want to talk.*
And allow me to assist others
* who now find it hard to walk.*
I know You have a busy schedule,
* but You always find the time*
To listen when I pray about the
* problems of others and mine.*
Everyone seems to be in such a hurry—
* too busy to stop for a while.*
Many are too rushed to speak,
* let alone to try to share a smile.*
Now that I am getting older,
* my feet falter when I walk.*
I know that I often must think first
* for the words when I want to talk.*
So please Dear Lord, help me be kinder
* for I don't mean to scold.*
I know how it feels to be hurried
* by others now that I am growing old.*
*   —Agnes Carrington McAndrews*

Acknowledgments

For helping me with yet another writing (and tasting) project, I want to thank:

My HE office helpers—Shirley, Jean, Gina, and Rita. Every noon that I was home, they would stop what they were doing and gather in my kitchen to taste and write down their evaluations!

My grandchildren—Zach, Josh, Aaron, Cheyanne, Spencer, Ellie, Abram, and Camryn. The happy smiles on their faces as they "taste-tested" for Grandma were worth more than gold!

My husband and business partner—Cliff. He wasn't too interested in any dishes featuring broccoli, but he sure enjoyed trying most all the rest of the recipes!

My writing partner—Barbara. Even though she was busy with grad school and teaching, she found the time to help me with yet another writing project.

My editor—John. He just keeps encouraging me to create those "common folk" recipes and sharing them in books such as this!

My Creator and Savior—God. I pray for the courage, determination, and strength to do what I'm to do each day and then trust in the Lord to see me through!

Contents

Turning Up the Heat—in Search of Your Best Self

Who was it who said, "If you can't stand the heat, stay out of the kitchen"? Hmm, I'll have to check on that and get back to you. But I'd like to offer a follow-up comment to that remark: "If you've got to be in the kitchen, find an easier way to handle the heat!"

Most of us have to spend some time preparing meals every day, for our families in many cases, and certainly for ourselves. We could choose to dine on microwaved frozen entrées for breakfast, lunch, and dinner, thanks to a host of manufacturers who've loaded our supermarket shelves with choices. But if you're one of the many who prefer home-cooked to defrosted most of the time, welcome to the club! We're busy, and when we've got little time on our hands, it becomes way too easy to eat in a way that adds to stress instead of helping us cope with it better.

The desire is there, though—I've seen and heard it wherever I've traveled across the nation. We want to make healthy eating choices, but with less time than ever before to get food on the table, we too often opt for handy takeout meals or heat up leftovers from the night before. Here's a little test: If you've got refrigerator magnets holding up a dozen delivery menus and your "before" picture looks a little too close to how you feel right now, help is on the way! All you need is a little counter space, an empty outlet, and a willingness to make a few changes in your kitchen.

The Appliance Glut

Let's talk for a moment about the twenty-first century American kitchen and its parade of machines designed to make life easy—and to make food delectable and quickly delivered. Whether you live in a tiny city apartment or a roomy farmhouse, a simple cottage or a four-bedroom house, your kitchen likely features a variety of appliances. Some, like the coffeemaker, you may use every single day. Others, like your bread machine or salad spinner, may be covered with a bit of dust and haven't been called into service for months. They seemed like a great idea at the time you bought them on sale or received them as gifts, but reality soon intervened, and far too many of our timesaving kitchen tools turn out to be underutilized counter "hogs."

Remember, I cook and create recipes for a living, so I experience this problem as much as anyone. And even though my current kitchen is much larger than the Pullman kitchen I labored in during twenty-plus years of marriage and while I raised my three children, I still regularly ask myself whether I really need a particular piece of kitchen equipment. Does that blender still earn its keep? Do I really want and need an electric carving knife? (Yes to the first, no to the second!)

One of my most recent cookbooks, which was dedicated to celebrating the slow cooker revival, meant making space for one and using it often. I also still use my microwave and toaster oven regularly, so those can stay where they are. But when, along with millions of Americans, I acquired a double-sided electric contact grill—the industry name for such machines as the George Foreman and Hamilton Beach grill—it became my passion and my mission to discover and perfect all kinds of recipes inspired by its unique talents.

Why Grill?

Grilling isn't a new cooking method; it's been around for centuries. But most of us associated grilling with barbecuing, an activity that took place outside—on porches and patios and in grassy backyards.

These outdoor grills required gas or charcoal briquets, cleanup was time-consuming, and heaven forbid the skies erupted in rain while your burgers were browning! If you didn't have the option of cooking outdoors, you could attempt what some intrepid apartment dwellers tried and grill on a rooftop or fire escape using a hibachi. Unfortunately, these methods proved unreliable, messy, and even slightly dangerous.

As kitchen stoves evolved and provided ever more elaborate features, some provided a built-in grill on the stovetop. If you were lucky enough to own one, you could provide your dinner guests with handsome-looking steaks and chops crisscrossed with the same kind of grill marks seen in the finest restaurants.

When one of the major fast-food chains created an entire ad campaign extolling the praises of burgers that were grilled, not fried, the bar was raised again. Grilling wasn't only good for the taste buds, it was viewed as a path to better health. The unwanted fat dripped away, saving calories and providing a cooking method that anyone concerned about cholesterol would cheer. Now all that remained was finding a way to bring this healthy cooking method into every kitchen in America!

It didn't take long for the double-sided electric contact grill to become one of the fastest-selling kitchen appliances of our time. With a nonstick coating that made cleanup a breeze, assorted sizes to fit every household, and a promise to put food on the table in five to ten minutes, these grills offered an exciting new food prep option for busy cooks. At last, the pleasures of grilling could be enjoyed indoors, year round, with a minimum of fuss. All that, and good health, too? It sounded like the answer to a dream!

Getting It Right

The new grills looked just about perfect, but home cooks still needed help figuring out how to prepare truly delicious meals using them. Some complained that food stuck or the sauce ran out along with the fat; others quickly got bored using the grill to make an endless quantity of burgers and grilled chicken breasts. Before long, many grill owners found themselves in a grilling rut. The booklets that came with the grills provided only a few cooking tips and recipes. People wanted and needed more and better advice to take full advantage of their newest appliances.

Sounds like a job for JoAnna Lund, right? Well, I thought so, and so did the people who publish and sell my books. I've spent the past few months grilling like crazy, testing and tasting and trying all kinds of recipes to find the tastiest and easiest to share with you. I've found wonderful ways to grill for breakfast and brunch; I've created some truly luscious lunches and suppers that sizzle; I've designed delectable dinner entrées good enough to serve to your family and your guests. And because none of my cookbooks go to press without some scrumptious desserts, this collection features festive and fun "happy endings" grilled to perfection!

Why Change Is Good

It's been more than a decade since I began eating healthy and created my first Healthy Exchanges recipes. In that time, I've lost a lot of weight, traveled from one end of the United States to the other, and spent countless hours on television and radio sharing my ideas for healthy living. I've become a grandmother eight times over, I've visited with people from all over the world who want to eat well and feel good, and I've created thousands of recipes to help make that goal possible.

Change has been part of my life, and learning to cope with change has been one of my greatest challenges and truest pleasures. Every time I found myself wondering how I'd handle the latest obstacle or the next professional or personal hurdle, I prayed to find the strength, courage, and determination to work toward it and the faith to believe I'd get where I was meant to go.

Writing this cookbook has coincided with a period of great change in my life, and it's been a good reminder that we must remain open to doing something new even when what we've been doing works just fine. As I've walked, ridden, and danced down the paths of my life, I've discovered that change is not only constant, but that change is *good*. Each day, our bodies create new cells to help us maintain good health; each day, our brains find cubbyholes to file the new knowledge we bring them.

To live the healthy lives we are capable of, to continue to grow and evolve all our lives long, we must embrace change and welcome the chaos it often brings into our lives. Even when these changes include having to cope with illness or financial difficulties, we can choose how we respond—and in choosing, shape our lives.

In the simplest sense, accepting change means considering new ways to prepare foods, trying new ingredients, tasting new spices, even risking a little embarrassment by attempting new activities (anyone for tango dancing or tackling a rock climbing wall?). If your goal is to find a way to live healthy for a lifetime, you need more than a diet plan, more than another piece of exercise equipment—you need a willingness to keep updating and revising what you're doing.

Other Changes to Think About

When I think back over how the world has transformed itself during my lifetime, I am reminded yet again that we are shaped by the changes we dare to choose.

When I was a child, I was surrounded by caring, accomplished women who had succeeded in their lives on their terms—raising children, running homes, even making a business like my grandmother's boardinghouse work. But the women who raised me also gave me the stamina, the will, and the courage to reach for even greater dreams. As I set goals and then worked to achieve them, I felt their approving eyes on me.

When I decided to attend college while raising my children and working full-time, I was taking a risk—and making an important change. When I rose in my profession and discovered that not everyone was happy for me, I began to understand that choosing to change might have a price. But I also learned that it could be one worth paying.

Perhaps the greatest change I ever made was deciding to live healthy after so many years of choosing not to take care of myself. By giving birth to Healthy Exchanges, I was making a statement to myself and others: I was admitting that I *could* change. Accepting that I had the power meant taking the responsibility as well, and that had its terrifying moments. But it was also an incredibly liberating experience—one that I hope you will choose for yourself.

The Gift That Keeps on Giving

Choosing to be healthy is a gift you give yourself, but more than that, it's a gift that you give to all those who love you and all those who count on you each and every day. But don't try to do it alone.

Asking for help is one way we let others share in our lives, and it offers a wonderful opportunity for both to acknowledge that we depend on each other to be well and to be happy.

And, speaking of gifts—I'm confident that a double-sided electric contact grill makes a terrific gift for anyone and everyone in your life who needs to know how special they are to you—and how much you want them to be healthy. If there's an occasion coming up, consider gifting someone you care for with a grill and a cookbook (I recommend this one, of course!) brimming with easy, healthy recipes that do more than satisfy the tummy. Each day, as your gift keeps on giving, that person will be celebrating life and thanking you for the chance to eat well and feel great!

Food Exchanges and Weight Loss Choices™

If you've ever been on one of the national weight-loss programs like Weight Watchers or Diet Center, you've already been introduced to the concept of measured portions of different food groups that make up your daily food plan. If you are not familiar with such a system of weight-loss choices or exchanges, here's a brief explanation. (If you want or need more detailed information, you can write to the American Dietetic Association or the American Diabetes Association for comprehensive explanations.)

The idea of food exchanges is to divide foods into basic food groups. The foods in each group are measured in servings that have comparable values. These groups include Proteins / Meats, Breads / Starches, Vegetables, Fats, Fruits, Fat-Free Milk, Free Foods, and Optional Calories.

Each choice or exchange included in a particular group has about the same number of calories and a similar carbohydrate, protein, and fat content as the other foods in that group. Because any food on a particular list can be "exchanged" for any other food in that group, it makes sense to call the food groups *exchanges* or *choices*.

I like to think we are also "exchanging" bad habits and food choices for good ones!

By using Weight Loss Choices or exchanges, you can choose from a variety of foods without having to calculate the nutrient value of each one. This makes it easier to include a wide variety of foods in your daily menus and gives you the opportunity to tailor your choices to your unique appetite.

If you want to lose weight, you should consult your physician or other weight-control expert regarding the number of servings that would be best for you from each food group. Since men generally require more calories than women, and since the requirements for growing children and teenagers differ from those of adults, the right number of exchanges for any one person is a personal decision.

I have included a suggested plan of weight-loss choices in the pages following the exchange lists. It's a program I used to lose 130 pounds, and it's the one I still follow today.

(If you are a diabetic or have been diagnosed with heart problems, it is best to meet with your physician before using this or any other food program or recipe collection.)

Food Group Weight Loss Choices/Exchanges

Not all food group exchanges are alike. The ones that follow are for anyone who's interested in weight loss or maintenance. If you are a diabetic, you should check with your health-care provider or dietitian to get the information you need to help you plan your diet. Diabetic exchanges are calculated by the American Diabetic Association, and information about them is provided in *The Diabetic's Healthy Exchanges Cookbook* (Perigee Books).

Every Healthy Exchanges recipe provides calculations in three ways:

- Weight Loss Choices/Exchanges

- Calories, Fat, Protein, Carbohydrates, and Fiber in grams, and Sodium and Calcium in milligrams

- Diabetic Exchanges calculated for me by a registered dietitian

Healthy Exchanges recipes can help you eat well and recover your health, whatever your health concerns may be. Please take a few minutes to review the exchange lists and the suggestions that follow on how to count them. You have lots of great eating in store for you!

Proteins

Meat, poultry, seafood, eggs, cheese, and legumes. One exchange of Protein is approximately 60 calories. Examples of one Protein choice or exchange:

1 ounce cooked weight of lean meat, poultry, or seafood
2 ounces white fish
1½ ounces 97% fat-free ham
1 egg (limit to no more than 4 per week)
¼ cup egg substitute
3 egg whites
¾ ounce reduced-fat cheese
½ cup fat-free cottage cheese
2 ounces cooked or ¾ ounces uncooked dry beans
1 tablespoon peanut butter (also count 1 fat exchange)

Breads

Breads, crackers, cereals, grains, and starchy vegetables. One exchange of Bread is approximately 80 calories. Examples of one Bread choice or exchange:

1 slice bread or 2 slices reduced-calorie bread (40 calories or less)
1 roll, any type (1 ounce)
½ cup cooked pasta or ¾ ounce uncooked (scant ½ cup)
½ cup cooked rice or 1 ounce uncooked (⅓ cup)
3 tablespoons flour
¾ ounce cold cereal
½ cup cooked hot cereal or ¾ ounce uncooked (2 tablespoons)
½ cup corn (kernels or cream-style) or peas
4 ounces white potato, cooked, or 5 ounces uncooked
3 ounces sweet potato, cooked, or 4 ounces uncooked

3 cups air-popped popcorn
7 fat-free crackers (¾ ounce)
3 (2½-inch squares) graham crackers
2 (¾ ounce) rice cakes or 6 mini
1 tortilla, any type (6-inch diameter)

Fruits

All fruits and fruit juices. One exchange of Fruit is approximately 60 calories. Examples of one Fruit choice or exchange:

1 small apple or ½ cup slices
1 small orange
½ medium banana
¾ cup berries (except strawberries and cranberries)
1 cup strawberries or cranberries
½ cup canned fruit, packed in fruit juice or rinsed well
2 tablespoons raisins
1 tablespoon spreadable fruit spread
½ cup apple juice (4 fluid ounces)
½ cup orange juice (4 fluid ounces)
½ cup applesauce

Fat-Free Milk

Milk, buttermilk, and yogurt. One exchange of Fat-Free Milk is approximately 90 calories. Examples of one Fat-Free Milk choice or exchange:

1 cup fat-free milk
½ cup evaporated fat-free milk
1 cup low-fat buttermilk
¾ cup plain fat-free yogurt
⅓ cup nonfat dry milk powder

Vegetables

All fresh, canned, or frozen vegetables other than the starchy vegetables. One exchange of Vegetables is approximately 30 calories. Examples of one Vegetable choice or exchange:

½ cup vegetables
¼ cup tomato sauce
1 medium fresh tomato
½ cup vegetable juice
1 cup shredded lettuce or cabbage

Fats

Margarine, mayonnaise, vegetable oils, salad dressings, olives, and nuts. One exchange of Fat is approximately 40 calories. Examples of one Fat choice or exchange:

1 teaspoon margarine or 2 teaspoons reduced-calorie margarine
1 teaspoon butter
1 teaspoon vegetable oil
1 teaspoon mayonnaise or 2 teaspoons reduced-calorie mayonnaise
1 teaspoon peanut butter
1 ounce olives
¼ ounce pecans or walnuts

Free Foods

Foods that do not provide nutritional value but are used to enhance the taste of foods are included in the Free Foods group. Examples of these are spices, herbs, extracts, vinegar, lemon juice, mustard, Worcestershire sauce, and soy sauce. Cooking sprays and artificial sweeteners used in moderation are also included in this group. However, you'll see that I include the caloric value of artificial sweeteners in the Optional Calories of the recipes.

You may occasionally see a recipe that lists "free food" as part of the portion. According to the published exchange lists, a free food contains fewer than 20 calories per serving. Two or three servings per day of free foods/drinks are usually allowed in a meal plan.

Optional Calories

Foods that do not fit into any other group but are used in moderation in recipes are included in Optional Calories. Foods that are counted in this way include sugar-free gelatin and puddings, fat-free mayonnaise and dressings, reduced-calorie whipped toppings, reduced-calorie syrups and jams, chocolate chips, coconut, and canned broth.

Sliders™

These are 80 Optional Calorie increments that do not fit into any particular category. You can choose which food group to *slide* these into. It is wise to limit this selection to approximately three to four per day to ensure the best possible nutrition for your body while still enjoying an occasional treat.

Sliders may be used in either of the following ways:

1. If you have consumed all your Protein, Bread, Fruit, or Fat-Free Milk Weight Loss Choices for the day, and you want to eat additional foods from those food groups, you simply use a Slider. It's what I call "healthy horse trading." Remember that Sliders may not be traded for choices in the Vegetables or Fats food groups.

2. Sliders may also be deducted from your Optional Calories for the day or week. One-quarter Slider equals 20 Optional Calories; ½ Slider equals 40 Optional Calories; ¾ Slider equals 60 Optional Calories; and 1 Slider equals 80 Optional Calories.

Healthy Exchanges
Weight Loss Choices

My original Healthy Exchanges program of Weight Loss Choices was based on an average daily total of 1,400 to 1,600 calories per day. That was what I determined was right for my needs, and for those of most women. Because men require additional calories (about 1,600 to 1,900), here are my suggested plans for women and men. (*If you require more or fewer calories, please revise this plan to meet your individual needs.*)

Each day, women should plan to eat:

2 Fat-Free Milk choices, 90 calories each
2 Fat choices, 40 calories each
3 Fruit choices, 60 calories each
4 Vegetable choices or more, 30 calories each
5 Protein choices, 60 calories each
5 Bread choices, 80 calories each

Each day, men should plan to eat:

2 Fat-Free Milk choices, 90 calories each
4 Fat choices, 40 calories each
3 Fruit choices, 60 calories each
4 Vegetable choices or more, 30 calories each
6 Protein choices, 60 calories each
7 Bread choices, 80 calories each

Young people should follow the program for men but add 1 Fat-Free Milk choice for a total of 3 servings.

You may also choose to add up to 100 Optional Calories per day, and up to 21 to 28 Sliders per week at 80 calories each. If you choose to include more Sliders in your daily or weekly totals, deduct those 80 calories from your Optional Calorie "bank."

A word about Sliders: These are to be counted toward your totals after you have used your allotment of choices of Fat-Free Milk, Protein, Bread, and Fruit for the day. By "sliding" an additional choice into one of these groups, you can meet your individual needs for that day. Sliders are especially helpful when traveling, stressed-out, eating out, or for special events. I often use mine so I can enjoy my favorite Healthy Exchanges desserts. Vegetables are not to be counted as Sliders. Enjoy as many Vegetable choices as you need to feel satisfied. Because we want to limit our fat intake to moderate amounts, additional Fat choices should not be counted as Sliders. If you choose to include more fat on an *occasional* basis, count the extra choices as Optional Calories.

Keep a daily food diary of your Weight Loss Choices, checking off what you eat as you go. If, at the end of the day, your required selections are not 100 percent accounted for, but you have done the best you can, go to bed with a clear conscience. There will be days when you have ¼ Fruit or ½ Bread left over. What are you going to do—eat two slices of an orange or half a slice of bread and throw the rest out? I always say, "Nothing in life comes out exact." Just do the best you can . . . *the best you can.*

Try to drink at least eight 8-ounce glasses of water a day. Water truly is the "nectar" of good health.

As a little added insurance, I take a multivitamin each day. It's not essential, but if my day's worth of well-planned meals "bites the dust" when unexpected events intrude on my regular routine, my body still gets its vital nutrients.

The calories listed in each group of Choices are averages. Some choices within each group may be higher or lower, so it's important to select a variety of different foods instead of eating the same three or four all the time.

Use your Optional Calories! They are what I call "life's little extras." They make all the difference in how you enjoy your food and appreciate the variety available to you. Yes, we can get by without them, but do you really want to? Keep in mind that you should be using all your daily Weight Loss Choices first to ensure you are getting the basics of good nutrition. But I guarantee that Optional Calories will keep you from feeling deprived—and help you reach your weight-loss goals.

JoAnna's Ten Commandments of Successful Cooking

A very important part of any journey is knowing where you are going and the best way to get there. If you plan and prepare before you start to cook, you should reach mealtime with foods to write home about!

1. **Read the entire recipe from start to finish** and be sure you understand the process involved. Check that you have all the equipment you will need *before* you begin.

2. **Check the ingredient list** and be sure you have *everything* and in the amounts required. Keep cooking sprays handy—while they're not listed as ingredients, I use them all the time (just a quick squirt!).

3. **Set out *all* the ingredients and equipment needed** to prepare the recipe on the counter near you *before* you start. Remember that old saying *A stitch in time saves nine*? It applies in the kitchen, too.

4. **Do as much advance preparation as possible** before actually cooking. Chop, cut, grate, or do whatever is needed to prepare the ingredients and have them ready

before you start to mix. Turn the oven on at least ten minutes before putting food in to bake, to allow the oven to preheat to the proper temperature.

5. **Use a kitchen timer** to tell you when the cooking or baking time is up. Because stove temperatures vary slightly by manufacturer, you may want to set your timer for five minutes less than the suggested time just to prevent overcooking. Check the progress of your dish at that time, then decide if you need the additional minutes or not.

6. **Measure carefully.** Use glass measures for liquids and metal or plastic cups for dry ingredients. My recipes are based on standard measurements. Unless I tell you it's a scant or full cup, measure the cup level.

7. **For best results, follow the recipe instructions exactly.** Feel free to substitute ingredients that *don't tamper* with the basic chemistry of the recipe, but be sure to leave key ingredients alone. For example, you could substitute sugar-free instant chocolate pudding for sugar-free instant butterscotch pudding, but if you used a six-serving package when a four-serving package was listed in the ingredients, or you used instant when cook-and-serve is required, you won't get the right result.

8. **Clean up as you go.** It is much easier to wash a few items at a time than to face a whole counter of dirty dishes later. The same is true for spills on the counter or floor.

9. **Be careful about doubling or halving a recipe.** Though many recipes can be altered successfully to serve more or fewer people, *many cannot*. This is especially true when it comes to spices and liquids. If you try to double a recipe that calls for 1 teaspoon pumpkin-pie spice, for example, and you double the spice, you may end up with a too-spicy taste. I usually suggest increasing spices or liquid by $1\frac{1}{2}$ times when doubling a recipe. If it tastes a little bland to you, you can increase the spice to $1\frac{3}{4}$ times the original amount the next time you prepare the dish. Remember:

You can always add more, but you can't take it out after it's stirred in.

The same is true with liquid ingredients. If you wanted to **triple** a main dish recipe because you were planning to serve a crowd, you might think you should use three times as much of every ingredient. Don't, or you could end up with soup instead! If the original recipe calls for 1¾ cup tomato sauce, I'd suggest using 3½ cups when you **triple** the recipe (or 2¾ cups if you **double** it). You'll still have a good-tasting dish that won't run all over the plate.

10. **Write your reactions next to each recipe once you've served it**. Yes, that's right, I'm giving you permission to write in this book. It's yours, after all. Ask yourself: Did everyone like it? Did you have to add another half teaspoon of chili seasoning to please your family, who like to live on the spicier side of the street? You may even want to rate the recipe on a scale of 1☆ to 4☆, depending on what you thought of it. (Four stars would be the top rating—and I hope you'll feel that way about many of my recipes.) Jotting down your comments while they are fresh in your mind will help you personalize the recipe to your own taste the next time you prepare it.

The "Grilling Goddess"'s Cook's Tips

1. **Remember that every grill works a little differently, and keep notes about what works for you.**

    The basic construction of double-sided home grills is very similar, no matter what brand you purchase. But— every home appliance (and even professional equipment) has its quirks, issues, and limitations. Get a pretty notebook, preferably one that is sturdy enough to survive the occasional spill, and keep an ongoing journal of what you learn as you go. Feel free to write notes on recipe pages, of course, but you may find a separate cook's diary helpful.

2. **Keep your grill clean between uses with the help of the right tools.**

    Not every grill can be taken apart for cleaning like the Hamilton Beach Contact Grill, which allows the cleaning surfaces to be removed and washed in the sink. But keeping your grill clean is important to producing the best results. Most grills come with a tool or two to help with maintenance. The plastic scraper that accompanied the George Foreman Grill does its job extremely well, but I also like to use a nylon scrubbing pad designed for Teflon surfaces to clean off bits of cooked-on food. Some cooks prefer paper towels, while others use and reuse kitchen wipes for this purpose.

3. **Spray, spray, and spray again as needed**.

   Follow recipe directions about spraying your grill prior to heating and cooking your food. But if you can't fit the entire recipe on your grill or if you choose to make more than one batch, briefly spray the surfaces again before each use.

4. **Every grill heats up on a different schedule**.

   I know you've carefully read the directions that came with your grill (of course you did, right?), but I want to suggest rereading the section on how to heat your grill before cooking. I've based my recipe directions on my experience testing recipes on several different kinds of grills, but just because I say preheat for five minutes doesn't mean that your grill will be ready then. It may heat more quickly, or it may heat on a slower schedule. For best results, experiment until you are confident that you're preheating for exactly the right time for *you*.

5. **For safety's sake, plug your grill directly into a wall socket**.

   Most appliances work best plugged directly into the wall, not into an extension cord or even a power strip. Confirm this advice with the instructions that came with your grill, of course, but professionals that I've consulted agree with this advice.

6. **Use a wooden spoon or mallet to press down on your grill cover if pressure is needed**.

   Depending on the grill you've purchased, you may find that you want or need to apply some pressure to compress the ingredients in a sandwich. Try using a wooden utensil to "push" down on the top grill lid. It's usually sufficient to do this right at the beginning of cooking. I find that it can help the foods "join hands" faster. The result? A tastier sandwich!

7. **Position your grill so that it doesn't interfere with other appliances**.

   We all struggle to find room on our countertops for the appliances we use most often, but it's important to consider the traffic patterns in your kitchen when placing your grill. Is there any danger of the grill tumbling to the floor when someone reaches into a cabinet? Is there a risk of getting burned while working near the grill? Answering these questions early on will help you cook up a storm without getting into trouble.

8. **Treat yourself to a pair of tongs for turning and removing items on the grill**.

   Sure, you could keep using a fork to spear and turn meat on the grill, but why not celebrate yourself as a "common folk" chef and pick up a pair of cooking tongs? They're perfect for lifting a sandwich from grill to plate or platter; they're wonderful for flipping a chicken breast from side to side without making lots of holes in it; and they're longer (and thus safer) for you to use around a hot appliance. My friend Barbara has a pair with a little push-pull knob that holds the tongs closed in storage but easily lets them open up for use.

9. **Don't "cut corners" by placing food on the grill before it's properly preheated**.

   So many people live life on the run, and this tip is for those of you who tend to try and hurry everything along. I give preheating instructions for every recipe, and it's important that your grill be sufficiently warmed up before you start cooking. Otherwise, the food just sits on a cold grill and your finished dish won't be as good.

10. **Grill your food when you're ready, and not a moment before**.

    The key to enjoying the most delicious grilled food possible is to serve your grilled food at once. You can just about always do all the "prep" work before you plug in your grill, but I've discovered it's best not to do the actual cooking until you're ready to serve.

HELP ME COOK HEALTHY: My Best Healthy Exchanges® Cooking Tips

Measurements, General Cooking Tips, and Basic Ingredients

The word *moderation* best describes my use of **fats, sugar substitutes,** and **sodium** in these recipes. Wherever possible, I've used cooking spray for sautéing and for browning meats and vegetables. I also use reduced-calorie margarine and fat-free mayonnaise and salad dressings. Lean ground turkey *or* ground beef can be used in the recipes. Just be sure whatever you choose is at least *90 percent lean.*

Sugar Substitutes

I've also included **small amounts of sugar substitutes as the sweetening agent** in many of the recipes. I don't drink a hundred cans of soda a day or eat enough artificially sweetened foods in a 24-hour time period to be troubled by sugar substitutes. But if this is a concern of yours and you *do not* need to watch your sugar intake, you can always replace the sugar substitutes with processed sugar and the sugar-free products with regular ones.

I created my recipes knowing they would also be used by hypoglycemics, diabetics, and those concerned about triglycerides. If you choose to use sugar instead, be sure to count the additional calories.

A word of caution when cooking with **sugar substitutes:** Use **sucralose** or **saccharin**-based sweeteners when **heating or baking**. In recipes that **don't require heat, aspartame** (known as NutraSweet) works well in uncooked dishes but leaves an aftertaste in baked products.

Splenda and **Sugar Twin** are my best choices for sugar substitutes. They measure like sugar, you can cook and bake with them, they're inexpensive, and they are easily poured from their boxes. (If you can't find **Splenda** in your store yet, try their Website: http://www.splenda.com to order directly.)

Many of my recipes for quick breads, muffins, and cakes include a package of sugar-free instant pudding mix, which is sweetened with NutraSweet. Yet we've been told that NutraSweet breaks down under heat. I've tested my recipes again and again, and here's what I've found: baking with a NutraSweet product sold for home sweetening doesn't work, but baking with NutraSweet-sweetened instant pudding mixes turns out great. I choose not to question why this is, but continue to use these products in creating my Healthy Exchanges recipes.

How much sweetener is the right amount? I use pourable Splenda, Sugar Twin, Brown Sugar Twin, and Sprinkle Sweet in my recipes because they measure just like sugar. What could be easier? I also use them because they work wonderfully in cooked and baked products.

If you are using a brand other than these, you need to check the package to figure out how much of your sweetener will equal what's called for in the recipe.

If you choose to use real sugar or brown sugar, then you would use the same amount the recipe lists for pourable Splenda, Sugar Twin, or Brown Sugar Twin.

You'll see that I list only the specific brands when the recipe preparation involves heat. In a salad or other recipe that doesn't require cooking, I will list the ingredient as "sugar substitute to equal 2 tablespoons sugar." You can then use any sweetener you choose—Equal, Sweet'n Low, Sweet Ten, or any other aspartame-based sugar substitute. Just check the label so you'll be using the right amount to equal those 2 tablespoons of sugar. Or, if you choose, you can use regular sugar.

With Healthy Exchanges recipes, the "sweet life" is the only life for me!

Pan Sizes

I'm often asked why I use an **8-by-8-inch baking dish** in my recipes. It's for portion control. If the recipe says it serves 4, just cut down the center, turn the dish, and cut again. Like magic, there's your serving. Also, if this is the only recipe you are preparing requiring an oven, the square dish fits into a tabletop toaster oven easily and energy can be conserved.

While many of my recipes call for an 8-by-8-inch baking dish, others ask for a 9-by-9-inch cake pan. If you don't have a 9-inch-square pan, is it all right to use your 8-inch dish instead? In most cases, the small difference in the size of these two pans won't significantly affect the finished product, so until you can get your hands on the right size pan, go ahead and use your baking dish.

However, since the 8-inch dish is usually made of glass, and the 9-inch cake pan is made of metal, you will want to adjust the baking temperature. If you're using a glass baking dish in a recipe that calls for a 9-inch pan, be sure to lower your baking temperature by 15 degrees *or* check your finished product at least 6 to 8 minutes before the specified baking time is over.

But it really is worthwhile to add a 9-by-9-inch pan to your collection, and if you're going to be baking lots of my Healthy

Exchanges cakes, you'll definitely use it frequently. A cake baked in this pan will have a better texture, and the servings will be a little larger. Just think of it—an 8-by-8-inch pan produces 64 square inches of dessert, while a 9-by-9-inch pan delivers 81 square inches. Those 17 extra inches are too tasty to lose!

To make life even easier, **whenever a recipe calls for ounce measurements** (other than raw meats) I've included the closest cup equivalent. I need to use my scale daily when creating recipes, so I've measured for you at the same time.

Freezing Leftovers

Most of the recipes are for **4 to 8 servings.** If you don't have that many to feed, do what I do: freeze individual portions. Then all you have to do is choose something from the freezer and take it to work for lunch or have your evening meals prepared in advance for the week. In this way, I always have something on hand that is both good to eat and good for me.

Unless a recipe includes hard-boiled eggs, cream cheese, mayonnaise, or a raw vegetable or fruit, **the leftovers should freeze well.** (I've marked recipes that freeze well with the symbol of a **snowflake✳.**) This includes most of the cream pies. Divide any recipe up into individual servings and freeze for your own "TV" dinners.

Another good idea is **cutting leftover pie into individual pieces and freezing each one separately** in a small Ziploc freezer bag. Once you've cut the pie into portions, place them on a cookie sheet and put it in the freezer for 15 minutes. That way, the creamy topping won't get smashed and your pie will keep its shape.

When you want to thaw a piece of pie for yourself, you don't have to thaw the whole pie. You can practice portion control at the same time, and it works really well for brown-bag lunches. Just pull a piece out of the freezer on your way to work and by lunchtime you will have a wonderful dessert waiting for you.

Why do I so often recommend freezing leftover desserts? One reason is that if you leave baked goods made with sugar substitute out on the counter for more than a day or two, they get moldy. Sugar is a preservative and retards the molding process. It's actually what's called an antimicrobial agent, meaning it works against microbes such as molds, bacteria, fungi, and yeasts that grow in foods and can cause food poisoning. Both sugar and salt work as antimicrobial agents to withdraw water from food. Since microbes can't grow without water, food protected in this way doesn't spoil.

So what do we do if we don't want our muffins to turn moldy, but we also don't want to use sugar because of the excess carbohydrates and calories? Freeze them! Just place each muffin or individually sliced bread serving into a Ziploc sandwich bag, seal, and toss into your freezer. Then, whenever you want one for a snack or a meal, you can choose to let it thaw naturally or "zap" it in the microwave. If you know that baked goods will be eaten within a day or two, packaging them in a sealed plastic container and storing in the refrigerator will do the trick.

Unless I specify **"covered" for simmering or baking,** prepare my recipes **uncovered.** Occasionally you will read a recipe that asks you to cover a dish for a time, then to uncover, so read the directions carefully to avoid confusion—and to get the best results.

Cooking Spray

Low-fat cooking spray is another blessing in a Healthy Exchanges kitchen. It's currently available in three flavors:

- **OLIVE OIL or GARLIC FLAVORED** when cooking Mexican, Italian, or Greek dishes

- **BUTTER or LEMON FLAVORED** when a hint of butter or lemon is desired

- **REGULAR** for everything else

A quick spray of butter flavored makes air-popped popcorn a low-fat taste treat, or try it as a butter substitute on steaming hot corn on the cob. One light spray of the skillet when browning meat will convince you that you're using "old-fashioned fat," and a quick coating of the casserole dish before you add the ingredients will make serving easier and cleanup quicker.

Baking Times

Sometimes I give you a range as a **baking time**, such as 22 to 28 minutes. Why? Because every kitchen, every stove, and every chef's cooking technique is slightly different. On a hot and humid day in Iowa, the optimum cooking time won't be the same as on a cold, dry day. Some stoves bake hotter than the temperature setting indicates; other stoves bake cooler. Electric ovens usually are more temperamental than gas ovens. If you place your baking pan on a lower shelf, the temperature is warmer than if you place it on a higher shelf. If you stir the mixture more vigorously than I do, you could affect the required baking time by a minute or more.

The best way to gauge the heat of your particular oven is to purchase an oven temperature gauge that hangs in the oven. These can be found in any discount store or kitchen equipment store, and if you're going to be cooking and baking regularly, it's a good idea to own one. Set the oven to 350 degrees and when the oven indicates that it has reached that temperature, check the reading on the gauge. If it's less than 350 degrees, you know your oven cooks cooler, and you need to add a few minutes to the cooking time *or* set your oven at a higher temperature. If it's more than 350 degrees, then your oven is warmer and you need to subtract a few minutes from the cooking time. In any event, always treat the suggested baking time as approximate. Check on your baked product at the earliest suggested time. You can always continue baking a few minutes more if needed, but you can't unbake it once you've cooked it too long.

Miscellaneous Ingredients and Tips

I use reduced-sodium **canned chicken broth** in place of dry bouillon to lower the sodium content. The intended flavor is still present in the prepared dish. As a reduced-sodium beef broth is not currently available (at least not in DeWitt, Iowa), I use the canned regular beef broth. The sodium content is still lower than regular dry bouillon.

Whenever **cooked rice or pasta** is an ingredient, follow the package directions, but eliminate the salt and/or margarine called for. This helps lower the sodium and fat content. It tastes just fine; trust me on this.

Here's another tip: When **cooking rice or noodles,** why not cook extra "for the pot"? After you use what you need, store leftover rice in a covered container (where it will keep for a couple of days). With noodles like spaghetti or macaroni, first rinse and drain as usual, then measure out what you need. Put the leftovers in a bowl covered with water, then store in the refrigerator, covered, until they're needed. Then, measure out what you need, rinse and drain them, and they're ready to go.

Does your **pita bread** often tear before you can make a sandwich? Here's my tip to make them open easily: cut the bread in half, put the halves in the microwave for about 15 seconds, and they will open up by themselves. *Voilà!*

When **chunky salsa** is listed as an ingredient, I leave the degree of "heat" up to your personal taste. In our house, I'm considered a wimp. I go for the "mild" while Cliff prefers "extra-hot." How do we compromise? I prepare the recipe with mild salsa because he can always add a spoonful or two of the hotter version to his serving, but I can't enjoy the dish if it's too spicy for me.

You can make purchased **fat-free salad dressings** taste **more like the "real thing"** by adding a small amount of fat-free mayonnaise and a pinch of sugar substitute to the diet dressing. Start with 2 tablespoons of salad dressing (such as ranch), add 1 teaspoon fat-free mayo and sugar substitute to equal ½ teaspoon sugar. Mix well and spoon over your salad. Unless you remind yourself you're eating the fat-free version, you may just fool yourself into thinking you've reached for the high-fat counterpart instead!

Milk, Yogurt, and More

Take it from me—nonfat dry milk powder is great! I *do not* use it for drinking, but I *do* use it for cooking. Three good reasons why:

1. It is very **inexpensive.**

2. It does not **sour** because you use it only as needed. Store the box in your refrigerator or freezer and it will keep almost forever.

3. You can easily **add extra calcium** to just about any recipe without added liquid.

I consider nonfat dry milk powder one of Mother Nature's modern-day miracles of convenience. But do purchase a good national name brand (I like Carnation), and keep it fresh by proper storage.

I've said many times, "Give me my mixing bowl, my wire whisk, and a box of nonfat dry milk powder, and I can conquer the world!" Here are some of my favorite ways to use dry milk powder:

1. You can make a **pudding** with the nutrients of 2 cups fat-free milk, but the liquid of only 1¼ to 1½ cups by using ⅔ cup nonfat dry milk powder, a 4-serving package of sugar-free instant pudding, and the lesser amount of water. This makes the pudding taste much creamier and more like homemade. Also, pie filling made my way will set up in minutes. If company is knocking at your door, you can prepare a pie for them almost as fast as you can open the door and invite them in. And if by chance you have leftovers, the filling will not separate the way it does when you use the 2 cups fat-free milk suggested on the package. (If you absolutely refuse to use this handy powdered milk, you can substitute fat-free milk in the amount of water I call for. Your pie won't be as creamy, and will likely get runny if you have leftovers.)

2. You can make your own **"sour cream"** by combining ¾ cup plain fat-free yogurt with ⅓ cup nonfat dry milk powder. What you do by doing this is fourfold: (1) The dry milk stabilizes the yogurt and keeps the whey from separating. (2) The dry milk slightly helps to cut the tartness of the yogurt. (3) It's still virtually fat-free. (4) The calcium has been increased by 100 percent. Isn't it great how we can make that distant relative of sour cream a first kissin' cousin by adding the nonfat dry milk powder? Or, if you place 1 cup plain fat-free yogurt in a sieve lined with a coffee filter, and place the sieve over a small bowl and refrigerate for about 6 hours, you will end up with a very good

alternative for sour cream. To **stabilize yogurt** when cooking or baking with it, just add 1 teaspoon cornstarch to every ¾ cup yogurt.

3. You can make **evaporated fat-free milk** by using ⅓ cup nonfat dry milk powder and ½ cup water for every ½ cup evaporated fat-free milk you need. This is handy to know when you want to prepare a recipe calling for evaporated fat-free milk and you don't have any in the cupboard. And if you are using a recipe that requires only 1 cup evaporated fat-free milk, you don't have to worry about what to do with the leftover milk in the can.

4. You can make **sugar-free and fat-free sweetened condensed milk** by using 1⅓ cups nonfat dry milk powder mixed with ½ cup cold water, microwaved on HIGH until the mixture is hot but not boiling. Then stir in ½ cup Splenda or pourable Sugar Twin. Cover and chill at least 4 hours.

5. For any recipe that calls for **buttermilk,** you might want to try **JO's Buttermilk:** Blend 1 cup water and ⅔ cup nonfat dry milk powder (the nutrients of 2 cups of fat-free milk). It'll be thicker than this mixed-up milk usually is, because it's doubled. Add 1 teaspoon white vinegar and stir, then let it sit for at least 10 minutes.

What else? Nonfat dry milk powder adds calcium without fuss to many recipes, and it can be stored for months in your refrigerator or freezer.

And for **a different taste when preparing sugar-free instant pudding mixes,** use ¾ cup plain fat-free yogurt for one of the required cups of milk. Blend as usual. It will be thicker and creamier—and no, it doesn't taste like yogurt.

Another **variation for the sugar-free instant vanilla pudding** is to use 1 cup fat-free milk and 1 cup crushed pineapple with juice. Mix as usual.

Soup Substitutes

One of my subscribers was looking for a way to further restrict salt intake and needed a substitute for **cream of mushroom soup**. For many of my recipes, I use Healthy Request Cream of Mushroom Soup, as it is a reduced-sodium product. The label suggests two servings per can, but I usually incorporate the soup into a recipe serving at least four. By doing this, I've reduced the sodium in the soup by half again.

But if you must restrict your sodium even more, try making my Healthy Exchanges **Creamy Mushroom Sauce**. Place 1½ cups evaporated fat-free milk and 3 tablespoons flour in a covered jar. Shake well and pour the mixture into a medium saucepan sprayed with butter-flavored cooking spray. Add ½ cup canned sliced mushrooms, rinsed and drained. Cook over medium heat, stirring often, until the mixture thickens. Add any seasonings of your choice. You can use this sauce in any recipe that calls for one 10¾-ounce can of cream of mushroom soup.

Why did I choose these proportions and ingredients?

- 1½ cups evaporated fat-free milk is the amount in one (12-ounce) can.

- It's equal to three Fat-Free Milk choices or exchanges.

- It's the perfect amount of liquid and flour for a medium cream sauce.

- 3 tablespoons flour is equal to one Bread/Starch choice or exchange.

- Any leftovers will reheat beautifully with a flour-based sauce, but not with a cornstarch base.

- The mushrooms are one Vegetable choice or exchange.

- This sauce is virtually fat-free, sugar-free, and sodium-free.

Proteins

Eggs

I use eggs in moderation. I enjoy the real thing on an average of three to four times a week. So, my recipes are calculated on using whole eggs. However, if you choose to use egg substitute in place of the egg, the finished product will turn out just fine and the fat grams per serving will be even lower than those listed.

If you like the look, taste, and feel of **hard-boiled eggs** in salads but haven't been using them because of the cholesterol in the yolk, I have a couple of alternatives for you. (1) Pour an 8-ounce carton of egg substitute into a medium skillet sprayed with cooking spray. Cover the skillet tightly and cook over low heat until substitute is just set, about 10 minutes. Remove from heat and let set, still covered, for 10 minutes more. Uncover and cool completely. Chop the set mixture. This will make about 1 cup of chopped egg. (2) Even easier is to hard-boil "real eggs," toss the yolk away, and chop the white. Either way, you don't deprive yourself of the pleasure of egg in your salad.

In most recipes calling for **egg substitutes**, you can use 2 egg whites in place of the equivalent of 1 egg substitute. Just break the eggs open and toss the yolks away. I can hear some of you already saying, "But that's wasteful!" Well, take a look at the price on the egg substitute package (which usually has the equivalent of 4 eggs in it), then look at the price of a dozen eggs, from which you'd get the equivalent of 6 egg substitutes. Now, what's wasteful about that?

Meats

Whenever I include **cooked chicken** in a recipe, I use roasted white meat without skin. Whenever I include **roast beef or pork** in a recipe, I use the loin cuts because they are much leaner. However, most of the time, I do my roasting of all these meats at the local deli. I just ask for a chunk of their lean roasted meat, 6 or 8 ounces, and ask them not to slice it. When I get home, I cube or dice the meat and am ready to use it in my recipe. The reason I do this is threefold: (1) I'm getting just the amount I need without leftovers; (2) I don't have the expense of heating the oven; and (3) I'm not throwing away the bone, gristle, and fat I'd be cutting off the meat. Overall, it is probably cheaper to "roast" it the way I do.

Did you know that you can make an acceptable meatloaf without using egg for the binding? Just replace every egg with ¼ cup of liquid. You could use beef broth, tomato sauce, even applesauce, to name just a few. For a meatloaf to serve 6, I always use 1 pound of extra-lean ground beef or turkey, 6 tablespoons of dried fine bread crumbs, and ¼ cup of the liquid, plus anything else healthy that strikes my fancy at the time. I mix well and place the mixture in an 8-by-8-inch baking dish or 9-by-5-inch loaf pan sprayed with cooking spray. Bake uncovered at 350 degrees for 35 to 50 minutes (depending on the added ingredients). You will never miss the egg.

Any time you are **browning ground meat** for a casserole and want to get rid of almost all the excess fat, just place the uncooked meat loosely in a plastic colander. Set the colander in a glass pie plate. Place in microwave and cook on HIGH for 3 to 6 minutes (depending on the amount being browned), stirring often. Use as you would for any casserole. You can also chop up onions and brown them with the meat if you want.

To **brown meat for any Italian dish** (and add some extra "zip"), simply pour a couple of tablespoons of fat-free Italian dressing into a skillet and add your ingredients to be browned. The dressing acts almost like olive oil in the process and adds a touch of flavor as well. And to make an **Italian Sloppy Joe**, brown 16 ounces extra-lean ground meat and 1 cup chopped onion in ¼ cup fat-free Italian dressing, then add 1 cup tomato sauce, lower heat, and simmer for 10 minutes. *Bravo!*

Remember, always opt for the leanest ground beef or turkey you can find. Here in DeWitt, we can buy 95% extra-lean ground sirloin, which provides about 8 to 10 grams fat in a 2 to 3 ounce serving. Lean ground turkey provides about 5 to 7 grams of fat. But cheaper cuts can "cost" you up to 20 grams of fat per serving. It's standard practice to grind the skin into inexpensive ground turkey found in most one-pound frozen packages, so beware.

Gravy and Mashed Potatoes

For **gravy** with all the "old time" flavor but without the extra fat, try this almost effortless way to prepare it. First, pour your pan drippings (from roasted turkey, roast beef, or roast pork) into a large cake pan and set the pan in your freezer for at least 15 to 20 minutes so that the fat can congeal on the top and be skimmed off. Use a large pan even if you only have a small amount of drippings so that you get maximum air exposure for quick congealing. (If you prefer, you can purchase one of those fat separator pitchers that separates the fat from the juice.)

Pour your defatted juice into a large skillet. This recipe begins with about one cup of "stock." Now, pour either one cup of potato water (water that potatoes were boiled in before mashing) or regular water into a large jar. Potato water is my first choice because it's loaded with nutrients so I use it whenever I'm making fresh mashed potatoes to go with my homemade gravy. Add 3 tablespoons of all-purpose flour, screw the lid on, and shake until the mixture is well-blended. This easy step assures that you won't get lumps in your gravy!

Pour the mixture into the skillet with defatted stock and add any seasonings you like. Cook over medium heat, stirring constantly with a wire whisk, until mixture thickens and starts to boil. (The whisk is another "secret" for lump-free gravy.) Now pour the gravy into your prettiest gravy bowl and serve with pride!

Why did I use flour instead of cornstarch? Because any leftovers will reheat nicely with the flour base and would not with a cornstarch base. Also, 3 tablespoons of flour works out to 1 Bread/Starch exchange. This virtually fat-free gravy makes about 2 cups, so you could spoon about ½ cup gravy on your low-fat mashed potatoes and only have to count your gravy as ¼ Bread/Starch exchange.

Here's how to make the **best mashed potatoes**: For a 6-serving batch, quarter 6 medium potatoes and boil until they are tender in just enough water to cover them. Drain the potatoes, but *do not* throw the water away. Return the potatoes to the saucepan, whip them gently with an electric mixer, then add about ½ cup of the reserved potato water, ⅓ cup Carnation nonfat dry milk powder, and 2 tablespoons fat-free sour cream. Continue whipping with the mixer until smooth. You're sure to be begged to share the "secret" of your creamy mashed potatoes!

Fruits and Vegetables

If you want to enjoy a **"fruit shake"** with some pizzazz, just combine soda water and unsweetened fruit juice in a blender. Add crushed ice. Blend on HIGH until thick. Refreshment without guilt.

You'll see that many recipes use ordinary **canned vegetables**. They're much cheaper than reduced-sodium versions, and once you rinse and drain them, the sodium is reduced anyway. I believe in saving money wherever possible so we can afford the best fat-free and sugar-free products as they come onto the market.

All three kinds of **vegetables—fresh, frozen, and canned—** have their place in a healthy diet. My husband, Cliff, hates the taste of frozen or fresh green beans and thinks the texture is all wrong, so I use canned green beans instead. In this case, canned vegetables have their proper place when I'm feeding my husband. If someone in your family has a similar concern, it's important to respond to it so everyone can be happy and enjoy the meal.

When I use **fruits or vegetables** like apples, cucumbers, and zucchini, I wash them really well and **leave the skin on**. It provides added color, fiber, and attractiveness to any dish. And, because I use processed flour in my cooking, I like to increase the fiber in my diet by eating my fruits and vegetables in their closest-to-natural state.

To help **keep fresh fruits and veggies fresh**, just give them a quick "shower" with lemon juice. The easiest way to do this is to pour purchased lemon juice into a kitchen spray bottle and store in the refrigerator. Then, every time you use fresh fruits or vegetables in a salad or dessert, simply give them a quick spray with your "lemon spritzer." You just might be amazed by how this little trick keeps your produce from turning brown so fast.

Another great way to **keep fruits from turning brown**: try dipping them in Diet Mountain Dew!

Here's a way to enjoy **cranberries** all year round: buy a few extra bags while they are in season and freeze them for future use. By the way, cranberries chop better when frozen!

The next time you warm canned vegetables such as carrots or green beans, drain and heat the vegetables in ¼ cup beef or chicken broth. It gives a nice variation to an old standby. Here's a simple white sauce for vegetables and casseroles without using added fat that can be made by spraying a medium saucepan with butter-flavored cooking spray. Place 1½ cups evaporated fat-free milk and 3 tablespoons flour in a covered jar. Shake well. Pour into the sprayed saucepan and cook over medium heat until thick, stirring constantly. Add salt and pepper to taste. You can also add ½ cup canned drained mushrooms and/or 3 ounces (¾ cup) shredded reduced-fat cheese. Continue cooking until the cheese melts.

Zip up canned or frozen green beans with chunky salsa: ½ cup to 2 cups beans. Heat thoroughly. Chunky salsa also makes a wonderful dressing on lettuce salads. It only counts as a vegetable, so enjoy.

Another wonderful South of the Border dressing can be stirred up by using ½ cup of chunky salsa and ¼ cup fat-free ranch dressing. Cover and store in your refrigerator. Use as a dressing for salads or as a topping for baked potatoes.

To "roast" green or red peppers, pierce a whole pepper in four or six places with the tines of a fork, then place the pepper in a glass pie plate and microwave on HIGH for 10 to 12 minutes, turning after every 4 minutes. Cover and let set for 5 minutes. Then, remove the seeds and peel the skin off and cut into strips. Use right away or freeze for future use.

Delightful Dessert Ideas

For a special treat that tastes anything but "diet," try placing spreadable fruit in a container and microwave for about 15 seconds. Then pour the melted fruit spread over a serving of nonfat ice cream or frozen yogurt. One tablespoon of spreadable fruit is equal to 1 Fruit choice or exchange. Some combinations to get you started are apricot over chocolate ice cream, strawberry over strawberry ice cream, or any flavor over vanilla.

Another way I use spreadable fruit is to make a delicious topping for a cheesecake or angel food cake. I take ½ cup fruit and ½ cup Cool Whip Lite and blend the two together with a teaspoon of coconut extract.

Here's a really good topping for the fall of the year. Place 1½ cups unsweetened applesauce in a medium saucepan or 4-cup glass measure. Stir in 2 tablespoons raisins, 1 teaspoon apple pie spice, and 2 tablespoons Cary's Sugar Free Maple Syrup. Cook over medium heat on the stovetop or microwave on HIGH until warm. Then spoon about ½ cup of the warm mixture over pancakes, French toast, or sugar- and fat-free vanilla ice cream. It's as close as you will get to guilt-free apple pie!

Do you love hot fudge sundaes as much as I do? Here's my secret for making **Almost Sinless Hot Fudge Sauce**. Just combine the contents of a 4-serving package of JELL-O sugar-free chocolate cook-and-serve pudding with ⅔ cup Carnation Nonfat Dry Milk Powder in a medium saucepan. Add 1¼ cups water. Cook over medium heat, stirring constantly with a wire whisk, until the mixture thickens and starts to boil. Remove from heat and stir in 1 teaspoon vanilla extract, 2 teaspoons reduced-calorie margarine, and ½ cup miniature marshmallows. This makes six ¼ cup servings. Any leftovers can be refrigerated and reheated later in the microwave. Yes, you can buy fat-free chocolate syrup nowadays, but have you checked the sugar content? For a ¼-cup serving of store-bought syrup (and you show me any true hot fudge sundae lover who would settle for less than ¼ cup) it clocks in at over 150 calories with 39 grams of sugar! Hershey's Lite Syrup, while better, still has 100 calories and 10 grams of sugar. But this "homemade" version costs you only 60 calories, less than ½ gram of fat, and just 6 grams of sugar for the same ¼-cup serving. For an occasional squirt on something where 1 teaspoon is enough, I'll use Hershey's Lite Syrup. But when I crave a hot fudge sundae, I scoop out some sugar- and fat-free ice cream, then spoon my Almost Sinless Hot Fudge Sauce over the top and smile with pleasure.

A quick yet tasty way to prepare **strawberries for shortcake** is to place about ¾ cup sliced strawberries, 2 tablespoons Diet Mountain Dew, and sugar substitute to equal ¼ cup sugar in a blender container. Process on BLEND until mixture is smooth. Pour the mixture into bowl. Add 1¼ cup sliced strawberries and mix well. Cover and refrigerate until ready to serve with shortcakes. This tastes just like the strawberry sauce I remember my mother making when I was a child.

Here's a wonderful secret for **making shortcakes**: just follow the recipe for shortcakes on the Bisquick Reduced Fat Baking Mix box, but substitute Splenda or pourable Sugar Twin for the sugar, fat-free milk for the regular milk, and fat-free sour cream for the margarine. When you serve these light and tasty shortcakes to your loved ones, I defy any of them to notice the difference between your version and the original!

Have you tried **thawing Cool Whip Lite** by stirring it? Don't! You'll get a runny mess and ruin the look and taste of your dessert. You can *never* treat Cool Whip Lite the same way you did regular Cool Whip because the "lite" version just doesn't contain enough fat. Thaw your Cool Whip Lite by placing it in your refrigerator at least two hours before you need to use it. When they took the excess fat out of Cool Whip to make it "lite," they replaced it with air. When you stir the living daylights out of it to hurry up the thawing, you also stir out the air. You also can't thaw your Cool Whip Lite in the microwave, or you'll end up with Cool Whip Soup!

Always have a thawed container of Cool Whip Lite in your refrigerator, as it keeps well for up to two weeks. It actually freezes and thaws and freezes and thaws again quite well, so if you won't be using it soon, you could refreeze your leftovers. Just remember to take it out a few hours before you need it, so it'll be creamy and soft and ready to use.

Remember, anytime you see the words *fat-free* or *reduced-fat* on the labels of cream cheese, sour cream, or whipped topping, handle it gently. The fat has been replaced by air or water, and the product has to be treated with special care.

How can you **frost an entire pie with just ½ cup of whipped topping?** First, don't use an inexpensive brand. I use Cool Whip Lite or La Creme Lite. Make sure the topping is fully thawed. Always spread from the center to the sides using a rubber spatula. This way, ½ cup topping will cover an entire pie. Remember, the operative word is *frost*, not pile the entire container on top of the pie!

Here's my vote for the easiest **crumb topping** ever! Simply combine 3 tablespoons of purchased graham cracker crumbs (or three 2½-inch squares made into fine crumbs) with 2 teaspoons reduced-calorie margarine and 1 tablespoon (if desired) chopped nuts. Mix this well and sprinkle evenly over the top of your fruit pie and bake as you normally would. You can use either a purchased graham cracker piecrust or an unbaked refrigerated regular piecrust. Another almost effortless crumb topping can be made by combining 6 tablespoons Bisquick Reduced-Fat Baking Mix and 2 tablespoons Splenda or pourable Sugar Twin with 2 teaspoons of reduced-calorie margarine until the mixture becomes crumbly. Again, you can stir in 1 tablespoon of chopped nuts if you wish. Evenly sprinkle this mixture over your fruit filling and bake as usual. This works best with a purchased unbaked refrigerated pie crust.

Another trick I often use is to include tiny amounts of "real people" food, such as coconut, but **extend the flavor by using extracts**. Try it—you will be surprised by how little of the real thing you can use and still feel you are not being deprived.

If you are preparing a pie filling that has ample moisture, just line the bottom of a 9-by-9-inch cake pan with **graham crackers**. Pour the filling over the top of the crackers. Cover and refrigerate until the moisture has enough time to soften the crackers. Overnight is best. This eliminates the added **fats and sugars of a piecrust**.

One of my readers provided a smart and easy way to enjoy a **two-crust pie** without all the fat that usually comes along with those two crusts. Just use one Pillsbury refrigerated piecrust. Let it set at room temperature for about 20 minutes. Cut the crust in half on the folded line. Gently roll each half into a ball. Wipe your counter with a wet cloth and place a sheet of wax paper on it. Put one of the balls on the wax paper, then cover with another piece of wax paper, and roll it out with your rolling pin. Carefully remove the wax paper on one side and place that side into your 8- or 9-inch pie plate. Fill with your usual pie filling, then repeat the process for the top crust. Bake as usual. Enjoy!

Here's a good tip for **avoiding a "doughy" taste when using a refrigerated piecrust**. Make sure you take the piecrust out of the refrigerator and let it sit on the counter for at least 10 minutes before putting it in the pie plate and baking it. If you put the piecrust into the plate before it has a chance to "warm up," it will be stiffer than if you let it come to room temperature before using. This means that the tiny amount of flour clinging to the crust doesn't have a chance to become "one" with the crust, making the finished product "doughier."

When you are preparing a pie that uses a purchased piecrust, simply tear out the paper label on the plastic cover (but do check it for a coupon good on a future purchase) and turn the cover upside down over the prepared pie. You now have a cover that protects your beautifully garnished pie from having anything fall on top of it. It makes the pie very portable when it's your turn to bring dessert to a get-together.

And for **"picture-perfect" presentation** when using a purchased piecrust, just remove the protective plastic cover, place a pizza pan over the top of the crust, invert the "tin pan" and carefully remove it so the bottom of the crust is exposed. Then, replace the "tin pan" with an attractive pottery pie plate and, with one hand holding each pan in place, flip the piecrust so that the piecrust is now sitting securely in the pottery plate. Remove the pizza pan and fill with your favorite Healthy Exchanges pie filling. This is easier than it sounds, and it makes your dessert look extra-special!

Did you know you can make your own **fruit-flavored yogurt?** Mix 1 tablespoon of any flavor of spreadable fruit with ¾ cup plain yogurt. It's every bit as tasty and much cheaper. You can also make your own **lemon yogurt** by combining 3 cups plain fat-free yogurt with 1 tub Crystal Light lemonade powder. Mix well, cover, and store in the refrigerator. I think you will be pleasantly surprised by the ease, cost, and flavor of this "made from scratch" calcium-rich treat. P.S.: You can make any flavor you like by using any of the Crystal Light mixes—Cranberry? Iced Tea? You decide.

Other Smart Substitutions

Many people have inquired about **substituting applesauce and artificial sweetener for butter and sugar**, but what if you aren't satisfied with the result? One woman wrote to me about a recipe for her grandmother's cookies that called for 1 cup of butter and 1½ cups of sugar. Well, any recipe that depends on as much butter and sugar as that one does is generally not a good candidate for "healthy exchanges." The original recipe needed a large quantity of fat to produce a crisp cookie just like Grandma made.

Applesauce can often be used instead of vegetable oil but generally doesn't work well as a replacement for butter, margarine, or lard. If a recipe calls for ½ cup of vegetable oil or less and your recipe is for a bar cookie, quick bread, muffin, or cake mix, you can try substituting an equal amount of unsweetened applesauce. If the recipe calls for more, try using ½ cup applesauce and the rest oil. You're cutting down the fat but shouldn't end up with a taste disaster! This "applesauce shortening" works great in many recipes, but so far I haven't been able to figure out a way to deep-fat fry with it!

Another rule for healthy substitution: up to ½ cup sugar or less can be replaced by *an artificial sweetener that can withstand the heat of baking*, like Splenda Granular or Sugar Twin. If it requires more than ½ cup sugar, cut the amount needed by 75 percent and use ½ cup sugar substitute and sugar for the rest. Other options: Reduce the butter and sugar by 25 percent and see if the finished product still satisfies you in taste and appearance. Or, make the cookies just like Grandma did, realizing they are part of your family's holiday tradition. Enjoy a *moderate* serving of a couple of cookies once or twice during the season, and just forget about them the rest of the year.

Did you know that you can replace the fat in many quick breads, muffins, and shortcakes with **fat-free mayonnaise** or **fat-free sour cream?** This can work if the original recipe doesn't call for a lot of fat *and* sugar. If the recipe is truly fat and sugar dependent, such as traditional sugar cookies, cupcakes, or pastries, it won't work. Those recipes require the large amounts of sugar and fat to make love in the dark of the oven to produce a tender finished product. But if you have a favorite quick bread that doesn't call for a lot of sugar or fat, why don't you give one of these substitutes a try?

If you enjoy beverage mixes like those from Alba, here are my Healthy Exchanges versions:

For **chocolate flavored**, use ⅓ cup nonfat dry milk powder and 2 tablespoons Nestlé Sugar-Free Chocolate Flavored Quik. Mix well and use as usual. Or, use ⅓ cup nonfat dry milk powder, 1 teaspoon unsweetened cocoa, and sugar substitute to equal 3 tablespoons sugar. Mix well and use as usual.

For **vanilla flavored**, use ⅓ cup nonfat dry milk powder, sugar substitute to equal 2 tablespoons sugar, and add 1 teaspoon vanilla extract when adding liquid.

For **strawberry flavored**, use ⅓ cup nonfat dry milk powder, sugar substitute to equal 2 tablespoons sugar, and add 1 teaspoon strawberry extract and 3–4 drops red food coloring when adding liquid.

Each of these makes one packet of drink mix. If you need to double the recipe, double everything but the extract. Use 1½ teaspoons of extract or it will be too strong. Use 1 cup cold water with one recipe mix to make a glass of flavored milk. If you want to make a shake, combine the mix, water, and 3–4 ice cubes in your blender, then process on BLEND till smooth.

A handy tip when making **healthy punch** for a party: Prepare a few extra cups of your chosen drink, freeze it in cubes in a couple of ice trays, then keep your punch from "watering down" by cooling it with punch cubes instead of ice cubes.

What should you do if you can't find the product listed in a Healthy Exchanges recipe? You can substitute in some cases—use Lemon JELL-O if you can't find Hawaiian Pineapple, for example. But if you're determined to track down the product you need, and your own store manager hasn't been able to order it for you, why not use one of the new online grocers and order exactly what you need, no matter where you live? Try **http://www.netgrocer.com**

Not all low-fat cooking products are interchangeable, as one of my readers recently discovered when she tried to cook pancakes on her griddle using I Can't Believe It's Not Butter! spray—and they stuck! This butter-flavored spray is wonderful for a quick squirt on air-popped popcorn or corn on the cob, and it's great for topping your pancakes once they're cooked. In fact, my taste buds have to check twice because it tastes so much like real butter! (And this is high praise from someone who once thought butter was the most perfect food ever created.)

But I Can't Believe It's Not Butter! doesn't work well for sautéing or browning. After trying to fry an egg with it and cooking up a disaster, I knew this product had its limitations. So I decided to continue using Pam or Weight Watchers butter-flavored cooking spray whenever I'm browning anything in a skillet or on a griddle.

Many of my readers have reported difficulty finding a product I use in many recipes: JELL-O cook-and-serve puddings. I have three suggestions for those of you with this problem:

1. **Work with your grocery store manager to get this product into your store,** and then make sure you and everyone you know buys it by the bagful! Products that sell well are reordered and kept in stock, especially with today's com-

puterized cash registers that record what's purchased. You may also want to write or call Kraft General Foods and ask for their help. They can be reached at (800) 431-1001 weekdays from 9 A.M. to 4 P.M. (EST).

2. **You can prepare a recipe that calls for cook-and-serve pudding by using instant pudding of the same flavor.** Yes, that's right, you **can** cook with the instant when making my recipes. The finished product won't be quite as wonderful, but still at least a 3 on a 4-star scale. You can never do the opposite—never use cook-and-serve in a recipe that calls for instant! One time at a cooking demonstration, I could not understand why my Blueberry Mountain Cheesecake never did set up. Then I spotted the box in the trash and noticed I'd picked the wrong type of pudding mix. Be careful—the boxes are both blue, but the instant has pudding on a silver spoon, and the cook-and-serve has a stream of milk running down the front into a bowl with a wooden spoon.

3. **You can make JO's Sugar-Free Vanilla Cook-and-Serve Pudding Mix instead of using JELL-O's.** Here's my recipe: 2 tablespoons cornstarch, ½ cup Splenda Granular or Sugar Twin, ⅔ cup Carnation Nonfat Dry Milk Powder, 1½ cups water, 2 teaspoons vanilla extract, and 4 to 5 drops yellow food coloring. Combine all this in a medium saucepan and cook over medium heat, stirring constantly, until the mixture comes to a full boil and thickens. This is for basic cooked vanilla sugar-free pudding. For a chocolate version, the recipe is 2 tablespoons cornstarch, ¼ cup pourable Sugar Twin or Splenda, 2 tablespoons sugar-free chocolate-flavored Nestlé Quik, 1½ cups water, and 1 teaspoon vanilla extract. Follow the same cooking instructions as for the vanilla.

If you're preparing this as part of a recipe that also calls for adding a package of gelatin, just stir that into the mix.

Adapting a favorite family cake recipe? Here's something to try: Replace an egg and oil in the original with ⅓ cup fat-free yogurt and ¼ cup fat-free mayonnaise. Blend these two ingredients with your liquids in a separate bowl, then add the yogurt mixture to the flour mixture and mix gently just to combine. (You don't want to overmix or you'll release the gluten in the batter and end up with a tough batter.)

Want a tasty coffee creamer without all the fat? You could use Carnation's Fat Free Coffee-Mate, which is 10 calories per teaspoon, but if you drink several cups a day with several teaspoons each, that adds up quickly to nearly 100 calories a day! Why not try my version? It's not quite as creamy, but it is good. Simply combine ⅓ cup Carnation Nonfat Dry Milk Powder and ¼ cup Splenda or pourable Sugar Twin. Cover and store in your cupboard or refrigerator. At 3 calories per teaspoon, you can enjoy three teaspoons for less than the calories of one teaspoon of the purchased variety.

Some Helpful Hints

Sugar-free puddings and gelatins are important to many of my recipes, but if you prefer to avoid sugar substitutes, you could still prepare the recipes with regular puddings or gelatins. The calories would be higher, but you would still be cooking low-fat.

When a recipe calls for **chopped nuts** (and you only have whole ones), who wants to dirty the food processor just for a couple of tablespoonsful? You could try to chop them using your cutting board, but be prepared for bits and pieces to fly all over the kitchen. I use "Grandma's food processor." I take the biggest nuts I can find, put them in a small glass bowl, and chop them into chunks just the right size using a metal biscuit cutter.

To quickly **toast nuts** without any fuss, spread about ½ cup of nuts (any kind) in a glass pie plate and microwave on HIGH (100% power) for 6 to 7 minutes or until golden. Stir after the first 3 minutes, then after each minute until done. Store them in an airtight container in your refrigerator. Toasting nuts really brings out their flavor, so it seems as if you used a whole treeful instead of tiny amounts.

A quick hint about **reduced-fat peanut butter:** Don't store it in the refrigerator. Because the fat has been reduced, it won't spread as easily when it's cold. Keep it in your cupboard and a little will spread a lot further.

Crushing **graham crackers** for topping? A self-seal sandwich bag works great!

An eleven-year-old fan e-mailed me with a great tip recently: if you can't find the **mini chocolate chips** I use in many recipes, simply purchase the regular size and put them in a nut grinder to coarsely chop them.

If you have a **leftover muffin** and are looking for something a little different for breakfast, you can make **a "breakfast sundae."** Crumble the muffin into a cereal bowl. Sprinkle a serving of fresh fruit over it and top with a couple of tablespoons of plain fat-free yogurt sweetened with sugar substitute and your choice of extract. The thought of it just might make you jump out of bed with a smile on your face. (Speaking of muffins, did you know that if you fill the unused muffin wells with water when baking muffins, you help ensure more even baking and protect the muffin pan at the same time?) Another muffin hint: Lightly spray the inside of paper baking cups with butter-flavored cooking spray before spooning the muffin batter into them. Then you won't end up with paper clinging to your fresh-baked muffins.

The secret of making **good meringues** without sugar is to use 1 tablespoon of Splenda or pourable Sugar Twin for every egg white, and a small amount of extract. Use ½ to 1 teaspoon for the batch. Almond, vanilla, and coconut are all good choices. Use the same amount of cream of tartar you usually do. Bake the meringue in the same old way. Even if you can't eat sugar, you can enjoy a healthy meringue pie when it's prepared the *Healthy Exchanges Way*. (Remember that egg whites whip up best at room temperature.)

Try **storing your Bisquick Reduced Fat Baking Mix** in the freezer. It won't freeze, and it *will* stay fresh much longer. (It works for coffee, doesn't it?)

To check if your **baking powder** is fresh, put 1 teaspoonful in a bowl and pour 2 tablespoons of very hot tap water over it. If it's fresh, it will bubble very actively. If it doesn't bubble, then it's time to replace your old can with a new one.

If you've ever wondered about **changing ingredients** in one of my recipes, the answer is that some things can be changed to suit your family's tastes, but others should not be tampered with. **Don't change**: the amount of flour, bread crumbs, reduced-fat baking mix, baking soda, baking powder, or liquid or dry milk powder. And if I include a small amount of salt, it's necessary for the recipe to turn out correctly. **What you can change:** an extract flavor (if you don't like coconut, choose vanilla or almond instead); a spreadable fruit flavor; the type of fruit in a pie filling (but be careful about substituting fresh for frozen and vice versa—sometimes it works, but it may not); the flavor of pudding or gelatin. As long as package sizes and amounts are the same, go for it. It will never hurt my feelings if you change a recipe, so please your family—don't worry about me!

Because I always say that "good enough" isn't good enough for me anymore, here's a way to make your cup of **fat-free and sugar-free hot cocoa** more special. After combining the hot chocolate mix and hot water, stir in ½ teaspoon vanilla extract and a light sprinkle of cinnamon. If you really want to feel decadent, add a tablespoon of Cool Whip Lite. Isn't life grand?

If you must limit your sugar intake, but you love the idea of sprinkling **powdered sugar** on dessert crepes or burritos, here's a pretty good substitute: Place 1 cup Splenda or pourable Sugar Twin and 1 teaspoon cornstarch in a blender container, then cover and process on HIGH until the mixture resembles powdered sugar in texture, about 45 to 60 seconds. Store in an airtight container and use whenever you want a dusting of "powdered sugar" on any dessert.

Want my "almost instant" pies to set up even more quickly? Do as one of my readers does: freeze your Keebler piecrusts. Then, when you stir up one of my pies and pour the filling into the frozen crust, it sets up within seconds.

Some of my "island-inspired" recipes call for **rum or brandy extracts**, which provide the "essence" of liquor without the real thing. I'm a teetotaler by choice, so I choose not to include real liquor in any of my recipes. They're cheaper than liquor and you won't feel the need to shoo your kids away from the goodies. If you prefer not to use liquor extracts in your cooking, you can always substitute vanilla extract.

Did you know you can make your own single-serving bags of microwave popcorn? Spoon 2 tablespoons of popping kernels into a paper lunch bag, folding the top over twice to seal and placing the sealed bag in the microwave. Microwave on HIGH for 2 to 3 minutes, or until the popping stops. Then pour the popcorn into a large bowl and lightly spritz with I Can't Believe It's Not Butter! Spray. You'll have 3 cups of virtually fat-free popcorn to munch on at a fraction of the price of purchased microwave popcorn.

Some Healthy Cooking Challenges and How I Solved 'Em

When you stir up one of my pie fillings, do you ever have a problem with **lumps?** Here's an easy solution for all of you "careful" cooks out there. Lumps occur when the pudding starts to set up before you can get the dry milk powder incorporated into the mixture. I always advise you to dump, pour, and stir fast with that wire whisk, letting no more than 30 seconds elapse from beginning to end.

But if you are still having problems, you can always combine the dry milk powder and the water in a separate bowl before adding the pudding mix and whisking quickly. Why don't I suggest this right from the beginning? Because that would mean an extra dish to wash every time—and you know I hate to wash dishes!

With a little practice and a light touch, you should soon get the hang of my original method. But now you've got an alternative way to lose those lumps!

I love the chemistry of foods, and so I've gotten great pleasure from analyzing what makes fat-free products tick. By dissecting these "miracle" products, I've learned how to make them work best. They require different handling than the high-fat products we're used to, but if treated properly, these slimmed-down versions can produce delicious results!

Fat-free sour cream: This product is wonderful on a hot baked potato, but have you noticed that it tends to be much gummier than regular sour cream? If you want to use it in a stroganoff dish or baked product, you must stir a tablespoon or two of fat-free milk into the fat-free sour cream before adding it to other ingredients.

Cool Whip Free: When the fat went out of the formula, air was stirred in to fill the void. So, if you stir it too vigorously, you release the air and *decrease* the volume. Handle it with kid gloves—gently. Since the manufacturer forgot to ask for my input, I'll share with you how to make it taste almost the same as it used to. Let the container thaw in the refrigerator, then ever so gently stir in 1 teaspoon vanilla extract. Now, put the lid back on and enjoy it a tablespoon at a time, the same way you did Cool Whip Lite.

Fat-free cream cheese: When the fat was removed from this product, water replaced it. So don't ever use an electric mixer on the fat-free version, or you risk releasing the water and having your finished product look more like dip than cheesecake! Stirring it gently with a sturdy spoon in a glass bowl with a handle will soften it just as much as it needs to be. (A glass bowl with a handle lets you see what's going on; the handle gives you control as you stir. This "user-friendly" method is good for tired cooks, young cooks, and cooks with arthritis!) And don't be alarmed if the cream cheese gets caught in your wire whisk when you start combining the pudding mix and other ingredients. Just keep knocking it back down into the bowl by hitting the whisk against the rim of the bowl, and as you continue blending, it will soften even more and drop off the whisk. When it's time to pour the filling into your crust, your whisk shouldn't have anything much clinging to it.

Reduced-fat margarine: Again, the fat was replaced by water. If you try to use the reduced-fat kind in your cookie recipe spoon for spoon, you will end up with a cakelike cookie instead of the crisp kind most of us enjoy. You have to take into consideration that some water will be released as the product bakes. Use less liquid than the recipe calls for (when re-creating family recipes *only*—I've figured that into Healthy Exchanges recipes). And never, never, never use fat-*free* margarine and expect anyone to ask for seconds!

When every minute counts, and you need 2 cups cooked noodles for a casserole, how do you **figure out how much of a box of pasta to prepare?** Here's a handy guide that should help. While your final amount might vary slightly because of how loosely or tightly you "stuff" your measuring cup, this will make life easier.

Type	Start with this amount uncooked	If you want this amount cooked
Noodles (thin, medium,wide, and mini lasagne)	1 cup 1¼ cups 1¾ cups 2¼ cups 2½ cups	1 cup 1½ cups 2 cups 2½ cups 3 cups
Macaroni (medium shells and elbow)	⅓ cup ⅔cup 1 cup 1 1⅓ cups 2 cups	½ cup 1 cup 1½ cups 2 cups 3 cups
Spaghetti, fettuccine, and rotini pasta	¾ cup 1 cup 1½ cups 2½ cups	1 cup 1½ cups 2 cups 3 cups
Rice (instant)	⅓ cup ⅔ cup 1 cup 1⅓ cups 2 cups	½ cup 1 cup 1½ cups 2 cups 3 cups
Rice (regular)	¼ cup ½ cup 1 cup 1½ cups	½ cup 1 cup 2 cups 3 cups

Here's a handy idea for **keeping your cookbooks open** to a certain page while cooking: use two rubber bands, one wrapped vertically around the left side of the book, another on the right side. And to **keep your cookbooks clean**, try slipping the rubber-banded book into a gallon-sized Ziploc bag. (Though I'd consider it a compliment to know that the pages of my cookbooks were all splattered, because it would mean that you are really using the recipes!)

Homemade or Store-Bought?

I've been asked which is better for you: homemade from scratch, or purchased foods. My answer is *both*! Each has a place in a healthy lifestyle, and what that place is has everything to do with you.

Take **piecrusts**, for instance. If you love spending your spare time in the kitchen preparing foods, and you're using low-fat, low-sugar, and reasonably low-sodium ingredients, go for it! But if, like so many people, your time is limited and you've learned to read labels, you could be better off using purchased foods.

I know that when I prepare a pie (and I experiment with a couple of pies each week, because this is Cliff's favorite dessert), I use a purchased crust. Why? Mainly because I can't make a good-tasting piecrust that is lower in fat than the brands I use. Also, purchased piecrusts fit my rule of "If it takes longer to fix than to eat, forget it!"

I've checked the nutrient information for the purchased piecrusts against recipes for traditional and "diet" piecrusts, using my computer software program. The purchased crust calculated lower in both fat and calories! I have tried some low-fat and low-sugar recipes, but they just didn't spark my taste buds, or were so complicated you needed an engineering degree just to get the crust in the pie plate.

I'm very happy with the purchased piecrusts in my recipes, because the finished product rarely, if ever, has more than 30 percent of total calories coming from fats. I also believe that we have to prepare foods our families and friends will eat with us on a regular basis and not feel deprived, or we've wasted time, energy, and money.

I could use a purchased "lite" **pie filling,** but instead I make my own. Here I can save both fat and sugar, and still make the filling almost as fast as opening a can. The bottom line: Know what you have to spend when it comes to both time and fat/sugar calories, then make the best decision you can for you and your family.

And don't go without an occasional piece of pie because you think it isn't *necessary*. A delicious pie prepared in a healthy way is one of the simple pleasures of life. It's a little thing, but it can make all the difference between just getting by with the bare minimum and living a full and healthy lifestyle.

I'm sure you'll add to this list of cooking tips as you begin preparing Healthy Exchanges recipes and discovering how easy it can be to adapt your own favorite recipes using these ideas and your own common sense.

A Peek into My Pantry and My Favorite Brands

Everyone asks me what foods I keep on hand and what brands I use. There are lots of good products on the grocery shelves today—many more than we dreamed about even a year or two ago. And I can't wait to see what's out there twelve months from now. The following are my staples and, where appropriate, my favorites *at this time.* I feel these products are healthier, tastier, easy to get—and deliver the most flavor for the least amount of fat, sugar, or calories. If you find others you like as well *or better,* please use them. This is only a guide to make your grocery shopping and cooking easier.

Fat-free plain yogurt (*Dannon*)
Nonfat dry milk powder (*Carnation*)
Evaporated fat-free milk (*Carnation*)
Fat-free cottage cheese
Fat-free cream cheese (*Philadelphia*)
Fat-free mayonnaise (*Kraft*)
Fat-free salad dressings (*Kraft and Hendrickson's*)
No-fat sour cream (*Land O Lakes*)
Reduced-calorie margarine (*I Can't Believe It's Not Butter Light*)
Cooking sprays
   Olive oil–flavored (*Pam*)
   Butter-flavored (*Pam*)

Butter-flavored for spritzing *after* cooking (*I Can't Believe It's Not Butter!*)

Cooking oil (*Puritan Canola Oil*)

Reduced-calorie whipped topping (*Cool Whip Lite or Cool Whip Free*)

Sugar substitute

   White sugar substitute (*Splenda*)

   Brown sugar substitute (*Brown Sugar Twin*)

Sugar-free gelatin and pudding mixes (*JELL-O*)

Baking mix (*Bisquick Reduced Fat*)

Pancake mix (*Aunt Jemima Reduced Calorie*)

Sugar-free pancake syrup (*Log Cabin or Cary's*)

Parmesan cheese (*Kraft Reduced Fat Parmesan Style Grated Topping*)

Reduced-fat cheese (shredded and sliced) (*Kraft 2% Reduced Fat*)

Shredded frozen potatoes (*Mr. Dell's or Ore Ida*)

Spreadable fruit spread (*Welch's or Smucker's*)

Peanut butter (*Peter Pan reduced-fat, Jif reduced-fat, or Skippy reduced-fat*)

Chicken broth (*Healthy Request*)

Beef broth (*Swanson*)

Tomato sauce (*Hunt's*)

Canned soups (*Healthy Request*)

Reduced sodium tomato juice

Reduced sodium ketchup

Piecrust

   Unbaked (*Pillsbury—in dairy case*)

   Graham cracker, shortbread, and chocolate (*Keebler*)

Crescent rolls (*Pillsbury Reduced Fat*)

Pastrami and corned beef (*Carl Buddig Lean*)

Luncheon meats (*Healthy Choice or Oscar Mayer*)

Ham (*Dubuque 97% fat-free and reduced-sodium or Healthy Choice*)

Bacon bits (*Hormel or Oscar Mayer*)

Kielbasa sausage and frankfurters (*Healthy Choice or Oscar Mayer Light*)

Canned white chicken, packed in water (*Swanson*)

Canned tuna, packed in water (*Starkist*)

95 to 97% ground sirloin beef or turkey breast
Crackers (*Nabisco Soda Fat Free and Ritz Reduced Fat*)
Reduced-calorie bread—40 calories per slice or less
Small hamburger buns—80 calories per bun
Rice—instant, regular, brown, and wild (*Minute Rice*)
Instant potato flakes
Noodles, spaghetti, macaroni, and rotini pasta
Salsa
Pickle relish—dill, sweet, and hot dog
Mustard—Dijon, prepared yellow, and spicy
Unsweetened apple and orange juice
Reduced-calorie cranberry juice cocktail (*Ocean Spray*)
Unsweetened applesauce (*Musselman's*)
Fruit—fresh, frozen (no sugar added), and canned in juice
Pie filling (*Lucky Leaf No Sugar Added Cherry and Apple*)
Spices—-JO's Spices or any national brand
Vinegar—cider and distilled white
Lemon and lime juice (in small plastic fruit-shaped bottles
    found in the produce section)
Instant fruit beverage mixes (*Crystal Light*)
Sugar-free hot chocolate beverage mixes (*Swiss Miss or
    Nesquik*)
Sugar-free and fat-free ice cream (*Wells' Blue Bunny*)

The items on my shopping list are everyday foods found in just about any grocery store in America. But all are as low in fat, sugar, calories, and sodium as I can find—and still taste good! I can make any recipe in my cookbooks and newsletters as long as I have my cupboards and refrigerator stocked with these items. Whenever I use the last of any one item, I just make sure I pick up another supply the next time I'm at the store.

If your grocer does not stock these items, why not ask if they can be ordered on a trial basis? If the store agrees to do so, be sure to tell your friends to stop by, so that sales are good enough to warrant restocking the new products. Competition for shelf space is fierce, so only products that sell well stay around.

The Healthy
Exchanges Kitchen

When I first started creating Healthy Exchanges recipes, I had a tiny galley kitchen with room for only one person. But it never stopped me from feeling the sky was the limit when it came to seeking out great healthy taste! Even though I have a bigger home kitchen now, what I learned in those early days still holds true. I'll say it again: Don't waste space on equipment you don't really need. Here's a list of what I consider worth having (in addition to your double-sided electric contact grill, of course!) You can probably find most of what you need at a local discount store or garage sale. You'll find you can prepare healthy, quick, and delicious food with just the "basics."

Kitchen Equipment Recommendations

Good-quality nonstick skillet (10-inch with a lid)
Good-quality nonstick saucepans (small, medium, large, with lids)—if you choose all Teflon-coated pans and skillets, your cleanup time will be greatly reduced
An electric skillet is a nice addition
8-by-8-inch baking dish
Disposable aluminum 9-by-9-inch baking pans
Rimmed cookie sheet (make sure it fits into YOUR oven with room to spare)
Heavy-duty plastic set of 3 mixing bowls (the kind that nest inside each other)

Empty Cool Whip Lite containers and lids for refrigerator
  food storage
Plastic liquid measuring cups (1-cup and 4-cup)
Sharp knives (paring and butcher)
Cutting board
Rubber spatulas
Wire whisk
Measuring spoons
Dry measuring cups
Large slotted spoon
Teakettle
Vegetable parer
Wire racks
Covered jar
Kitchen timer
Can opener

You're stocked, you're set—let's go!

The Recipes

How to Read a Healthy Exchanges Recipe

The Healthy Exchanges Nutritional Analysis

Before using these recipes, you may wish to consult your physician or health-care provider to be sure they are appropriate for you. The information in this book is not intended to take the place of any medical advice. It reflects my experiences, studies, research, and opinions regarding healthy eating.

Each recipe includes nutritional information calculated in three ways:

> Healthy Exchanges Weight Loss Choices™ or Exchanges
> Calories; Fat, Protein, Carbohydrates, and Fiber in grams;
>   Sodium and Calcium in milligrams
> DIABETIC EXCHANGES

In every Healthy Exchanges recipe, the DIABETIC EXCHANGES have been calculated by a registered dietitian. All the other calculations were done by computer, using the Food Processor II software. When the ingredient listing gives more than one choice, the first ingredient listed is the one used in the recipe analysis. Due to inevitable variations in the ingredients you choose to use, the nutritional values should be considered approximate.

The annotation "(limited)" following Protein counts in some recipes indicates that consumption of whole eggs should be limited to four per week.

Please note the following symbols:

☆ This star means read the recipe's directions carefully for special instructions about **division** of ingredients.

❋ This symbol indicates **FREEZES WELL.**

Sizzling

Side Dishes

I was never one of those people who eat their way around the plate one item at a time. I prefer a bite of this, then a bite of that, until the meal is through. So while I truly enjoy a hearty entrée, I've always been a fan of the numerous side dishes that are a Midwestern tradition. My garden contributes a variety of colorful vegetables to my table in late spring and through the summer, but for much of the year, I serve veggie dishes based on the best canned and frozen vegetables I can find. And both Cliff and I enjoy the healthy starches—potatoes, rice, and pasta—so you'll always find those somewhere on our plates. Maybe the right term for these delights isn't "side dishes" but "co-stars"!

In honor of my husband, Cliff, I've created some terrific new green bean dishes: **Georgia-Style Green Beans, Grilled Green Beans and Walnuts,** and **German Grilled Potatoes and Green Beans**. In honor of my Iowa heritage, I always include some special ways to serve our state vegetable, corn: **Farmland Corn Fritters, Grilled Squaw Corn,** and **Mexican Corn**. And for those of you who never met a potato you didn't like: **Catalina Potatoes and Veggies, Fried Sweet Potato Cakes,** and **Mexican Grilled Hash Browns**.

Grilled Asparagus in Mustard Butter

I know that a lot of my readers don't cook fresh asparagus very often, even when it's green and gorgeous in the local market, especially during the May and June harvest time. If it's always seemed like too much trouble, here's a simple yet festive way to discover what's wonderful about this particular veggie!

 Serves 4 (full ½ cup)

> 2 tablespoons + 2 teaspoons I Can't Believe It's Not Butter! Light
>   Margarine, melted
> 1 tablespoon Grey Poupon Country Dijon Mustard
> ⅛ teaspoon black pepper
> 3 cups chopped fresh asparagus

Plug in and generously spray both sides of double-sided electric contact grill with butter-flavored cooking spray and preheat for 5 minutes. Meanwhile, in a medium bowl, combine melted margarine, mustard, and black pepper. Add asparagus. Mix well to coat. Evenly arrange asparagus mixture on prepared grill. Lightly spray top of asparagus mixture with butter-flavored cooking spray. Close lid and grill for 10 to 12 minutes or until asparagus is tender. Serve at once.

Each serving equals:

HE: 1½ Vegetable • 1 Fat

---

64 Calories • 4 g Fat • 3 g Protein •
4 g Carbohydrate • 183 mg Sodium •
24 mg Calcium • 1 g Fiber

DIABETIC: 1 Vegetable • 1 Fat

Grilled Celery au French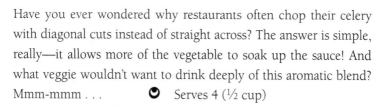

Have you ever wondered why restaurants often chop their celery with diagonal cuts instead of straight across? The answer is simple, really—it allows more of the vegetable to soak up the sauce! And what veggie wouldn't want to drink deeply of this aromatic blend? Mmm-mmm . . . ☻ Serves 4 (½ cup)

¼ cup Kraft Fat Free French Dressing
1 (2-ounce) jar chopped pimiento, drained
1 teaspoon dried parsley flakes
3 cups chopped celery
½ cup finely chopped onion

Plug in and generously spray both sides of double-sided electric contact grill with butter-flavored cooking spray and preheat for 5 minutes. Meanwhile, in a large bowl, combine French dressing, pimiento, and parsley flakes. Add celery and onion. Mix well to coat. Evenly arrange vegetable mixture on prepared grill. Lightly spray top of vegetable mixture with butter-flavored cooking spray. Close lid and grill for 16 to 18 minutes or until vegetables are tender. Serve at once.

Each serving equals:

HE: 1¾ Vegetable • ¼ Slider • 5 Optional Calories

52 Calories • 0 g Fat • 1 g Protein •
12 g Carbohydrate • 231 mg Sodium •
41 mg Calcium • 2 g Fiber

DIABETIC: 1½ Vegetable

Grilled Cauliflower with Tomato-Cheese Sauce

Well, now, I know that almost any vegetable tastes better with cheese sauce, but the combination of flavors and textures in this grilled dish will delight and surprise you. If you like things spicier, experiment with a bit more pepper, or even some crushed red pepper to heat things up. ☻ Serves 4

> 1 tablespoon + 1 teaspoon I Can't Believe It's Not Butter!
>   Light Margarine, melted
> 1 teaspoon dried parsley flakes
> 3 cups chopped fresh cauliflower
> ½ cup chopped onion
> ½ cup chopped green bell pepper
> 1 (10¾-ounce) can Healthy Request
>   Tomato Soup
> ¾ cup (3 ounces) shredded Kraft reduced-fat
>   Cheddar cheese
> ⅛ teaspoon black pepper

Plug in and generously spray both sides of double-sided electric contact grill with butter-flavored cooking spray and preheat for 5 minutes. Meanwhile, in a large bowl, combine melted margarine and parsley flakes. Add cauliflower, onion, and green pepper. Mix well to coat. Evenly arrange vegetable mixture evenly on prepared grill. Lightly spray top of vegetable mixture with butter-flavored cooking spray. Close lid and grill for 7 to 8 minutes. Meanwhile, in a medium saucepan, combine tomato soup, Cheddar cheese, and black pepper. Cook over medium-low heat while cauliflower mixture grills, stirring occasionally. For each serving, place ½ cup cauliflower mixture on a plate and spoon about ¼ cup tomato sauce over top.

Each serving equals:

HE: 2 Vegetable • 1 Protein • ½ Fat • ½ Slider •
5 Optional Calories

---

154 Calories • 6 g Fat • 8 g Protein •
17 g Carbohydrate • 518 mg Sodium •
163 mg Calcium • 3 g Fiber

DIABETIC: 1 Vegetable • 1 Meat • ½ Fat •
½ Starch / Carbohydrate

French Grilled Zucchini Slices

Some foods go from good-looking to gorgeous on the grill, and I think zucchini is one of those that truly improves when you see those luscious grill marks on each succulent piece. But looks aren't everything, so you'll be pleased to know that these taste as yummy as they look! ◐ Serves 4 (½ cup)

⅓ cup Kraft Fat Free French Dressing
2 teaspoons dried parsley flakes
½ cup finely chopped onion
4 cups sliced zucchini

Plug in and generously spray both sides of double-sided electric contact grill with butter-flavored cooking spray and preheat for 5 minutes. Meanwhile, in a large bowl, combine French dressing, parsley flakes, and onion. Add zucchini. Mix well to coat. Evenly arrange zucchini mixture on prepared grill. Lightly spray top of vegetable mixture with butter-flavored cooking spray. Close lid and grill for 7 to 8 minutes. Serve at once.

Each serving equals:

HE: 2¼ Vegetable • ¼ Slider • 13 Optional Calories

52 Calories • 0 g Fat • 1 g Protein •
12 g Carbohydrate • 203 mg Sodium •
21 mg Calcium • 2 g Fiber

DIABETIC: 1½ Vegetable

Grilled Italian Zucchini and Tomato

So much of Italian cooking is about the spices—especially that magical herb called basil. With just a sprinkling over this recipe's super-fresh tomatoes, you will be transported to the hills of Tuscany! ☻ Serves 4 (½ cup)

¼ cup Kraft Fat Free Italian Dressing
2 teaspoons Splenda Granular
½ teaspoon dried basil
2 cups thinly sliced unpeeled zucchini
1 cup chopped fresh mushrooms
½ cup chopped onion
1 cup peeled and coarsely chopped fresh tomatoes

Plug in and generously spray both sides of double-sided electric contact grill with olive oil–flavored cooking spray and preheat for 5 minutes. Meanwhile, in a large bowl, combine Italian dressing, Splenda, and basil. Add zucchini, mushrooms, and onion. Mix well to combine. Stir in tomatoes. Evenly arrange vegetables on prepared grill. Lightly spray top of vegetable mixture with olive oil–flavored cooking spray. Close lid and grill for 5 minutes. Gently stir vegetables. Re-cover and continue grilling for 3 minutes. Serve at once.

Each serving equals:

HE: 2¼ Vegetable • 9 Optional Calories

36 Calories • 0 g Fat • 2 g Protein •
7 g Carbohydrate • 232 mg Sodium •
23 mg Calcium • 2 g Fiber

DIABETIC: 1½ Vegetable

Savory Tomato Side Dish

I've always had a tomato patch, whether it was just a few plants outside my kitchen or dozens more in an elevated garden (to keep animals away!). When summer comes, my harvest is more appealing to Cliff and me than a plate of rubies!

☻ Serves 4 (full ½ cup)

> 4 cups peeled and chopped fresh tomatoes
> 2 tablespoons Splenda Granular
> 1 teaspoon dried basil
> ⅛ teaspoon black pepper
> 1 cup chopped onion
> ¼ cup Hormel Bacon Bits

Plug in and generously spray both sides of double-sided electric contact grill with butter-flavored cooking spray and preheat for 5 minutes. Meanwhile, in a large bowl, combine tomatoes, Splenda, basil, and black pepper. Stir in onion and bacon bits. Evenly arrange mixture on prepared grill. Lightly spray top of vegetable mixture with butter-flavored cooking spray. Close lid and grill for 5 minutes or just until the tomatoes start to soften. Serve at once.

Each serving equals:

HE: 1½ Vegetable • ¼ Slider • 8 Optional Calories

94 Calories • 2 g Fat • 5 g Protein •
14 g Carbohydrate • 267 mg Sodium •
30 mg Calcium • 3 g Fiber

DIABETIC: 2 Vegetable • ½ Meat

Italian Grilled Tomato Slices

If you want to bring out the best in your rosy summer harvest of ripe tomatoes, here's a fresh approach that is a delectable accompaniment to any meat-and-potatoes meal. It brings color to the plate and invites you to savor every bite.   ❍   Serves 4

2 tablespoons Kraft Fat Free Italian Dressing
3 tablespoons all-purpose flour
1 teaspoon dried parsley flakes
⅛ teaspoon salt
⅛ teaspoon black pepper
2 (medium-sized) firm red tomatoes, cut into ¾-inch slices

Plug in and generously spray both sides of double-sided electric contact grill with butter-flavored cooking spray and preheat for 5 minutes. Meanwhile, pour Italian dressing in a shallow saucer. In another shallow saucer, combine flour, parsley flakes, salt, and black pepper. First, dip tomato slices into Italian dressing, then into flour mixture to coat both sides. Evenly arrange coated tomato slices on prepared grill. Lightly spray top of tomato slices with butter-flavored cooking spray. Close lid and grill for 3 to 4 minutes. Evenly divide into 4 servings. Serve at once.

HINTS: 1. Grilled tomato slices will be soft, but good!
2. Green tomatoes may be used in place of ripe tomatoes.

Each serving equals:

HE: 1 Vegetable • ¼ Bread • 4 Optional Calories

44 Calories • 0 g Fat • 2 g Protein •
9 g Carbohydrate • 80 mg Sodium • 6 mg Calcium •
1 g Fiber

DIABETIC: 1 Vegetable

Island Grilled Carrots

When I say "island," do you close your eyes and imagine lying on white sand beneath palm trees, while delectable aromas try to persuade you that it's dinnertime? Food has a wonderful ability to take us on journeys to faraway lands, even if it's just in our imaginations!

● Serves 4 (½ cup)

> 2 tablespoons reduced-sodium ketchup
> 2 tablespoons white distilled vinegar
> 2 tablespoons Splenda Granular
> ⅛ teaspoon ground ginger
> 1 teaspoon dried parsley flakes
> 3 cups frozen sliced carrots, thawed
> 1 cup chopped green bell pepper

Plug in and generously spray both sides of double-sided electric contact grill with butter-flavored cooking spray and preheat for 5 minutes. Meanwhile, in a large bowl, combine ketchup, vinegar, Splenda, ginger, and parsley flakes. Add carrots and green peppers. Mix well to coat. Evenly arrange vegetable mixture on prepared grill. Lightly spray top of vegetable mixture with butter-flavored cooking spray. Close lid and grill for 12 to 15 minutes. Serve at once.

HINT: Thaw carrots by placing in a colander and rinsing under hot water for 1 minute.

Each serving equals:

HE: 2 Vegetable • 11 Optional Calories

60 Calories • 0 g Fat • 1 g Protein •
14 g Carbohydrate • 65 mg Sodium •
38 mg Calcium • 4 g Fiber

DIABETIC: 2 Vegetable

Carrots and Cabbage Combo ❄

What a terrific last-minute triumph this recipe provides, since most supermarkets offer packages of cabbage and carrots already shredded! You may never have imagined grilling these particular vegetables, but the results are bound to convince you this "couple" is forever. ☻ Serves 4 (¾ cup)

> 1 tablespoon + 1 teaspoon I Can't Believe It's Not Butter! Light
>   Margarine, melted
> 1 tablespoon Splenda Granular
> ⅛ teaspoon black pepper
> 3 cups shredded cabbage
> 2 cups shredded carrots

Plug in and generously spray both sides of double-sided electric contact grill with butter-flavored cooking spray and preheat for 5 minutes. Meanwhile, in a large bowl, combine melted margarine, Splenda, and black pepper. Add cabbage and carrots. Mix well to coat. Evenly arrange vegetable mixture on prepared grill. Lightly spray top of vegetable mixture with butter-flavored cooking spray. Close lid and grill for 6 to 7 minutes. Serve at once.

Each serving equals:

HE: 1¾ Vegetable • ½ Fat • 1 Optional Calorie

---

62 Calories • 2 g Fat • 2 g Protein •
9 g Carbohydrate • 77 mg Sodium • 47 mg Calcium •
3 g Fiber

DIABETIC: 2 Vegetable • ½ Fat

Dutch Carrots and Peas

Peas and carrots might just be the most popular combination ever invented for vegetables, but something as superb as that duo can still be improved. Here, a little onion and bacon makes for a piquant, tangy side dish that can't be beat!

● Serves 4 (¾ cup)

> *4 cups frozen peas and carrots, thawed*
> *½ cup chopped onion*
> *¼ cup Hormel Bacon Bits*

Plug in and generously spray both sides of double-sided electric contact grill with butter-flavored cooking spray and preheat for 5 minutes. Meanwhile, in a large bowl, combine peas and carrots and onion. Stir in bacon bits. Evenly arrange mixture on prepared grill. Lightly spray top of vegetable mixture with butter-flavored cooking spray. Close lid and grill for 7 to 8 minutes. Serve at once.

HINT: Thaw peas and carrots by placing in a colander and rinsing under hot water for 1 minute.

Each serving equals:

HE: 1¼ Vegetable • 1 Bread • ¼ Slider • 5 Optional Calories

122 Calories • 2 g Fat • 8 g Protein • 18 g Carbohydrate • 361 mg Sodium • 42 mg Calcium • 5 g Fiber

DIABETIC: 1 Vegetable • 1 Starch • ½ Meat

Georgia-Style Green Beans

Oh, those Southern cooks knew what they were doing when they cooked up a pot of green beans to please a family of ravenous men! You'll be amazed by what a difference a bit of bacon and a sprinkle of nuts make in this special side dish.

● Serves 4 (¾ cup)

> 2 tablespoons white distilled vinegar
> 2 tablespoons Splenda Granular
> 4 cups frozen cut green beans, thawed
> ½ cup chopped onion
> ¼ cup Hormel Bacon Bits
> ¼ cup coarsely chopped dry-roasted peanuts

Plug in and generously spray both sides of double-sided electric contact grill with butter-flavored cooking spray and preheat for 5 minutes. Meanwhile, in a large bowl, combine vinegar and Splenda. Stir in green beans, onion, and bacon bits. Add peanuts. Mix well to combine. Evenly arrange vegetable mixture on prepared grill. Lightly spray top of vegetable mixture with butter-flavored cooking spray. Close lid and grill for 7 to 8 minutes. Serve at once.

HINT: Thaw green beans by placing in a colander and rinsing under hot water for 1 minute.

Each serving equals:

HE: 2¼ Vegetable • ½ Fat • ¼ Protein • ¼ Slider • 8 Optional Calories

153 Calories • 5 g Fat • 7 g Protein • 20 g Carbohydrate • 261 mg Sodium • 62 mg Calcium • 4 g Fiber

DIABETIC: 2 Vegetable • 1 Fat • ½ Meat

Grilled Green Beans and Walnuts

Cliff loved this recipe when I served it to him one evening for supper, maybe because he loves green beans best, and he also enjoys the crunchiness of nuts. Grilled, two of his favorites combined to make a third!   ☻   Serves 4 (¾ cup)

> 2 tablespoons Kraft Fat Free Catalina Dressing
> 1 teaspoon dried parsley flakes
> 4 cups frozen cut green beans, thawed
> ¼ cup (1 ounce) chopped walnuts

Plug in and generously spray both sides of double-sided electric contact grill with butter-flavored cooking spray and preheat for 5 minutes. In a large bowl, combine Catalina dressing, parsley flakes, and green beans. Add walnuts. Mix well to coat. Evenly arrange green bean mixture on prepared grill. Lightly spray top of green bean mixture with butter-flavored cooking spray. Close lid and grill for 7 to 8 minutes. Serve at once.

HINT: Thaw green beans by placing in a colander and rinsing under hot water for 1 minute.

Each serving equals:

> HE: 2 Vegetable • ½ Fat • ¼ Protein •
> 12 Optional Calories
>
> ---
>
> 109 Calories • 5 g Fat • 3 g Protein •
> 13 g Carbohydrate • 94 mg Sodium •
> 59 mg Calcium • 4 g Fiber
>
> ---
>
> DIABETIC: 2 Vegetable • 1 Fat

Tex-Mex Veggie Grill

Here's a fun fact: Frozen vegetables may be the healthiest best choice for us if we can't pick the veggies fresh from our own gardens. Because vegetables start losing nutrients as soon as they are picked, those we purchase in markets may have sat on train cars for days, even weeks. But when they are frozen moments after picking, they retain all those great vitamins and minerals until you cook them!   ☺   Serves 4 (¾ cup)

¼ cup Kraft Fat Free Catalina Dressing
½ teaspoon chili seasoning
2 cups frozen cut carrots, thawed
1½ cups frozen cut green beans, thawed
1 cup frozen whole-kernel corn, thawed
½ cup chopped onion

Plug in and generously spray both sides of double-sided electric contact grill with butter-flavored cooking spray and preheat for 5 minutes. Meanwhile, in a large bowl, combine Catalina dressing and chili seasoning. Add carrots, green beans, corn, and onion. Mix well to coat. Evenly arrange vegetable mixture on prepared grill. Lightly spray top of vegetable mixture with butter-flavored cooking spray. Close lid and grill for 9 to 10 minutes. Serve at once.

HINT: Thaw frozen vegetables by placing in a colander and rinsing under hot water for 1 minute.

Each serving equals:

HE: 2 Vegetable • ½ Bread • ¼ Slider •
5 Optional Calories

112 Calories • 0 g Fat • 3 g Protein •
25 g Carbohydrate • 224 mg Sodium •
46 mg Calcium • 5 g Fiber

DIABETIC: 2 Vegetable • ½ Starch

Cajun Grilled Mixed Vegetables

Let the good times—and the good tastes—roll with this spicy veggie dish that is great for using up your summer zucchini harvest! If you love that Louisiana heat, get out the grill!

○ Serves 4 (¾ cup)

> ¼ cup Kraft Fat Free French Dressing
> 1½ teaspoons Cajun seasoning
> 1½ cups diced unpeeled zucchini
> 1 cup chopped onion
> 1 cup chopped green bell pepper
> 1½ cups peeled and chopped fresh tomatoes

Plug in and generously spray both sides of double-sided electric contact grill with butter-flavored cooking spray and preheat for 5 minutes. Meanwhile, in a large bowl, combine French dressing and Cajun seasoning. Add zucchini, onion, and green pepper. Mix well to coat. Stir in tomatoes. Evenly arrange vegetable mixture on prepared grill. Lightly spray top of vegetable mixture with butter-flavored cooking spray. Close lid and grill for 7 to 8 minutes. Serve at once.

Each serving equals:

HE: 2½ Vegetable • ¼ Slider • 5 Optional Calories

---

72 Calories • 0 g Fat • 2 g Protein •
16 g Carbohydrate • 367 mg Sodium •
22 mg Calcium • 3 g Fiber

DIABETIC: 2 Vegetable

Italian Garden Sauté

This dish is all about the glories of color on the plate—golden yellow corn, deep green zucchini, and lush red tomatoes! What meal wouldn't be made even more delightful with this seductive addition? ☾ Serves 4

> 1/4 cup Kraft Fat Free Italian Dressing
> 1 tablespoon chopped fresh parsley or 1 teaspoon dried parsley flakes
> 1/8 teaspoon black pepper
> 1/2 cup chopped onion
> 1 1/2 cups sliced zucchini
> 1 1/2 cups fresh or frozen whole-kernel corn, thawed
> 1 1/2 cups chopped fresh tomatoes
> 1/2 cup + 1 tablespoon (2 1/4 ounces) shredded Kraft reduced-fat mozzarella cheese

Plug in and generously spray both sides of double-sided electric contact grill with olive oil–flavored cooking spray and preheat for 5 minutes. Meanwhile, in a large bowl, combine Italian dressing, parsley, and black pepper. Add onion, zucchini, and corn. Mix well to combine. Stir in tomatoes. Evenly arrange vegetable mixture on prepared grill. Lightly spray top of vegetable mixture with olive oil–flavored cooking spray. Close lid and grill for 10 minutes. For each serving, place 3/4 cup hot vegetable mixture on a plate and spoon a full 2 tablespoons mozzarella cheese over top. Serve at once.

Each serving equals:

HE: 1 3/4 Vegetable • 3/4 Bread • 3/4 Protein •
8 Optional Calories

139 Calories • 3 g Fat • 8 g Protein •
20 g Carbohydrate • 340 mg Sodium •
122 mg Calcium • 3 g Fiber

DIABETIC: 1 Vegetable • 1 Starch • 1/2 Meat

Corn and Celery Sauté ❄

Talk about crunchy and sweet all at once! I think celery tastes good raw, but it takes on a whole new flavor when it's introduced to Iowa's proudest farm product.   ☯   Serves 4 (¾ cup)

> 2 cups chopped celery
> 2 cups frozen whole-kernel corn, thawed
> 1 (2-ounce) jar chopped pimiento, drained
> 2 teaspoons dried onion flakes
> ⅛ teaspoon black pepper

Plug in and generously spray both sides of double-sided electric contact grill with butter-flavored cooking spray and preheat for 5 minutes. Meanwhile, in a large bowl, combine celery, corn, pimiento, onion flakes, and black pepper. Evenly arrange vegetable mixture on prepared grill. Lightly spray top of vegetable mixture with butter-flavored cooking spray. Close lid and grill for 10 to 12 minutes. Serve at once.

HINT: Thaw corn by placing in a colander and rinsing under hot water for 1 minute.

Each serving equals:

HE: 1 Bread • 1 Vegetable

---

92 Calories • 0 g Fat • 3 g Protein •
20 g Carbohydrate • 56 mg Sodium •
29 mg Calcium • 3 g Fiber

DIABETIC: 1 Starch • ½ Vegetable

Mexican Corn

From a kitchen tradition that features grilled vegetables in many of its best-known dishes, here is a tangy way to serve good old corn. It's remarkable how much flavor is provided by the addition of olives. ◐ Serves 4 (full ⅓ cup)

> 2 teaspoons I Can't Believe It's Not Butter! Light Margarine,
>   melted
> 2 cups fresh or frozen whole-kernel corn, thawed
> 2 tablespoons chopped fresh parsley
> 1 (2-ounce) jar chopped pimiento, drained
> ¼ cup chopped ripe olives

Plug in and generously spray both sides of double-sided electric contact grill with butter-flavored cooking spray and preheat for 5 minutes. Meanwhile, in a large bowl, combine melted margarine and corn. Add parsley, pimiento, and olives. Mix well to combine. Evenly arrange corn mixture on prepared grill. Lightly spray top of corn mixture with butter-flavored cooking spray. Close lid and grill for 7 minutes. Serve at once.

Each serving equals:

HE: 1 Bread • ½ Fat

---

102 Calories • 2 g Fat • 3 g Protein •
18 g Carbohydrate • 90 mg Sodium •
13 mg Calcium • 2 g Fiber

DIABETIC: 1 Starch • ½ Fat

Grilled Squaw Corn

I've made squaw corn in a variety of ways, so when I decided to write a grilling cookbook, I knew I had to create another splendid heartland standby. This is one of the best yet!

◐ Serves 4 (½ cup)

> 1 tablespoon + 1 teaspoon I Can't Believe It's Not Butter! Light
>   Margarine, melted
> ½ teaspoon Worcestershire sauce
> 1 teaspoon dried parsley flakes
> 2 cups fresh or frozen whole-kernel corn, thawed
> 1 cup chopped onion
> ½ cup chopped green bell pepper
> ¼ cup Hormel Bacon Bits

Plug in and generously spray both sides of double-sided electric contact grill with butter-flavored cooking spray, and preheat for 5 minutes. Meanwhile, in a large bowl, combine margarine, Worcestershire sauce, and parsley flakes. Add corn, onion, and green pepper. Mix well to combine. Stir in bacon bits. Evenly arrange corn mixture on prepared grill. Lightly spray top of corn mixture with butter-flavored cooking spray. Close lid and grill for 8 to 10 minutes. Serve at once.

HINT: Thaw corn by placing in a colander and rinsing under hot water for 1 minute.

Each serving equals:

> HE: 1 Bread • ¾ Vegetable • ½ Fat • ¼ Slider •
> 5 Optional Calories
> ___
> 136 Calories • 4 g Fat • 5 g Protein •
> 20 g Carbohydrate • 306 mg Sodium •
> 11 mg Calcium • 3 g Fiber
> ___
> DIABETIC: 1 Starch • ½ Vegetable • ½ Fat • ½ Meat

Chuck Wagon Corn Cakes

Here's an old-timey favorite made quick and tasty on your handy grill. It's a good idea to try when you've got some leftover rice and a few pantry basics! ☻ Serves 6

> 6 tablespoons Bisquick Reduced Fat Baking Mix
> ½ cup cold cooked rice
> 1½ cups frozen whole-kernel corn, thawed
> 1 egg, beaten, or equivalent in egg substitute
> ¼ cup fat-free milk
> 1 teaspoon dried parsley flakes

Plug in and generously spray both sides of double-sided electric contact grill with butter-flavored cooking spray and preheat for 5 minutes. Meanwhile, in a large bowl, combine baking mix, rice, and corn. Add egg, milk, and parsley flakes. Mix well to combine. Using a ⅓ cup measuring cup as a guide, drop batter onto prepared grill to form 6 cakes. Lightly spray tops with butter-flavored cooking spray. Close lid and grill for 7 to 8 minutes. Serve at once.

HINTS: 1. Usually ⅓ cup uncooked instant rice cooks to about ½ cup.
2. Thaw corn by placing in a colander and rinsing under hot water for 1 minute.

Each serving equals:

HE: 1 Bread • 14 Optional Calories

89 Calories • 1 g Fat • 3 g Protein •
17 g Carbohydrate • 104 mg Sodium •
27 mg Calcium • 1 g Fiber

DIABETIC: 1 Starch

Cabbage and Noodle Side Dish ❄

This pasta dish has a bit of Asian influence and it's a great way to use up some leftover cold spaghetti. Did you ever think you'd be grilling noodles when you first purchased your electric grill? Life is full of tasty surprises! ☺ Serves 4 (¾ cup)

¼ cup Kraft Fat Free Catalina Dressing

1 tablespoon reduced-sodium soy sauce

1 teaspoon Oriental seasoning

1 teaspoon dried parsley flakes

2 cups chopped cabbage

½ cup shredded carrots

½ cup finely chopped onion

2 cups cooked spaghetti

Plug in and generously spray both sides of double-sided electric contact grill with butter-flavored cooking spray and preheat for 5 minutes. Meanwhile, in a large bowl, combine Catalina dressing, soy sauce, Oriental seasoning, and parsley flakes. Add cabbage, carrots, and onion. Mix well to combine. Stir in spaghetti. Evenly arrange mixture on prepared grill. Lightly spray top of mixture with butter-flavored cooking spray. Close lid and grill for 8 to 10 minutes. Serve at once.

HINT: Usually 1½ cups broken uncooked spaghetti cooks to about 2 cups.

Each serving equals:

HE: 1 Bread • 1 Vegetable • ¼ Slider •
5 Optional Calories

136 Calories • 0 g Fat • 4 g Protein •
30 g Carbohydrate • 194 mg Sodium •
34 mg Calcium • 3 g Fiber

DIABETIC: 1 Starch • 1 Vegetable

Italian Carrots and Potatoes Side Dish

Italian dressing is a grill cook's really good friend—it lends the kind of flavor to grilled meats and veggies you used to be able to get only from a marinade used for hours. Try this dish with red-skinned new potatoes if they're available. ☻ Serves 4 (¾ cup)

> ⅓ cup Kraft Fat Free Italian Dressing
> 1 tablespoon Splenda Granular
> 1 teaspoon dried parsley flakes
> ⅛ teaspoon black pepper
> 2 cups shredded carrots
> 1½ cups (8 ounces) diced cooked potatoes
> ½ cup finely chopped onion
> ½ cup finely chopped green bell pepper

Plug in and generously spray both sides of double-sided electric contact grill with olive oil–flavored cooking spray and preheat for 5 minutes. Meanwhile, in a large bowl, combine Italian dressing, Splenda, parsley flakes, and black pepper. Add carrots, potatoes, onion, and green pepper. Mix well to combine. Evenly arrange vegetable mixture on prepared grill. Lightly spray top of vegetable mixture with olive oil–flavored cooking spray. Close lid and grill for 6 to 8 minutes. Serve at once.

Each serving equals:

HE: 1½ Vegetable • ½ Bread • 12 Optional Calories

96 Calories • 0 g Fat • 2 g Protein •
22 g Carbohydrate • 298 mg Sodium •
24 mg Calcium • 3 g Fiber

DIABETIC: 1½ Vegetable • 1 Starch

Catalina Potatoes and Veggies

This is a wonderfully hearty grilled vegetable combo, perfect for dinner when you're eating less meat but still want your family's tummies to be satisfied. These veggies reminded me of what you get when you order fajitas in a Mexican restaurant—heat, crunch, sweetness, mmm-mmm. ☻ Serves 4 (1 cup)

¼ cup Kraft Fat Free Catalina Dressing
1 teaspoon dried parsley flakes
½ teaspoon chili seasoning
1½ cups (8 ounces) diced cooked potatoes
1½ cups coarsely chopped onion
1½ cups coarsely chopped green bell pepper
1 cup peeled and chopped fresh tomatoes

Plug in and generously spray both sides of double-sided electric contact grill with butter-flavored cooking spray and preheat for 5 minutes. Meanwhile, in a large bowl, combine Catalina dressing, parsley flakes, and chili seasoning. Add potatoes, onion, and green pepper. Mix well to combine. Stir in tomatoes. Evenly arrange mixture on prepared grill. Lightly spray top of vegetable mixture with butter-flavored cooking spray. Close lid and grill for 10 minutes. Serve at once.

Each serving equals:

HE: 2 Vegetable • ½ Bread • ¼ Slider •
5 Optional Calories

120 Calories • 0 g Fat • 2 g Protein •
28 g Carbohydrate • 192 mg Sodium •
24 mg Calcium • 4 g Fiber

DIABETIC: 1½ Vegetable • 1 Starch

German Grilled Potatoes and Green Beans

Even if you never get a chance to visit Germany and taste the "real thing," this recipe will convince your taste buds you're sitting with friends in a beer garden enjoying the intriguing flavors of olden days. I like cut green beans in this dish, but you can also try it with whole green beans, too.   ♥   Serves 4 (1 cup)

¼ cup white distilled vinegar
¼ cup Splenda Granular
¼ cup Hormel Bacon Bits
1 teaspoon dried parsley flakes
⅛ teaspoon black pepper

1½ cups (8 ounces) diced
  cooked potatoes
3 cups frozen cut green beans,
  thawed
½ cup chopped onion

Plug in and generously spray both sides of double-sided electric contact grill with butter-flavored cooking spray and preheat for 5 minutes. Meanwhile, in a large bowl, combine vinegar, Splenda, bacon bits, parsley flakes, and black pepper. Add potatoes, green beans, and onion. Mix well to coat. Evenly arrange mixture on prepared grill. Lightly spray top of vegetable mixture with butter-flavored cooking spray. Close lid and grill for 8 to 10 minutes. Serve at once.

HINT: Thaw green beans by placing in a colander and rinsing under hot water for 1 minute.

Each serving equals:

HE: 1¾ Vegetable • ½ Bread • ¼ Slider •
11 Optional Calories

178 Calories • 2 g Fat • 6 g Protein •
34 g Carbohydrate • 268 mg Sodium •
51 mg Calcium • 4 g Fiber

DIABETIC: 2 Vegetable • 1 Starch • ½ Meat

Daddy's Potato Patties

Yes, it's true—potato "burgers" are a delicious new way to enjoy our favorite spuds! These are a little like those hash brown patties you find in fast-food places, but with nowhere near the fat or calories, you get the pleasure with none of the pain.   ❤   Serves 4

> 1⅓ cups boiling water
> 1⅓ cups instant potato flakes
> 2 teaspoons dried onion flakes
> 1 teaspoon dried parsley flakes
> ⅛ teaspoon black pepper
> 1 egg or equivalent in egg substitute
> 1⅓ cups (1½ ounces) shredded Kraft reduced-fat Cheddar cheese

Plug in and generously spray both sides of double-sided electric contact grill with butter-flavored cooking spray and preheat for 5 minutes. Meanwhile, in a large bowl, combine boiling water and potato flakes. Mix well using a fork. Stir in onion flakes, parsley flakes, and black pepper. Let set for 1 to 2 minutes. Add egg and Cheddar cheese. Mix well to combine. Using a ½ cup measuring cup as a guide, form into 4 patties. Evenly arrange patties on prepared grill. Lightly spray tops with butter-flavored cooking spray. Close lid and grill for 5 to 6 minutes. Serve at once.

Each serving equals:

HE: 1 Bread • ¾ Protein

101 Calories • 1 g Fat • 4 g Protein •
19 g Carbohydrate • 61 mg Sodium • 9 mg Calcium •
1 g Fiber

DIABETIC: 1 Starch • 1 Meat

Mexican Grilled Hash Browns

I know a few people who could eat hash browns any time of the day or night—do you? Grilling these prepared potatoes with garlic and onion infuses them with tons of flavor, making them even better than at an old-fashioned diner! ☻ Serves 4 (¾ cup)

4½ cups (16 ounces) shredded loose-packed frozen potatoes
½ cup chopped onion
½ cup chopped green pepper
1 teaspoon dried minced garlic
1 (2-ounce) jar chopped pimiento, drained
2 tablespoons Hormel Bacon Bits

Plug in and generously spray both sides of double-sided electric contact grill with butter-flavored cooking spray and preheat for 5 minutes. Meanwhile, in a large bowl, combine potatoes, onion, and green pepper. Add garlic, pimiento, and bacon bits. Mix well to combine. Evenly arrange potato mixture on prepared grill. Lightly spray top of potato mixture with butter-flavored cooking spray. Close lid and grill for 9 to 10 minutes. Serve at once.

HINT: Mr. Dell's frozen shredded potatoes are a good choice or raw shredded potatoes, rinsed and patted dry, may be used in place of frozen potatoes.

Each serving equals:

HE: 1 Bread • ½ Vegetable • 12 Optional Calories

121 Calories • 1 g Fat • 5 g Protein •
23 g Carbohydrate • 128 mg Sodium •
18 mg Calcium • 4 g Fiber

DIABETIC: 1 Starch • ½ Vegetable

Grilled Potato Spears

Are you one of those people who never met a potato they didn't love at first bite? Here's another version to add to your list of favorites. It's both creamy and crisp!   ☻   Serves 4

> 4 (5-ounce) baking potatoes
> ¼ cup Kraft fat-free mayonnaise
> 1 teaspoon dried onion flakes
> 1 teaspoon dried parsley flakes
> ⅛ teaspoon black pepper

Plug in and generously spray both sides of double-sided electric contact grill with butter-flavored cooking spray and preheat for 5 minutes. Meanwhile, cut each potato lengthwise into 3-inch wedges. In a small bowl, combine mayonnaise, onion flakes, parsley flakes, and black pepper. Using a pastry brush, lightly coat potato wedges with mayonnaise mixture. Evenly arrange coated wedges on prepared grill. Lightly spray top of potato wedges with butter-flavored cooking spray. Close lid and grill for 16 to 18 minutes. Evenly divide into 4 servings. Serve at once.

Each serving equals:

HE: 1 Bread • 10 Optional Calories

112 Calories • 0 g Fat • 2 g Protein •
26 g Carbohydrate • 125 mg Sodium •
9 mg Calcium • 2 g Fiber

DIABETIC: 1½ Starch

Ranch Hand Potatoes

Anywhere you travel throughout the West, ranch-style dressing is often the first offered by any restaurant server. Maybe it's the cowboy heritage of the name, or the rich flavor that brings to mind golden sunsets, but it's a splendid way to make potatoes special.

❍ Serves 4 (full ½ cup)

> ¼ cup Kraft Fat Free Ranch Dressing
> 1 teaspoon dried parsley flakes
> ⅛ teaspoon black pepper
> 2 full cups (12 ounces) diced cooked potatoes
> 1 cup chopped onion
> ¼ cup Hormel Bacon Bits

Plug in and generously spray both sides of double-sided electric contact grill with butter-flavored cooking spray and preheat for 5 minutes. Meanwhile, in a large bowl, combine ranch dressing, parsley flakes, and black pepper. Add potatoes, onion, and bacon bits. Mix well to combine. Evenly arrange potato mixture on prepared grill. Lightly spray top of potato mixture with butter-flavored cooking spray. Close lid and grill for 5 to 6 minutes. Serve at once.

Each serving equals:

HE: ¾ Bread • ½ Vegetable • ½ Slider •
10 Optional Calories

137 Calories • 1 g Fat • 5 g Protein •
27 g Carbohydrate • 435 mg Sodium •
13 mg Calcium • 3 g Fiber

DIABETIC: 1½ Starch/Carbohydrate • ½ Vegetable

O'Brien Potatoes

If you love a lot of onions in your hash browns, this recipe will make you smile in anticipation! If your grill can't hold the entire recipe, divide the blended potatoes in half and keep the first half warm in the oven on low heat. ☻ Serves 4 (1 cup)

4½ cups (16 ounces) shredded loose-packed frozen potatoes, thawed
1 cup chopped onion
½ cup chopped green bell pepper
1 teaspoon dried parsley flakes
½ teaspoon lemon pepper

Plug in and generously spray both sides of double-sided electric contact grill with butter-flavored cooking spray and preheat for 5 minutes. Meanwhile, in a large bowl, combine potatoes, onion, and green pepper. Add parsley flakes and lemon pepper. Mix well to combine. Evenly arrange potato mixture on prepared grill. Lightly spray top of potato mixture with butter-flavored cooking spray. Close lid and grill for 10 to 12 minutes. Serve at once.

Each serving equals:

HE: 1 Bread • ¾ Vegetable

112 Calories • 0 g Fat • 3 g Protein •
25 g Carbohydrate • 2 mg Sodium • 22 mg Calcium •
4 g Fiber

DIABETIC: 1 Starch • 1 Vegetable

Maple Sweet Potato Grill

If you're yearning for something sweet, you may be astonished to discover that sweet potatoes, especially when served with maple syrup, satisfy you! The nuts add a lively bit of extra crunch.

◑ Serves 4 (½ cup)

> ¼ cup Log Cabin Sugar Free Maple Syrup
> 1 teaspoon dried parsley flakes
> 1 teaspoon dried onion flakes
> ⅛ teaspoon black pepper
> 2 full cups (12 ounces) peeled and diced cooked sweet potatoes
> ¼ cup chopped walnuts

Plug in and generously spray both sides of double-sided electric contact grill with butter-flavored cooking spray and preheat for 5 minutes. Meanwhile, in a large bowl, combine maple syrup, parsley flakes, onion flakes, and black pepper. Add sweet potatoes and walnuts. Mix well to combine. Evenly arrange sweet potato mixture on prepared grill. Lightly spray sweet potato mixture with butter-flavored cooking spray. Close lid and grill for 6 to 8 minutes. Serve at once.

Each serving equals:

HE: 1 Bread • ½ Fat • ¼ Protein •
10 Optional Calories

153 Calories • 5 g Fat • 3 g Protein •
24 g Carbohydrate • 78 mg Sodium •
31 mg Calcium • 2 g Fiber

DIABETIC: 1½ Starch • 1 Fat

Sweet Potato Cakes

If you love sweet potatoes but tend to serve them only around Thanksgiving, it's time for a change. Try this sweet-and-savory way to prepare a healthy starchy vegetable so that it tastes like a true treat! ◐ Serves 4

> *2 full cups (12 ounces) diced cooked sweet potatoes*
> *½ cup finely chopped onion*
> *3 tablespoons purchased graham cracker crumbs or 3 (2½-inch)*
>   *graham cracker squares, made into crumbs*
> *2 tablespoons Splenda Granular*
> *1 teaspoon dried parsley flakes*

Plug in and generously spray both sides of double-sided electric contact grill with butter-flavored cooking spray and preheat for 5 minutes. Meanwhile, in a medium-large bowl, mash sweet potatoes with a potato masher or fork. Stir in onion, graham cracker crumbs, Splenda, and parsley flakes. Using a ½ cup measuring cup as a guide, form into 4 cakes. Evenly arrange cakes on prepared grill. Lightly spray top of cakes with butter-flavored cooking spray. Close lid and grill for 7 to 8 minutes.

HINT: A self-seal sandwich bag works great for crushing graham crackers.

Each serving equals:

HE: 1 Bread • ¼ Vegetable

121 Calories • 1 g Fat • 2 g Protein •
26 g Carbohydrate • 97 mg Sodium •
38 mg Calcium • 2 g Fiber

DIABETIC: 1½ Starch/Carbohydrate

Spectacular
Sandwiches
and Burgers

"*Spectacular*" *isn't an overstatement when it comes to making sand-wiches on the grill. There's nothing like the heat and compression the grill provides to make the flavors in a sandwich combine brilliantly. It seems that no matter what you spread or pile on the bread of your choice, the finished product will be better than you expected! As for hamburgers, the indoor grill does double duty—it cooks them beautifully and it gets rid of unwanted fat. That's why I just had to include a section of nothing but burgers and sandwiches. It's bound to be one of your most-used and best-loved recipe collections.*

Ever since childhood, most of us have loved grilled cheese sandwiches, so I've included many different versions of that lunch-time classic: **Chicken and Cheese Sandwiches, Grilled Bacon and Cheese Sandwich Deluxe,** and **Crunchy Tuna and Cheese Sandwiches,** for a start. But if your passion burns for burgers, I've featured some unusual combos that will give your burger habit a whole new lease on life! Try my **Bacon Dill Burgers, Fast Food Lane Burgers, Popeye Spinach Burgers, Pronto Pizza Burg-ers** . . . and so many more. And for more culinary sizzle, you can choose **Philly Steak Wraps; Peanut Butter, Jelly, and Banana Grilled Sandwiches;** or **German Pretzel Burgers.**

Sunshine Sandwiches

Are you one of those carrot-lovers who just can't get enough of your favorite veggie? The sweetness, the crunch—it's all there in every bite when you nibble them raw, but I decided to up the stakes a bit by adding sweet spreadable fruit and a sweet bread to boot. The only reaction you're likely to get when you serve this: YUM!

☻ Serves 4

> ¼ cup orange marmalade spreadable fruit
> ¼ cup Kraft fat-free mayonnaise
> 1 cup shredded carrots
> 8 slices cinnamon-raisin bread

Plug in and generously spray both sides of double-sided electric contact grill with butter-flavored cooking spray and preheat for 5 minutes. Meanwhile, in a medium bowl, combine spreadable fruit and mayonnaise. Stir in carrots. Evenly spread about ¼ cup carrot mixture on 4 slices of bread, then top each with another slice of bread. Evenly arrange sandwiches on prepared grill. Lightly spray top of sandwiches with butter-flavored cooking spray. Close lid and grill for 4 minutes or until bread is toasted and filling is hot. Serve at once.

Each serving equals:

HE: 2 Bread • 1 Fruit • ½ Vegetable • 10 Optional Calories

219 Calories • 3 g Fat • 6 g Protein • 42 g Carbohydrate • 343 mg Sodium • 8 mg Calcium • 3 g Fiber

DIABETIC: 2 Starch • 1 Fruit • ½ Vegetable

Peanut Butter, Jelly, and Banana Grilled Sandwiches

Wasn't it Elvis who loved grilled peanut butter and banana sandwiches? (Or so it was rumored!) I think the grill makes this kiddy fave a little more grown-up—but not too fancy to keep it fun and fresh anytime. My granddaughter Cheyanne thinks it's yummy!

❍ Serves 4

> ¼ cup Peter Pan reduced-fat peanut butter
> 8 slices reduced-calorie white bread
> ¼ cup grape spreadable fruit
> 1 cup (1 medium) sliced banana

Plug in and generously spray both sides of double-sided electric contact grill with butter-flavored cooking spray and preheat for 5 minutes. Meanwhile, spread 1 tablespoon peanut butter on 4 slices of bread. Spread 1 tablespoon spreadable fruit on remaining 4 slices of bread. Evenly arrange ¼ cup banana slices on each piece of bread with peanut butter. Place remaining 4 slices of bread (jelly side down) over bananas. Evenly arrange sandwiches on prepared grill. Lightly spray top of sandwiches with butter-flavored cooking spray. Close lid and grill for 4 minutes or until bread is toasted and filling is hot. Serve at once.

Each serving equals:

HE: 1½ Fruit • 1 Bread • 1 Protein • 1 Fat

---

246 Calories • 6 g Fat • 10 g Protein •
38 g Carbohydrate • 323 mg Sodium •
43 mg Calcium • 2 g Fiber

DIABETIC: 1½ Starch • 1 Fruit • ½ Meat • ½ Fat

Baked Bean Sandwiches

Some readers have called me the "Mother of Invention" because I often stir up surprising combos in my healthy recipes. Well, Mother had fun inventing this sandwich surprise from a few items I've always got in my cupboard—bet you will, too! ☻ Serves 4

1 (16-ounce) can pork and beans, fat removed and well drained
2 teaspoons dried onion flakes
½ teaspoon prepared yellow mustard
2 tablespoons Log Cabin Sugar Free Maple Syrup
2 tablespoons Hormel Bacon Bits
8 slices Healthy Choice Hearty 7-Grain Bread

Plug in and generously spray both sides of double-sided electric contact grill with butter-flavored cooking spray and preheat for 5 minutes. Meanwhile, in a medium bowl, combine pork and beans, onion flakes, mustard, and syrup. Stir in bacon bits. Evenly spread about ¼ cup bean mixture on 4 slices of bread, then top each with another slice of bread. Evenly arrange sandwiches on prepared grill. Lightly spray top of sandwiches with butter-flavored cooking spray. Close lid and grill for 4 to 5 minutes or until bread is toasted and filling is hot. Serve at once.

Each serving equals:

HE: 1½ Protein • 1 Bread • 18 Optional Calories

230 Calories • 2 g Fat • 11 g Protein •
42 g Carbohydrate • 857 mg Sodium •
92 mg Calcium • 9 g Fiber

DIABETIC: 1½ Starch • 1 Meat

Peanut Butter and Bacon Sandwiches

This American classic used to be reserved for special occasions, because making the bacon was always such an operation—the mess, the grease, the time you had to wait for it to be ready. But with real bacon bits handy, this sandwich is ready in a snap!

◐ Serves 4

¼ cup Peter Pan reduced-fat creamy peanut butter
8 slices Healthy Choice Hearty 7-Grain bread
¼ cup Hormel Bacon Bits

Plug in and generously spray both sides of double-sided electric contact grill with butter-flavored cooking spray and preheat for 5 minutes. Meanwhile, spread 1 tablespoon peanut butter on 4 slices of bread. Sprinkle 1 tablespoon bacon bits over peanut butter and top with another slice of bread. Evenly arrange sandwiches on prepared grill. Lightly spray top of sandwiches with butter-flavored cooking spray. Close lid and grill for 4 minutes or until bread is toasted and filling is hot. Serve at once.

Each serving equals:

HE: 1 Bread • 1 Protein • 1 Fat • ¼ Slider • 5 Optional Calories

203 Calories • 7 g Fat • 11 g Protein • 24 g Carbohydrate • 552 mg Sodium • 33 mg Calcium • 4 g Fiber

DIABETIC: 1½ Starch • 1½ Protein • ½ Fat

Grilled BLT Sandwiches

The standard dish is bacon, lettuce, and tomato on white toast, but here's the thing: those delectable ingredients never really get the chance to join hands and get to know each other! But when you add a rich dressing and the heat of your grill, you'll taste the tempting difference. ☻ Serves 4

2 tablespoons Kraft fat-free mayonnaise
2 tablespoons Kraft Fat Free Thousand Island Dressing
8 slices reduced-calorie white or whole wheat bread
2 cups finely shredded lettuce
½ cup peeled and finely chopped fresh tomato
¼ cup Hormel Bacon Bits

Plug in and generously spray both sides of double-sided electric contact grill with butter-flavored cooking spray and preheat for 5 minutes. In a small bowl, combine mayonnaise and Thousand Island dressing. Evenly spread 1½ teaspoons mayonnaise mixture on all slices of bread. In a medium bowl, combine lettuce, tomato, and bacon bits. Spoon a full ½ cup mixture on 4 slices of bread, then top each with another slice of bread, mayonnaise side down. Evenly arrange sandwiches on prepared grill. Lightly spray top of sandwiches with butter-flavored cooking spray. Close lid and grill for 4 to 5 minutes or until bread is toasted and filling is hot. Serve at once.

Each serving equals:

HE: 1 Bread • ¾ Vegetable • ½ Slider •
3 Optional Calories

155 Calories • 3 g Fat • 9 g Protein •
23 g Carbohydrate • 574 mg Sodium •
57 mg Calcium • 2 g Fiber

DIABETIC: 1 Starch • ½ Vegetable • ½ Meat

Cheese and Tomato Sandwiches

The trouble with most grilled cheese and tomato sandwiches, in my opinion, is that the cheese melts faster than the tomato gets warm and soft! But that's one of the flaws that the home grill addresses, I think—and you'll finally get a chance to taste this sandwich the way it was originally dreamed up! ("Mmm-mmm" was the vote of confidence I got from my grandson Spencer when he tasted this!).

☻ Serves 4

> 8 (¾-ounce) slices Kraft reduced-fat Cheddar cheese
> 8 slices reduced-calorie whole wheat or white bread
> 4 (¼-inch thick) ripe tomato slices

Plug in and generously spray both sides of double-sided electric contact grill with butter-flavored cooking spray and preheat for 5 minutes. Meanwhile, evenly arrange a slice of cheese on 4 slices of bread. Place a tomato slice over cheese and top each with another slice of cheese and bread. Evenly arrange sandwiches on prepared grill. Lightly spray top of sandwiches with butter-flavored cooking spray. Close lid and grill for 3 to 4 minutes or until bread is toasted and filling is hot. Serve at once.

Each serving equals:

HE: 2 Protein • 1 Bread • ¼ Vegetable

---

216 Calories • 8 g Fat • 16 g Protein •
20 g Carbohydrate • 588 mg Sodium •
316 mg Calcium • 1 g Fiber

DIABETIC: 1½ Meat • 1 Starch

Egg and Mushroom Sandwiches

I chose fresh mushrooms for this recipe because they're wonderful on the grill. Most other methods of cooking make them shrink too fast, but in a dish like this one, they retain size, shape, and flavor as long as possible.   ☻   Serves 4

4 hard-boiled eggs, chopped
¼ cup Kraft fat-free mayonnaise
½ teaspoon lemon pepper
½ cup chopped fresh mushrooms
8 slices reduced-calorie white bread

Plug in and generously spray both sides of double-sided electric contact grill with butter-flavored cooking spray and preheat for 5 minutes. Meanwhile, in a medium bowl, combine eggs, mayonnaise, and lemon pepper. Stir in mushrooms. Evenly spread about ¼ cup egg mixture on 4 slices of bread, then top each with another slice of bread. Evenly arrange sandwiches on prepared grill. Lightly spray top of sandwiches with butter-flavored cooking spray. Close lid and grill for 4 to 5 minutes or until bread is toasted and filling is hot. Serve at once.

Each serving equals:

HE: 1 Bread • 1 Protein • ¼ Vegetable • 10 Optional Calories

---

182 Calories • 6 g Fat • 12 g Protein • 20 g Carbohydrate • 470 mg Sodium • 62 mg Calcium • 1 g Fiber

---

DIABETIC: 1 Starch • 1 Meat

Deviled Egg Sandwiches

I'm such a fan of summer picnics and potlucks, I always seem to put a deviled egg recipe into each of my cookbooks (sometimes more than one!). This is a terrific way to serve your family and friends the taste of deviled eggs without the extra effort of stuffing the egg halves individually. And see if you don't agree that it's great on the grill!　●　Serves 4

  2 tablespoons Kraft fat-free mayonnaise
  2 tablespoons sweet pickle relish
  2 tablespoons prepared yellow mustard
  1 teaspoon Worcestershire sauce
  1 teaspoon dried parsley flakes
  4 hard-boiled eggs, finely chopped
  8 slices reduced-calorie white bread

Plug in and generously spray both sides of double-sided electric contact grill with butter-flavored cooking spray and preheat for 5 minutes. Meanwhile, in a medium bowl, combine mayonnaise, pickle relish, mustard, Worcestershire sauce, and parsley flakes. Add chopped eggs. Mix well to combine. Evenly spread about ⅓ cup egg mixture on 4 slices of bread, then top each with another slice of bread. Evenly arrange sandwiches on prepared grill. Lightly spray top of sandwiches with butter-flavored cooking spray. Close lid and grill for 4 minutes or until bread is toasted and filling is hot. Serve at once.

Each serving equals:

HE: 1 Bread • 1 Protein • 12 Optional Calories

199 Calories • 7 g Fat • 12 g Protein •
22 g Carbohydrate • 515 mg Sodium •
69 mg Calcium • 1 g Fiber

DIABETIC: 1 Starch • 1 Meat

Western Egg Salad Sandwiches

Here's a sort of omelet-in-a-sandwich idea, with some of your favorite breakfast flavors spread between two slices of bread and grilled until it's soooo good!   ●   Serves 4

1 tablespoon Kraft Fat Free Catalina Dressing
2 tablespoons Kraft fat-free mayonnaise
1 cup + 2 tablespoons (4½ ounces) shredded Kraft reduced-fat
    Cheddar cheese
¼ cup chopped green bell pepper
¼ cup chopped onion
¼ cup chopped ripe olives
2 hard-boiled eggs, chopped
8 slices reduced-calorie whole wheat or white bread

Plug in and generously spray both sides of double-sided electric contact grill with butter-flavored cooking spray and preheat for 5 minutes. Meanwhile, in a large bowl, combine Catalina dressing and mayonnaise. Add Cheddar cheese, green pepper, onion, and olives. Mix well to combine. Stir in chopped eggs. Evenly spread about ½ cup egg mixture on 4 slices of bread, then top each with another slice of bread. Evenly arrange sandwiches on prepared grill. Lightly spray top of sandwiches with butter-flavored cooking spray. Close lid and grill for 4 to 5 minutes or until bread is toasted and filling is hot. Serve at once.

Each serving equals:

HE: 2 Protein • 1 Bread • ¼ Vegetable •
11 Optional Calories

245 Calories • 9 g Fat • 17 g Protein •
24 g Carbohydrate • 652 mg Sodium •
268 mg Calcium • 1 g Fiber

DIABETIC: 2 Meat • 1 Starch

Terrific Tuna Sandwiches

When I think tuna and eggs, I think summertime, picnics under a beautiful tree, and loved ones all around me. (Amazing, isn't it, how food fills us with notions that have nothing to do with the taste!) This quick-and-easy recipe is an all-year-round wonder for feeding our tummies and our hearts. ❂ Serves 4

1 (6-ounce) can white tuna, packed in water, drained and flaked

¼ cup Kraft fat-free mayonnaise

2 teaspoons prepared yellow mustard

1 (2-ounce) jar chopped pimiento, drained

⅛ teaspoon black pepper

2 hard-boiled eggs, chopped

8 slices reduced-calorie whole wheat bread

Plug in and generously spray both sides of double-sided electric contact grill with butter-flavored cooking spray and preheat for 5 minutes. Meanwhile, in a medium bowl, combine tuna, mayonnaise, mustard, pimiento, and black pepper. Stir in chopped eggs. Evenly spread a full ⅓ cup tuna mixture on 4 slices of bread, then top each with another slice of bread. Evenly arrange sandwiches on prepared grill. Lightly spray top of sandwiches with butter-flavored cooking spray. Close lid and grill for 4 minutes or until bread is toasted and filling is hot. Serve at once.

Each serving equals:

HE: 1⅔ Protein • 1 Bread • 10 Optional Calories

201 Calories • 5 g Fat • 18 g Protein •
21 g Carbohydrate • 572 mg Sodium •
57 mg Calcium • 1 g Fiber

DIABETIC: 2 Meat • 1½ Starch

Tempting Tuna Sandwiches

There's a famous quotation that says "I can resist anything except temptation." (Thank you, Oscar Wilde!) I suspect that no one will be able to turn down a taste of tuna grilled to a tempting turn. Why eat everyday-style when you can delight in something this good?

⏺ Serves 4

1 (6-ounce) can white tuna, packed in water, drained and flaked
1/4 cup finely chopped onion
3/4 cup finely chopped celery
1/3 cup (1 1/2 ounces) shredded Kraft reduced-fat Cheddar cheese
1/4 cup chopped ripe olives
1/4 cup Kraft fat-free mayonnaise
1 teaspoon dried parsley flakes
1/8 teaspoon black pepper
8 slices reduced-calorie white or whole wheat bread

Plug in and generously spray both sides of double-sided electric contact grill with butter-flavored cooking spray and preheat for 5 minutes. Meanwhile, in a medium bowl, combine tuna, onion, celery, Cheddar cheese, and olives. Add mayonnaise, parsley flakes, and black pepper. Mix well to combine. Evenly spread about 1/2 cup tuna mixture on 4 slices of bread, then top each with another slice of bread. Evenly arrange sandwiches on prepared grill. Lightly spray top of sandwiches with butter-flavored cooking spray. Close lid and grill for 4 to 5 minutes or until bread is toasted and filling is hot. Serve at once.

Each serving equals:

HE: 1 2/3 Protein • 1 Bread • 1/2 Vegetable • 1/4 Fat • 10 Optional Calories

205 Calories • 5 g Fat • 18 g Protein • 22 g Carbohydrate • 681 mg Sodium • 130 mg Calcium • 1 g Fiber

DIABETIC: 2 Meat • 1 Starch • 1/2 Vegetable

Crunchy Tuna and Cheese Sandwiches

I love grilled cheese and tuna as much as the next person, but I also like a little c-r-u-n-c-h with mine. Even when it's grilled, the celery keeps its bite! ◐ Serves 4

1 (6-ounce) can white tuna, packed in water, drained and flaked
¼ cup Kraft Fat Free Thousand Island Dressing
2 tablespoons Kraft fat-free mayonnaise
½ cup finely chopped celery
1 (2-ounce) jar chopped pimiento, drained
1 teaspoon dried onion flakes
8 slices reduced-calorie bread
4 (¾-ounce) slices Kraft reduced-fat Swiss cheese

Plug in and generously spray both sides of double-sided electric contact grill with butter-flavored cooking spray and preheat for 5 minutes. Meanwhile, in a medium bowl, combine tuna, Thousand Island dressing, mayonnaise, celery, pimiento, and onion flakes. Evenly spread about ½ cup tuna mixture on 4 slices of bread. Place 1 slice Swiss cheese on each, then top each with another slice of bread. Evenly arrange sandwiches on prepared grill. Lightly spray top of sandwiches with butter-flavored cooking spray. Close lid and grill for 4 to 5 minutes or until bread is toasted and filling is hot. Serve at once.

Each serving equals:

HE: 2 Protein • 1 Bread • ¼ Vegetable • ¼ Slider • 7 Optional Calories

255 Calories • 7 g Fat • 21 g Protein •
27 g Carbohydrate • 901 mg Sodium •
239 mg Calcium • 2 g Fiber

DIABETIC: 2 Meat • 1½ Starch/Carbohydrate

Southern Grilled Chicken Salad Sandwich

Do you like surprises when you bite into a sandwich? I do! Well, if you were expecting a regular old chicken salad sandwich, and you found—what? A walnut!—you might wonder what exotic taste buds came up with this recipe. I'm the one, of course, who wondered how sweet apricot flavor would blend with crunchy walnuts into a chicken salad grilled to perfection. I think I got it right!

● Serves 2

2 tablespoons apricot spreadable fruit
2 tablespoons Kraft fat-free mayonnaise
½ teaspoon dried parsley flakes
1 cup (5 ounces) diced cooked chicken breast
2 tablespoons chopped walnuts
4 slices reduced-calorie whole wheat bread

Plug in and generously spray both sides of double-sided electric contact grill with butter-flavored cooking spray and preheat for 5 minutes. Meanwhile, in a medium bowl, combine spreadable fruit, mayonnaise, and parsley flakes. Add chicken and walnuts. Mix well to combine. Evenly spread about ½ cup chicken mixture on 2 slices of bread, then top each with another slice of bread. Evenly arrange sandwiches on prepared grill. Lightly spray top of sandwiches with butter-flavored cooking spray. Close lid and grill for 4 to 5 minutes or until bread is toasted and filling is hot. Serve at once.

Each serving equals:

HE: 2½ Protein • 1 Bread • 1 Fruit • ½ Fat • 10 Optional Calories

296 Calories • 8 g Fat • 27 g Protein • 29 g Carbohydrate • 406 mg Sodium • 55 mg Calcium • 1 g Fiber

DIABETIC: 2½ Meat • 1 Starch • 1 Fruit • 1 Fat

Chicken and Pineapple Salad Sandwiches

No, it's not true that *everything* in Hawaii is served with pineapple—but it does show up in a number of island recipes because it's grown there and tastes better there than just about anywhere in the world. This sandwich invites you to visit those exquisite isles in every bite, reminding us that paradise can taste as great as it looks!

◗ Serves 4

1 tablespoon Grey Poupon Country Dijon Mustard
¼ cup Kraft fat-free mayonnaise
1 (8-ounce) can crushed pineapple, packed in fruit juice, drained
2 teaspoons dried parsley flakes
1 teaspoon dried onion flakes
1 full cup (6 ounces) finely diced cooked chicken breast
8 slices reduced-calorie whole wheat bread

Plug in and generously spray both sides of double-sided electric contact grill with butter-flavored cooking spray and preheat for 5 minutes. Meanwhile, in a medium bowl, combine mustard, mayonnaise, pineapple, parsley flakes, and onion flakes. Stir in chicken. Evenly spread about ¼ cup chicken mixture on 4 slices of bread, then top each with another slice of bread. Evenly arrange sandwiches on prepared grill. Lightly spray top of sandwiches with butter-flavored cooking spray. Close lid and grill for 4 to 5 minutes or until bread is toasted and filling is hot. Serve at once.

Each serving equals:

HE: 1½ Protein • 1 Bread • ¼ Fruit •
10 Optional Calories

195 Calories • 3 g Fat • 18 g Protein •
24 g Carbohydrate • 472 mg Sodium •
53 mg Calcium • 1 g Fiber

DIABETIC: 1½ Meat • 1 Starch • ½ Fat

Chicken Almondine Salad Sandwiches

I have always loved almonds in hot dishes because they retain their special crunch longer than many other nuts you might add. They're also extra-good when paired with chicken, and this sandwich spotlights a delectable dining duo with real pizzazz!

☻ Serves 4

1 full cup (6 ounces) chopped cooked chicken breast
¼ cup finely chopped blanched almonds
¼ cup Kraft fat-free mayonnaise
1 teaspoon dried parsley flakes
⅛ teaspoon black pepper
8 slices reduced-calorie white bread

Plug in and generously spray both sides of double-sided electric contact grill with butter-flavored cooking spray and preheat for 5 minutes. Meanwhile, in a medium bowl, combine chicken, almonds, and mayonnaise. Add parsley flakes and black pepper. Mix well to combine. Evenly spread about ¼ cup chicken mixture on 4 slices of bread, then top each with another slice of bread. Evenly arrange sandwiches on prepared grill. Lightly spray top of sandwiches with butter-flavored cooking spray. Close lid and grill for 4 to 5 minutes or until bread is toasted and filling is hot. Serve at once.

Each serving equals:

HE: 1¾ Protein • 1 Bread • ½ Fat •
10 Optional Calories

218 Calories • 6 g Fat • 20 g Protein •
21 g Carbohydrate • 382 mg Sodium •
61 mg Calcium • 1 g Fiber

DIABETIC: 2 Meat • 1 Starch • 1 Fat

Country Club Chicken Sandwiches

There's a certain luxurious quality to foods served at a country club—maybe because they want you to know you're not dining at a diner! Here, the creamy chicken and sauce peek out of the bread and let you know that something good is on the way.

● Serves 4

¼ cup Land O Lakes no-fat sour cream

2 tablespoons Kraft fat-free mayonnaise

1 teaspoon lemon juice

1 cup (5 ounces) finely chopped cooked chicken breast

¼ cup chopped ripe olives

1 (2-ounce) jar chopped pimiento, drained

6 tablespoons finely chopped celery

2 tablespoons finely chopped onion

8 slices reduced-calorie white bread

Plug in and generously spray both sides of double-sided electric contact grill with butter-flavored cooking spray and preheat for 5 minutes. Meanwhile, in a medium bowl, combine sour cream, mayonnaise, and lemon juice. Stir in chicken, olives, and pimiento. Add celery and onion. Mix well to combine. Evenly spread about ⅓ cup chicken mixture on 4 slices of bread, then top each with another slice of bread. Evenly arrange sandwiches on prepared grill. Lightly spray top of sandwiches with butter-flavored cooking spray. Close lid and grill for 4 to 5 minutes or until bread is toasted and filling is hot. Serve at once.

Each serving equals:

HE: 1¼ Protein • 1 Bread • ¼ Fat • ¼ Vegetable • ¼ Slider

---

187 Calories • 3 g Fat • 17 g Protein •
23 g Carbohydrate • 396 mg Sodium •
73 mg Calcium • 1 g Fiber

DIABETIC: 1½ Starch • 1 Meat

Special Chicken Salad Sandwiches

What makes life truly special? Well, besides spending as much time as we can with the people we love and finding work that fulfills us, I think it means finding pleasure in each new day, new friend, new flavor. Here's a sandwich I thought was special enough to earn the name!   ☯   Serves 4

> 1 full cup (6 ounces) diced cooked chicken breast
> ¼ cup Hormel Bacon Bits
> ⅓ cup (1½ ounces) shredded Kraft reduced-fat Cheddar cheese
> ¼ cup Kraft fat-free mayonnaise
> 1 (2.5-ounce) jar sliced mushrooms, drained
> ¼ teaspoon lemon pepper
> 8 slices reduced-calorie white bread

Plug in and generously spray both sides of double-sided electric contact grill with butter-flavored cooking spray and preheat for 5 minutes. Meanwhile, in a medium bowl, combine chicken, bacon bits, and Cheddar cheese. Add mayonnaise, mushrooms, and lemon pepper. Mix well to combine. Evenly spread about ½ cup chicken mixture on 4 slices of bread, then top each with another slice of bread. Evenly arrange sandwiches on prepared grill. Lightly spray top of sandwiches with butter-flavored cooking spray. Close lid and grill for 4 to 5 minutes or until bread is toasted and filling is hot. Serve at once.

Each serving equals:

HE: 2 Protein • 1 Bread • ¼ Vegetable • ¼ Slider • 15 Optional Calories

---

238 Calories • 6 g Fat • 24 g Protein •
22 g Carbohydrate • 807 mg Sodium •
115 mg Calcium • 1 g Fiber

DIABETIC: 2 Meat • 1½ Starch/Carbohydrate

Chicken and Cheese Sandwiches

If you're a fan of chicken salad the way it's usually served—chilled, on a bed of lettuce—I bet you'll thrill to this warmed-up version made special with melted cheese! How can something so tasty and rich be good for you? Just one of those everyday miracles I love to share.   ☻   Serves 4

1 full cup (6 ounces) finely diced cooked chicken breast
½ cup finely chopped celery
⅓ cup Kraft fat-free mayonnaise
1 teaspoon lemon juice
8 slices reduced-calorie white bread
4 (¾-ounce) slices Kraft reduced-fat American cheese

Plug in and generously spray both sides of double-sided electric contact grill with butter-flavored cooking spray and preheat for 5 minutes. Meanwhile, in a medium bowl, combine chicken, celery, mayonnaise, and lemon juice. Evenly spread a full ¼ cup chicken mixture on 4 slices of bread. Top each with 1 slice of cheese and another slice of bread. Evenly arrange sandwiches on prepared grill. Lightly spray top of sandwiches with butter-flavored cooking spray. Close lid and grill for 4 to 5 minutes or until bread is toasted and filling hot. Serve at once.

Each serving equals:

HE: 2½ Protein • 1 Bread • ¼ Vegetable •
13 Optional Calories

---

230 Calories • 6 g Fat • 22 g Protein •
22 g Carbohydrate • 726 mg Sodium •
302 mg Calcium • 1 g Fiber

DIABETIC: 2½ Meat • 1 Starch

Ham and Chicken Salad Sandwiches

Can't decide between ham or chicken for lunch today? No problem! Have both, by blending these two favorites into one great grilled delight. ❂ Serves 4

> 1 cup (5 ounces) finely diced cooked chicken breast
> ½ cup finely chopped celery
> ¼ cup Kraft fat-free mayonnaise
> ⅛ teaspoon black pepper
> 1 (6-ounce) package Healthy Choice Deli Style Ham
> 8 slices reduced-calorie whole wheat or white bread

Plug in and generously spray both sides of double-sided electric contact grill with butter-flavored cooking spray and preheat for 5 minutes. Meanwhile, in a small bowl, combine chicken, celery, mayonnaise, and black pepper. Place about 2 slices of ham on all slices of bread. Top 4 slices with about ¼ cup chicken mixture. Cover with remaining bread slices, ham side down. Evenly arrange sandwiches on prepared grill. Lightly spray top of sandwiches with butter-flavored cooking spray. Close lid and grill for 3 to 4 minutes or until bread is toasted and filling is hot. Serve at once.

Each serving equals:

HE: 2¼ Protein • 1 Bread • ¼ Vegetable •
17 Optional Calories

208 Calories • 4 g Fat • 23 g Protein •
20 g Carbohydrate • 703 mg Sodium •
47 mg Calcium • 1 g Fiber

DIABETIC: 2 Meat • 1 Starch

Shanghai Salad Sandwiches

The culinary culture of China doesn't normally include sandwiches, but one of the ways we've made this country such a melting pot is taking elements of two different cuisines and blending them. The American sandwich, the Chinese bean sprout and soy sauce—and voilà, you've got something fun and new!   ☻   Serves 4

1 (16-ounce) can bean sprouts, rinsed and very well drained
½ cup (3 ounces) finely chopped Dubuque 97% fat-free ham
    or any extra-lean ham
1 cup (5 ounces) finely chopped cooked chicken breast
1 tablespoon reduced-sodium soy sauce
1 teaspoon white distilled vinegar
1 tablespoon Splenda Granular
8 slices reduced-calorie white bread

Plug in and generously spray both sides of double-sided electric contact grill with butter-flavored cooking spray and preheat for 5 minutes. Meanwhile, in a medium bowl, combine bean sprouts, ham, chicken, soy sauce, vinegar, and Splenda. Evenly spread a full ½ cup salad mixture on 4 slices of bread, then top each with another slice of bread. Evenly arrange sandwiches on prepared grill. Lightly spray top of sandwiches with butter-flavored cooking spray. Close lid and grill for 4 to 5 minutes or until bread is toasted and filling is hot. Serve at once.

Each serving equals:

HE: 1¾ Protein • 1 Bread • ½ Vegetable •
2 Optional Calories

199 Calories • 3 g Fat • 21 g Protein •
22 g Carbohydrate • 668 mg Sodium •
53 mg Calcium • 1 g Fiber

DIABETIC: 2 Meat • 1 Starch • ½ Vegetable

Ham–Veggie Salad Sandwiches

Don't believe anyone who says that looks aren't important when it comes to eating! This sandwich is as pretty as it is tasty, and that makes it a hit even before the first bite. ☻   Serves 4

> 2 full cups (12 ounces) finely chopped Dubuque 97% fat-free ham
>   or any extra-lean ham
> 6 tablespoons grated carrots
> 2 tablespoons finely chopped onion
> 2 tablespoons dill pickle relish
> ½ cup Kraft fat-free mayonnaise
> ⅛ teaspoon black pepper
> 8 slices reduced-calorie whole wheat bread

Plug in and generously spray both sides of double-sided electric contact grill with butter-flavored cooking spray and preheat for 5 minutes. Meanwhile, in a medium bowl, combine ham, carrots, onion, dill pickle relish, mayonnaise, and black pepper. Evenly spread about ½ cup ham mixture on 4 slices of bread, then top each with another slice of bread. Evenly arrange sandwiches on prepared grill. Lightly spray top of sandwiches with butter-flavored cooking spray. Close lid and grill for 4 to 5 minutes or until bread is toasted and filling is hot. Serve at once.

Each serving equals:

HE: 2¼ Protein • 1 Bread • ¼ Vegetable • ¼ Slider

220 Calories • 4 g Fat • 20 g Protein •
26 g Carbohydrate • 984 mg Sodium •
41 mg Calcium • 2 g Fiber

DIABETIC: 2 Meat • 1½ Starch/Carbohydrate

Ham and Cabbage Sandwiches

Grilled ham and cheese is a deli standard, but I decided to make a good thing so much better by adding the munchy magnificence of cabbage. This recipe works with all types of ham, but I thought it was especially good with the honey ham.   ☻   Serves 4

> 2 cups shredded cabbage
> ¼ cup Kraft fat-free mayonnaise
> ⅛ teaspoon black pepper
> 1 (6-ounce) package Healthy Choice Deli Sliced Honey Ham
> 4 (¾-ounce) slices Kraft reduced-fat Cheddar cheese
> 8 slices reduced-calorie rye bread

Plug in and generously spray both sides of double-sided electric contact grill with butter-flavored cooking spray and preheat for 5 minutes. Meanwhile, in a medium bowl, combine cabbage, mayonnaise, and black pepper. Evenly arrange 3 to 4 slices of ham on 4 slices of bread. Top each with ½ cup cabbage mixture, 1 slice Cheddar cheese, and another slice of bread. Lightly spray top of sandwiches with butter-flavored cooking spray. Evenly arrange sandwiches on prepared grill. Close lid and grill for 5 to 6 minutes or until bread is toasted and filling is hot. Serve at once.

Each serving equals:

HE: 2 Protein • 1 Bread • ½ Vegetable •
10 Optional Calories

---

239 Calories • 7 g Fat • 18 g Protein •
26 g Carbohydrate • 907 mg Sodium •
198 mg Calcium • 3 g Fiber

DIABETIC: 2 Meat • 1½ Starch/Carbohydrate •
½ Vegetable

Caribbean Ham Salad Sandwiches

Do you find that you're more adventurous on vacation than you usually are at home? When you're in a new place, you're more likely to risk a taste on a local favorite, even if the combination of ingredients is quirky or unusual. Well, pretend you're somewhere tropical when you bite into this ham-coconut-carrot extravaganza!

◑ Serves 4

> 1 full cup (6 ounces) finely diced Dubuque 97% fat-free ham or
> any extra-lean ham
> ¼ cup raisins
> 2 tablespoons flaked coconut
> ½ cup shredded carrots
> ¼ cup Kraft fat-free mayonnaise
> 8 slices reduced-calorie whole wheat bread
> 4 (¾-ounce) slices Kraft reduced-fat Cheddar cheese

Plug in and generously spray both sides of double-sided electric contact grill with butter-flavored cooking spray and preheat for 5 minutes. Meanwhile, in a medium bowl, combine ham, raisins, coconut, carrots, and mayonnaise. Evenly spread about ½ cup ham mixture on 4 slices of bread. Place 1 slice of Cheddar cheese over ham mixture, then top each with another slice of bread. Evenly arrange sandwiches on prepared grill. Lightly spray top of sandwiches with butter-flavored cooking spray. Close lid and grill for 4 to 5 minutes or until bread is toasted and filling is hot. Serve at once.

Each serving equals:

HE: 2 Protein • 1 Bread • ½ Fruit • ¼ Vegetable •
18 Optional Calories

259 Calories • 7 g Fat • 19 g Protein •
30 g Carbohydrate • 863 mg Sodium •
234 mg Calcium • 2 g Fiber

DIABETIC: 2 Meat • 1 Starch • ½ Fruit

Hawaiian Ham Salad Sandwiches

Something remarkable happens to pineapple on the grill, I discovered—it finds something extra when it's heated. Maybe it's the warmth of the sun that helped it grow so sweet, or maybe it's something that can't quite be explained. Whatever it is, it's delicious!

☻ Serves 4

> 1 (8-ounce) can crushed pineapple, packed in fruit juice, well drained
> ¼ cup Kraft fat-free mayonnaise
> 1 teaspoon dried parsley flakes
> 1 full cup (6 ounces) finely chopped Dubuque 97% fat-free ham or any extra-lean ham
> ¾ cup (3 ounces) shredded Kraft reduced-fat Cheddar cheese
> 8 slices reduced-calorie whole wheat bread

Plug in and generously spray both sides of double-sided electric contact grill with butter-flavored cooking spray and preheat for 5 minutes. Meanwhile, in a medium bowl, combine pineapple, mayonnaise, and parsley flakes. Add ham and Cheddar cheese. Mix well to combine. Evenly spread about ½ cup ham mixture on 4 slices of bread, then top each with another slice of bread. Evenly arrange sandwiches on prepared grill. Lightly spray top of sandwiches with butter-flavored cooking spray. Close lid and grill for 4 to 5 minutes or until bread is toasted and filling is hot. Serve at once.

Each serving equals:

HE: 2 Protein • 1 Bread • ½ Fruit • 10 Optional Calories

230 Calories • 6 g Fat • 18 g Protein • 26 g Carbohydrate • 803 mg Sodium • 185 mg Calcium • 1 g Fiber

DIABETIC: 2 Meat • 1 Starch • ½ Fruit

Italian Grilled Cheese and Pastrami Sandwiches

Break out of the bread rut, and bring home something a little different! The good news is, it'll still fit on your grill. And when you mingle pastrami, cheese, and those special seasonings Italians do best, you'll shout *"Belissima!"*   ♥   Serves 4

> 4 (¾-ounce) slices Kraft reduced-fat mozzarella cheese
> 8 slices reduced-calorie Italian bread
> 1 (2.5-ounce) package sliced Carl Buddig lean pastrami or extra-lean ham
> 2 tablespoons Kraft fat-free mayonnaise
> ½ teaspoon Italian seasoning

Plug in and generously spray both sides of double-sided electric contact grill with olive oil–flavored cooking spray and preheat for 5 minutes. Meanwhile, place 1 slice of mozzarella cheese on 4 slices of bread. Divide pastrami into 4 even portions and place on top of cheese slices. In a small bowl, combine mayonnaise and Italian seasoning. Evenly spread mixture on remaining 4 slices of bread. Place bread slices, mayonnaise side down, over pastrami. Evenly arrange sandwiches on prepared grill. Lightly spray top of sandwiches with olive oil–flavored cooking spray. Close lid and grill for 4 minutes. Serve at once.

Each serving equals:

HE: 1⅔ Protein • 1 Bread • 5 Optional Calories

177 Calories • 5 g Fat • 14 g Protein •
19 g Carbohydrate • 616 mg Sodium •
176 mg Calcium • 1 g Fiber

DIABETIC: 1½ Meat • 1 Starch

Cliff's Reuben Sandwiches

So many people order a Reuben when they're at a restaurant but have never attempted to make this favorite sandwich at home. I offer this handy recipe as a public service, then, so you can enjoy it anytime at all! ☻ Serves 4

2 tablespoons Kraft fat-free mayonnaise
2 tablespoons Kraft Fat Free Thousand Island Dressing
1 (8-ounce) can sauerkraut, well drained
2 (2.5-ounce) packages Carl Buddig 90% lean corned beef, shredded
8 slices reduced-calorie rye bread
4 (¾-ounce) slices Kraft reduced-fat mozzarella or Swiss cheese

Plug in and generously spray both sides of double-sided electric contact grill with butter-flavored cooking spray and preheat for 5 minutes. Meanwhile, in a medium bowl, combine mayonnaise, Thousand Island dressing, sauerkraut, and shredded corned beef. Evenly spread about ½ cup corned beef mixture on 4 slices of bread. Place 1 slice mozzarella cheese over corned beef mixture, then top each with another slice of bread. Evenly arrange sandwiches on prepared grill. Lightly spray top of sandwiches with butter-flavored cooking spray. Close lid and grill for 4 to 5 minutes or until bread is toasted and filling is hot. Serve at once.

Each serving equals:

HE: 2¼ Protein • 1 Bread • ½ Vegetable • 18 Optional Calories

235 Calories • 7 g Fat • 18 g Protein • 25 g Carbohydrate • 981 mg Sodium • 196 mg Calcium • 4 g Fiber

DIABETIC: 2 Meat • 1 Starch • ½ Vegetable

Hot Corned Beef Sandwiches

Another away-from-home dish now comes back to your kitchen, courtesy of the wondrous appliance called a two-sided grill. You don't have to give up enjoying this deli sandwich "out," but aren't you glad to know it can be yours to love at home, too?

◉ Serves 4

> 2 (2.5-ounce) packages Carl Buddig 90% lean corned beef,
>   shredded
> ¼ cup Kraft fat-free mayonnaise
> 2 tablespoons reduced-sodium ketchup
> 1 teaspoon prepared horseradish sauce
> 1 teaspoon prepared yellow mustard
> ½ cup + 1 tablespoon (2¼ ounces) shredded Kraft reduced-fat
>   Cheddar cheese
> 8 slices reduced-calorie white bread

Plug in and generously spray both sides of double-sided electric contact grill with butter-flavored cooking spray and preheat for 5 minutes. Meanwhile, in a medium bowl, combine shredded corned beef, mayonnaise, ketchup, horseradish sauce, and mustard. Stir in Cheddar cheese. Evenly spread about ⅓ cup mixture on 4 slices of bread, then top each with remaining 4 slices of bread. Evenly arrange sandwiches on prepared grill. Lightly spray top of sandwiches with butter-flavored cooking spray. Close lid and grill for 5 to 6 minutes or until bread is toasted and filling is hot. Serve at once.

Each serving equals:

HE: 2 Protein • 1 Bread • 18 Optional Calories

219 Calories • 7 g Fat • 16 g Protein •
23 g Carbohydrate • 976 mg Sodium •
151 mg Calcium • 1 g Fiber

DIABETIC: 2 Meat • 1 Starch

Veggie Pita Sandwiches

For years, you had to visit specialty food shops to find such exotic delicacies as feta cheese, but now we find these treats in nearly every supermarket across America. As times have changed, so have tastes, and feta has been welcomed in communities all over, so this delicately flavored vegetarian sandwich should find lots of fans!

◑ Serves 2

> 2 tablespoons Kraft Fat Free Italian Dressing
> 1 cup chopped onion
> 1 cup chopped fresh mushrooms
> 1 cup peeled and chopped fresh tomato
> 2 tablespoons Kraft fat-free mayonnaise
> 3 tablespoons crumbled feta cheese
> ½ teaspoon dried parsley flakes
> 1 pita bread round, halved

Plug in and generously spray both sides of double-sided electric contact grill with olive oil–flavored cooking spray and preheat for 5 minutes. Meanwhile, in a medium bowl, combine Italian dressing, onion, and mushrooms. Stir in tomato. Evenly arrange vegetable mixture on prepared grill. Close lid and grill for 6 to 7 minutes. Meanwhile, in a small bowl, combine mayonnaise, feta cheese, and parsley flakes. For each sandwich, spoon about ½ cup warm vegetable mixture into a pita half and top with 2 full tablespoons feta cheese mixture. Serve at once.

Each serving equals:

> HE: 3 Vegetable • 1 Bread • ½ Protein •
> 18 Optional Calories
>
> ---
>
> 192 Calories • 4 g Fat • 7 g Protein •
> 32 g Carbohydrate • 675 mg Sodium •
> 119 mg Calcium • 4 g Fiber
>
> ---
>
> DIABETIC: 2½ Vegetable • 1 Starch • ½ Meat

Pita Steak Sandwiches

I think these would make terrific party food—mostly because the ingredients mix up so easily, and you can prepare them ahead of time, grilling and stuffing once your guests arrive. Serving steak is always a good way to show your guests they're special . . . and your family, too! ☻ Serves 4

> 1 cup chopped onion
>
> 1 cup chopped fresh mushrooms
>
> 8 ounces tenderized round steak, cut into 28 pieces
>
> 2 tablespoons Kraft Fat Free Italian Dressing
>
> 2 tablespoons Kraft Fat Free Ranch Dressing
>
> 2 tablespoons Land O Lakes no-fat sour cream
>
> 1 cup chopped cucumber
>
> 1 cup chopped fresh tomato
>
> 2 pita bread rounds, halved

Plug in and generously spray both sides of double-sided electric contact grill with olive oil–flavored cooking spray and preheat for 5 minutes. Meanwhile, in a medium bowl, combine onion, mushrooms, steak pieces, and Italian dressing. Mix well to coat. Evenly arrange steak mixture on prepared grill. Close lid and grill for 7 to 8 minutes. Meanwhile, in a large bowl, combine Ranch dressing and sour cream. Add cucumber and tomato. Mix gently to combine. For each sandwich, stuff about ½ cup steak mixture into a pita half and top with ½ cup cucumber mixture. Serve at once.

Each serving equals:

HE: 2 Vegetable • 1½ Protein • 1 Bread • ¼ Slider

207 Calories • 3 g Fat • 18 g Protein • 27 g Carbohydrate • 405 mg Sodium • 54 mg Calcium • 2 g Fiber

DIABETIC: 1½ Vegetable • 1½ Meat • 1 Starch

Cabbage and More Sandwich Wraps

Cabbage really finds a home on a grill, I discovered, because the concentrated heat awakens its unique flavor but doesn't destroy all that lovely crunch!   ☺   Serves 2

2 tablespoons white distilled vinegar

2 tablespoons Splenda Granular

2 cups chopped cabbage

1/2 cup chopped onion

2 tablespoons Hormel Bacon Bits

2 (6-inch) flour tortillas

6 tablespoons (1 1/2 ounces) shredded Kraft reduced-fat Cheddar cheese

Plug in and generously spray both sides of double-sided electric contact grill with butter-flavored cooking spray and preheat for 5 minutes. Meanwhile, in a large bowl, combine vinegar and Splenda. Add cabbage, onion, and bacon bits. Mix well to combine. Evenly arrange cabbage mixture on prepared grill. Lightly spray top of cabbage mixture with butter-flavored cooking spray. Close lid and grill for 6 to 8 minutes. For each wrap, spoon about 3/4 cup cabbage mixture on a tortilla, sprinkle 3 tablespoons Cheddar cheese over top, and roll tortilla up tightly. Serve at once.

Each serving equals:

HE: 1 1/2 Vegetable • 1 Bread • 1 Protein • 1/4 Slider • 11 Optional Calories

235 Calories • 7 g Fat • 13 g Protein • 30 g Carbohydrate • 632 mg Sodium • 263 mg Calcium • 3 g Fiber

DIABETIC: 1 1/2 Vegetable • 1 Starch • 1 Meat

Philly Steak Wraps

The classic cheese steak is served on a bun, but that doesn't mean you're stuck with one version to eat all the rest of your life! Wraps are an easy way to whip up a quick and satisfying meal in a hurry without sacrificing any flavor. ☻ Serves 4

8 ounces tenderized round steak, cut into 36 pieces
½ cup chopped green bell pepper
1 cup chopped onion
¼ cup Kraft Fat Free Italian Dressing
4 (6-inch) flour tortillas
¾ cup (3 ounces) shredded Kraft reduced-fat mozzarella cheese

Plug in and generously spray both sides of double-sided electric contact grill with olive oil–flavored cooking spray and preheat for 5 minutes. Meanwhile, in a large bowl, combine steak pieces, green pepper, onion, and Italian dressing. Evenly arrange steak mixture on prepared grill. Close lid and grill for 8 to 10 minutes. For each sandwich, spoon a full ⅓ cup meat mixture in center of tortilla, sprinkle 3 tablespoons mozzarella cheese over top, and roll tortilla up tightly. Serve at once.

Each serving equals:

HE: 2½ Protein • 1 Bread • ¾ Vegetable •
8 Optional Calories

264 Calories • 8 g Fat • 23 g Protein •
25 g Carbohydrate • 578 mg Sodium •
222 mg Calcium • 1 g Fiber

DIABETIC: 2 Meat • 1 Starch • ½ Vegetable

Bandstand Cheese Steak Sandwiches

This recipe brings back those old-timey memories of summer concerts in the town square, when families relaxed under the stars and listened to a local band play. Put something peppy on the boom box, and your whole clan will enjoy the feast!   ☻   Serves 4

  2 cups chopped onion
  1 cup chopped green bell pepper
  ⅛ teaspoon black pepper
  2 teaspoons vegetable oil
  8 ounces tenderized round steak, cut into 32 pieces
  4 small French rolls, split in half
  4 (¾-ounce) slices Kraft reduced-fat mozzarella cheese

Plug in and generously spray both sides of double-sided electric contact grill with butter-flavored cooking spray and preheat for 5 minutes. Meanwhile, in a large bowl, combine onion, green pepper, black pepper, and vegetable oil. Add steak pieces. Mix well to combine. Evenly arrange steak mixture on prepared grill. Close lid and grill for 7 to 8 minutes. For each sandwich, spoon about ½ cup steak mixture on a French roll bottom, arrange a mozzarella cheese slice over steak mixture, and top with French roll top. Serve at once.

Each serving equals:

HE: 2½ Protein • 1½ Vegetable • 1 Bread • ½ Fat

300 Calories • 8 g Fat • 25 g Protein •
32 g Carbohydrate • 428 mg Sodium •
220 mg Calcium • 3 g Fiber

DIABETIC: 2½ Meat • 1 Starch • 1 Vegetable • ½ Fat

Tangy Tuna Burgers ❄

This is one of those "toss-it-in, toss-it-in" recipes, when lots of intriguing flavors are blended to create something truly memorable, but easy at the same time. These tuna patties simply sing with good-for-you flavor. ◐ Serves 4

> 1 (6-ounce) can white tuna, packed in water, drained and
>   flaked
> 2 slices reduced-calorie bread, made into crumbs
> ½ cup finely chopped celery
> 2 tablespoons dried onion flakes
> 2 tablespoons Kraft fat-free mayonnaise
> 2 tablespoons chili sauce
> 1 teaspoon lemon juice
> 1 cup diced fresh tomato
> ½ cup finely shredded lettuce
> 2 tablespoons Kraft Fat Free Italian Dressing
> 4 small hamburger buns

Plug in and generously spray both sides of double-sided electric contact grill with butter-flavored cooking spray and preheat for 5 minutes. Meanwhile, in a medium bowl, combine tuna, bread crumbs, celery, and onion flakes. Add mayonnaise, chili sauce, and lemon juice. Mix well to combine. Using a ⅓ cup measuring cup as a guide, form into 4 burgers. Evenly arrange burgers on prepared grill. Lightly spray top of burgers with butter-flavored cooking spray. Close lid and grill for 5 to 6 minutes. Meanwhile, in a small bowl, combine tomato, lettuce, and Italian dressing. For each sandwich, place a tuna burger on a hamburger bun bottom, top with ¼ cup lettuce mixture, and place bun top over all.

Each serving equals:

HE: 1¼ Bread • 1 Protein • 1 Vegetable •
16 Optional Calories

---

187 Calories • 3 g Fat • 14 g Protein •
26 g Carbohydrate • 642 mg Sodium •
36 mg Calcium • 3 g Fiber

DIABETIC: 1½ Starch/Carbohydrate • 1 Meat •
½ Vegetable

Greek Burgers

Cliff and I have never visited the Greek Isles, but as an avid cookbook reader and movie viewer, I've imagined just exactly what such a visit might be like—and how delicious the local food would taste. By blending a few unusual ingredients like the feta cheese, yogurt, and mint into the meat, you can be in Athens in just a few bites!

❤ Serves 6

> 16 ounces extra-lean ground sirloin beef or turkey breast
> ¾ cup finely chopped onion
> 1 tablespoon lemon juice
> 1 teaspoon finely chopped fresh mint or ⅓ teaspoon dried mint
> ¾ cup Dannon plain fat-free yogurt
> 6 tablespoons crumbled feta cheese
> 1½ cups finely chopped lettuce
> 6 small hamburger buns

Plug in and generously spray both sides of double-sided electric contact grill with olive oil–flavored cooking spray and preheat for 5 minutes. Meanwhile, in a large bowl, combine meat, onion, lemon juice, and mint. Using a ⅓ cup measuring cup as a guide, form into 6 burgers. Evenly arrange burgers on prepared grill. Close lid and grill for 5 to 7 minutes. Meanwhile, in a small bowl, combine yogurt and feta cheese. For each sandwich, sprinkle ¼ cup lettuce on a hamburger bun bottom, arrange burger over lettuce, spoon a full 2 tablespoons yogurt mixture over burger, and place hamburger bun top over all.

Each serving equals:

HE: 2¼ Protein • 1 Bread • ½ Vegetable •
15 Optional Calories

---

219 Calories • 7 g Fat • 20 g Protein •
19 g Carbohydrate • 337 mg Sodium •
121 mg Calcium • 2 g Fiber

DIABETIC: 2 Meat • 1 Starch • ½ Vegetable

Olive Burgers

It's probably one of the last ingredients you think about when creating a sandwich filling, maybe because olives are more commonly offered as an accompaniment or side dish. But oh, what they deliver in terms of tangy flavor when you weave them into this special burger blend. ☯ Serves 6

> 16 ounces extra-lean ground sirloin beef or turkey breast
> ½ cup chopped pimiento-stuffed green olives
> 6 tablespoons dried fine bread crumbs
> ¼ cup water
> 2 teaspoons prepared yellow mustard
> 6 small hamburger buns

Plug in and generously spray both sides of double-sided electric contact grill with olive oil–flavored cooking spray and preheat for 5 minutes. Meanwhile, in a large bowl, combine meat, olives, bread crumbs, water, and mustard. Using a ⅓ cup measuring cup as a guide, form into 6 burgers. Evenly arrange burgers on prepared grill. Close lid and grill for 5 to 7 minutes. Serve on hamburger buns.

Each serving equals:

HE: 2 Protein • 1⅓ Bread • ½ Fat

216 Calories • 8 g Fat • 17 g Protein •
19 g Carbohydrate • 490 mg Sodium •
22 mg Calcium • 1 g Fiber

DIABETIC: 2 Meat • 1 Starch • ½ Fat

Bacon Dill Burgers

When you get your fast-food burgers, they often slip in a sliver of pickle, but it doesn't deliver the culinary treat that just a bit of pickle relish can! Prepare this one on the grill, and you've got sizzle to burn. ❍ Serves 6

> 16 ounces extra-lean ground sirloin beef or turkey breast
> ¼ cup Hormel Bacon Bits
> ¼ cup dill pickle relish
> 2 tablespoons Kraft fat-free mayonnaise
> ⅛ teaspoon black pepper
> 6 small hamburger buns

Plug in and generously spray both sides of double-sided electric contact grill with butter-flavored cooking spray and preheat for 5 minutes. Meanwhile, in a large bowl, combine meat, bacon bits, pickle relish, mayonnaise, and black pepper. Using a ⅓ cup measuring cup as a guide, form into 6 burgers. Evenly arrange burgers on prepared grill. Close lid and grill for 5 to 7 minutes. Serve on hamburger buns.

Each serving equals:

HE: 2 Protein • 1 Bread • 19 Optional Calories

---

206 Calories • 6 g Fat • 19 g Protein •
19 g Carbohydrate • 510 mg Sodium •
3 mg Calcium • 1 g Fiber

DIABETIC: 2 Meat • 1 Starch

Popeye Spinach Burgers

Calling all sailor men—and women—to eat hearty and happily tonight! These burgers are bolstered by a vegetable that delivers both healthy iron and rich flavor all at once. Make sure you drain it well; these burgers are plenty moist on their own.   ☻   Serves 6

16 ounces extra-lean ground sirloin beef or turkey breast
1½ cups finely chopped fresh spinach leaves
½ cup + 1 tablespoon dried fine bread crumbs
¾ cup finely chopped onion
1 (2-ounce) jar chopped pimiento, undrained
¼ cup Grey Poupon Country Dijon Mustard
6 (¾-ounce) slices Kraft reduced-fat mozzarella cheese
6 small hamburger buns

Plug in and generously spray both sides of double-sided electric contact grill with olive oil–flavored cooking spray and preheat for 5 minutes. Meanwhile, in a large bowl, combine meat, spinach, bread crumbs, onion, undrained pimiento, and mustard. Using a ½ cup measuring cup as a guide, form into 6 burgers. Evenly arrange burgers on prepared grill. Close lid and grill for 8 to 9 minutes. For each sandwich, place a burger on a hamburger bun bottom, arrange 1 slice mozzarella cheese over burger, and place bun top over all.

Each serving equals:

HE: 3 Protein • 1½ Bread • ½ Vegetable

272 Calories • 8 g Fat • 25 g Protein • 25 g Carbohydrate • 706 mg Sodium • 218 mg Calcium • 3 g Fiber

DIABETIC: 2½ Meat • 1½ Starch • ½ Vegetable

Grilled Cheese Burgers ❄

Tired of the same old, same old? But a cheeseburger is just a cheese-burger, right? Not in my book! It's the sauce, the pepper, and the grill that will make this taste fresh and fun.   ☻   Serves 6

16 ounces extra-lean ground sirloin beef or turkey breast
³/₄ cup (3 ounces) shredded Kraft reduced-fat Cheddar cheese
1 tablespoon dried onion flakes
1¹/₂ teaspoons prepared yellow mustard
¹/₈ teaspoon black pepper
6 small hamburger buns

Plug in and generously spray both sides of double-sided electric contact grill with butter-flavored cooking spray and preheat for 5 minutes. Meanwhile, in a large bowl, combine meat, Cheddar cheese, onion flakes, mustard, and black pepper. Using a ¹/₃ cup measuring cup as a guide, form into 6 burgers. Evenly arrange burgers on prepared grill. Close lid and grill for 5 to 7 minutes. Serve on hamburger buns.

Each serving equals:

HE: 2¹/₂ Protein • 1 Bread

194 Calories • 6 g Fat • 20 g Protein •
15 g Carbohydrate • 309 mg Sodium •
65 mg Calcium • 1 g Fiber

DIABETIC: 2¹/₂ Meat • 1 Starch

Pineapple Burgers

What a great dish for a barbecue moved indoors because of bad weather! Of course, you don't need the excuse of a rainy night to choose these sweet-and-savory burgers—they're spectacular out of season and whenever you've got a hankering for a burger that's anything but ordinary. ☻ Serves 6

1 (8-ounce) can crushed pineapple, packed in fruit juice, well drained
¾ cup finely chopped green bell pepper
2 tablespoons reduced-sodium soy sauce
1 tablespoon Splenda Granular
16 ounces extra-lean ground sirloin beef or turkey breast
6 tablespoons purchased graham cracker crumbs or 6 (2½-inch) graham crackers, made into crumbs
6 small hamburger buns

Plug in and generously spray both sides of double-sided electric contact grill with butter-flavored cooking spray and preheat for 5 minutes. Meanwhile, in a large bowl, combine pineapple, green pepper, soy sauce, and Splenda. Add meat and graham cracker crumbs. Mix well to combine. Using a ½ cup measuring cup as a guide, form into 6 burgers. Evenly arrange burgers on prepared grill. Close lid and grill for 7 to 8 minutes. Serve on hamburger buns.

HINT: A self-seal sandwich bag works great for crushing graham crackers.

Each serving equals:

HE: 2 Protein • 1⅓ Bread • ⅓ Fruit • ¼ Vegetable • 1 Optional Calorie

218 Calories • 6 g Fat • 17 g Protein • 24 g Carbohydrate • 333 mg Sodium • 11 mg Calcium • 2 g Fiber

DIABETIC: 2 Meat • 1½ Starch/Carbohydrate

Gringo Chili Burgers

You can choose your favorite chili sauce and level of heat when you prepare these palate-pleasers. You may also want to experiment with just how "crushed" the cornflakes should be, as your family may like a slightly different texture. But I promise you, any way you do 'em will win their hearts! ☻ Serves 6

> 16 ounces extra-lean ground sirloin beef or turkey breast
> ¾ cup (1½ ounces) crushed cornflakes
> ¼ cup chili sauce
> 1 tablespoon Splenda Granular
> 2 tablespoons fat-free milk
> 6 small hamburger buns

Plug in and generously spray both sides of double-sided electric contact grill with butter-flavored cooking spray and preheat for 5 minutes. Meanwhile, in a large bowl, combine meat, cornflake crumbs, chili sauce, Splenda, and milk. Using a ⅓ cup measuring cup as a guide, form into 6 burgers. Evenly arrange burgers on prepared grill. Close lid and grill for 5 to 7 minutes. Serve on hamburger buns.

Each serving equals:

HE: 2 Protein • 1⅓ Bread • ¼ Slider •
9 Optional Calories

---

193 Calories • 5 g Fat • 17 g Protein •
20 g Carbohydrate • 393 mg Sodium •
17 mg Calcium • 1 g Fiber

DIABETIC: 2 Meat • 1 Starch

Tater Burgers

Love potatoes as much as you love your burgers? You're not alone! For you passionate potato fans, I decided to mix the two together and turn up the heat. The result: as Nat King Cole used to sing, "Unforgettable"! ● Serves 6

> 16 ounces extra-lean ground sirloin beef or turkey breast
> 1½ cups (5 ounces) shredded loose-packed frozen potatoes
> ¾ cup finely chopped onion
> 2 tablespoons reduced-sodium ketchup
> 1 teaspoon dried parsley flakes
> ⅛ teaspoon black pepper
> 6 small hamburger buns

Plug in and generously spray both sides of double-sided electric contact grill with butter-flavored cooking spray and preheat for 5 minutes. Meanwhile, in a large bowl, combine meat, potatoes, onion, ketchup, parsley flakes, and black pepper. Using a ½ cup measuring cup as a guide, form into 6 burgers. Evenly arrange burgers on prepared grill. Close lid and grill for 6 to 8 minutes. Serve on hamburger buns.

HINT: Mr. Dell's frozen shredded potatoes are a good choice or raw shredded potatoes, rinsed and patted dry, may be used in place of frozen potatoes.

Each serving equals:

HE: 2 Protein • 1 Bread • ¼ Vegetable •
18 Optional Calories

---

197 Calories • 5 g Fat • 18 g Protein •
20 g Carbohydrate • 210 mg Sodium •
10 mg Calcium • 2 g Fiber

DIABETIC: 2 Meat • 1½ Starch

Pronto Pizza Burgers

Don't dial up dinner—grill it instead! These pizza-flavored treats are man-pleasers and teen-pleasers, too, perfect for watching football or soccer on a cool fall evening. ☻ Serves 6

> 16 ounces extra-lean ground sirloin beef or turkey breast
> 6 tablespoons dried fine bread crumbs
> 1½ teaspoons pizza or Italian seasoning
> ½ cup finely chopped onion
> ¼ cup finely chopped green bell pepper
> ½ cup + 1 tablespoon (2¼ ounces) shredded Kraft reduced-fat
>   mozzarella cheese
> ¼ cup reduced-sodium ketchup
> 6 small hamburger buns

Plug in and generously spray on both sides of double-sided electric contact grill with olive oil–flavored cooking spray and preheat for 5 minutes. Meanwhile, in a large bowl, combine meat, bread crumbs, pizza seasoning, onion, green pepper, mozzarella cheese, and ketchup. Using a ½ cup measuring cup as a guide, form into 6 burgers. Evenly arrange burgers on prepared grill. Close lid and grill for 5 to 7 minutes. Serve on hamburger buns.

Each serving equals:

HE: 2½ Protein • 1⅓ Bread • ¼ Vegetable •
10 Optional Calories

---

239 Calories • 7 g Fat • 21 g Protein •
23 g Carbohydrate • 334 mg Sodium •
91 mg Calcium • 2 g Fiber

DIABETIC: 2½ Meat • 1½ Starch

Worcestershire Burgers

It's remarkable how one little bottle of sauce imported from England can transform a simple hamburger into a dining experience—but it will! There's a wondrous richness that weaves through every bite of the beef (or turkey) and provides true taste satisfaction.

❂ Serves 6

> 16 ounces extra-lean ground sirloin beef or turkey breast
> ¼ cup Worcestershire sauce
> 1 tablespoon dried parsley flakes
> ⅛ teaspoon black pepper
> 6 small hamburger buns

Plug in and generously spray both sides of double-sided electric contact grill with butter-flavored cooking spray and preheat for 5 minutes. Meanwhile, in a large bowl, combine meat, Worcestershire sauce, parsley flakes, and black pepper. Using a ⅓ cup measuring cup as a guide, form into 6 burgers. Evenly arrange burgers on prepared grill. Close lid and grill for 5 to 7 minutes. Serve on hamburger buns.

Each serving equals:

HE: 2 Protein • 1 Bread

165 Calories • 5 g Fat • 16 g Protein •
14 g Carbohydrate • 252 mg Sodium •
6 mg Calcium • 1 g Fiber

DIABETIC: 2 Meat • 1 Starch

Deviled Burgers

Heat and tangy zest are the secret sauce that goes into these unique burgers, and I hope you'll agree that saucy is splendid!

💿 Serves 6

> 1 tablespoon prepared yellow mustard
> ¼ cup reduced-sodium ketchup
> 1 teaspoon prepared horseradish sauce
> 1½ teaspoons Worcestershire sauce
> 16 ounces extra-lean ground sirloin beef or turkey breast
> ¾ cup finely chopped onion
> 6 small hamburger buns

Plug in and generously spray both sides of double-sided electric contact grill with butter-flavored cooking spray and preheat for 5 minutes. Meanwhile, in a large bowl, combine mustard, ketchup, horseradish sauce, and Worcestershire sauce. Add meat and onion. Mix well to combine. Using a ⅓ cup measuring cup as a guide, form into 6 burgers. Evenly arrange burgers on prepared grill. Close lid and grill for 5 to 7 minutes. Serve on hamburger buns.

Each serving equals:

HE: 2 Protein • 1 Bread • ¼ Vegetable •
10 Optional Calories

---

198 Calories • 6 g Fat • 17 g Protein •
19 g Carbohydrate • 235 mg Sodium •
11 mg Calcium • 1 g Fiber

DIABETIC: 2 Meat • 1 Starch

Mushroom Burgers

I still marvel how good no-fat sour cream is, and I regularly offer thanks to those inventive nutrition scientists who've figured out how to keep the good stuff and remove the less-healthy fat. This creamy concoction is sure to become a family favorite—at my house as well as yours!   ☻   Serves 6

> 16 ounces extra-lean ground sirloin beef or turkey breast
> ½ cup + 1 tablespoon dried fine bread crumbs
> 1 (2.5-ounce) jar sliced mushrooms, undrained
> ¼ cup finely chopped onion
> ¼ cup Land O Lakes no-fat sour cream
> ⅛ teaspoon black pepper
> 6 small hamburger buns

Plug in and generously spray both sides of double-sided electric contact grill with butter-flavored cooking spray and preheat for 5 minutes. Meanwhile, in a large bowl, combine meat, bread crumbs, undrained mushrooms, onion, sour cream, and black pepper. Using a ½ cup measuring cup as a guide, form into 6 burgers. Evenly arrange burgers on prepared grill. Close lid and grill for 6 to 8 minutes. Serve on hamburger buns.

Each serving equals:

HE: 2 Protein • 1½ Bread • ¼ Vegetable •
15 Optional Calories

230 Calories • 6 g Fat • 18 g Protein •
26 g Carbohydrate • 360 mg Sodium •
36 mg Calcium • 2 g Fiber

DIABETIC: 2 Meat • 1½ Starch

Porcupine Burgers ❄

I almost called these "porcupette burgers" because those baby porcupines are wonderfully soft and touchable for the first half hour of their lives. (Alas, the spiky spines are soon stiff and hard.) You'll love the rich tomato flavor of this dish, which reminds me a little of stuffed peppers. ☺ Serves 6

> 16 ounces extra-lean ground sirloin beef or turkey breast
> ½ cup cold cooked rice
> 2 teaspoons dried onion flakes ☆
> 1½ teaspoons dried parsley flakes ☆
> 2 teaspoons Worcestershire sauce
> 1 (10¾-ounce) can Healthy Request Tomato Soup ☆
> ¼ cup fat-free milk
> 6 small hamburger buns

Plug in and generously spray both sides of double-sided electric contact grill with butter-flavored cooking spray and preheat for 5 minutes. Meanwhile, in a large bowl, combine meat, rice, 1 teaspoon onion flakes, 1 teaspoon parsley flakes, Worcestershire sauce, and 2 tablespoons tomato soup. Using a ⅓ cup measuring cup as a guide, form into 6 burgers. Evenly arrange burgers on prepared grill. Close lid and grill for 6 to 7 minutes. Meanwhile, in a medium saucepan, combine remaining 1 teaspoon onion flakes, remaining ½ teaspoon parsley flakes, remaining tomato soup, and milk. Cook over medium-low heat while burgers are grilling, stirring often. For each serving, place a burger on a bun bottom, spoon a full 2 tablespoons sauce over burger, and place bun top over all.

HINT: Usually ⅓ cup uncooked instant rice cooks to about ½ cup.

Each serving equals:

HE: 2 Protein • 1 Bread • ½ Slider •
7 Optional Calories

---

230 Calories • 6 g Fat • 18 g Protein •
26 g Carbohydrate • 416 mg Sodium •
20 mg Calcium • 2 g Fiber

DIABETIC: 2 Meat • 1½ Starch

Tex-Mex Taco Burgers

You could call this version "taco-on-a-bun" and you'd be absolutely right—but the secret's in the seasoning of the burgers before they hit the grill. You may also want to serve these burgers with salsa as well as ketchup. ☻ Serves 6

16 ounces extra-lean ground sirloin beef or turkey breast

⅓ cup (1½ ounces) shredded Kraft reduced-fat Cheddar cheese

6 tablespoons dried fine bread crumbs

¼ cup reduced-sodium tomato juice

2 teaspoons taco seasoning

6 small hamburger buns

¾ cup finely shredded lettuce

½ cup finely chopped fresh tomato

6 tablespoons Land O Lakes no-fat sour cream

Plug in and generously spray both sides of double-sided electric contact grill with butter-flavored cooking spray and preheat for 5 minutes. Meanwhile, in a large bowl, combine meat, Cheddar cheese, bread crumbs, tomato juice, and taco seasoning. Using a ⅓ cup measuring cup as a guide, form into 6 burgers. Evenly arrange burgers on prepared grill. Close lid and grill for 5 to 7 minutes. For each sandwich, place a burger on a hamburger bun bottom, sprinkle 2 tablespoons lettuce over burger, spoon 1 full tablespoon tomato and 1 tablespoon sour cream over lettuce, and place bun top over all.

Each serving equals:

HE: 2⅓ Protein • 1⅓ Bread • ½ Vegetable • 15 Optional Calories

226 Calories • 6 g Fat • 20 g Protein • 23 g Carbohydrate • 364 mg Sodium • 89 mg Calcium • 1 g Fiber

DIABETIC: 2½ Meat • 1 Starch • ½ Vegetable

Barbecued Burgers

✻

You could try to invent your own way of infusing smoky barbecue flavor into burgers, but why bother when you can call on a healthy sauce to do the job? Feel free to add more onion if your family relishes that special flavor! ☻ Serves 6

> 16 ounces extra-lean ground sirloin beef or turkey breast
> ½ cup + 1 tablespoon dried fine bread crumbs
> ¼ cup Healthy Choice Barbecue Sauce
> 1 teaspoon dried onion flakes
> 1 teaspoon dried parsley flakes
> 6 small hamburger buns

Plug in and generously spray both sides of double-sided electric contact grill with butter-flavored cooking spray and preheat for 5 minutes. Meanwhile, in a large bowl, combine meat, bread crumbs, barbecue sauce, onion flakes, and parsley flakes. Using a ⅓ cup measuring cup as a guide, form into 6 burgers. Evenly arrange burgers on prepared grill. Close lid and grill for 5 to 7 minutes. Serve on hamburger buns.

Each serving equals:

HE: 2 Protein • 1½ Bread • 8 Optional Calories

214 Calories • 6 g Fat • 18 g Protein •
22 g Carbohydrate • 304 mg Sodium •
28 mg Calcium • 2 g Fiber

DIABETIC: 2 Meat • 1½ Starch

Veggie Meat Burgers

I didn't create this recipe as a simple timesaver, though I suppose it could be viewed as one since it combines the meat and vegetables into one handy patty! Let me assure you that I was only thinking of the irresistible flavors teamed up for taste when I created this dish. What you do with it on the nights you're really rushed is up to you!

● Serves 6

> 1 cup shredded carrots
> ½ cup finely chopped onion
> 1 cup finely chopped cabbage
> 16 ounces extra-lean ground sirloin beef or turkey breast
> ¼ cup reduced-sodium ketchup
> 1 teaspoon dried parsley flakes
> ⅛ teaspoon black pepper
> 6 small hamburger buns

Plug in and generously spray both sides of double-sided electric contact grill with butter-flavored cooking spray and preheat for 5 minutes. Meanwhile, in a large bowl, combine carrots, onion, and cabbage. Add meat, ketchup, parsley flakes, and black pepper. Mix well to combine. Using a ½ cup measuring cup as a guide, form into 6 burgers. Evenly arrange burgers on prepared grill. Close lid and grill for 7 to 9 minutes. Serve on hamburger buns.

Each serving equals:

HE: 2 Protein • 1 Bread • ⅔ Vegetable • 10 Optional Calories

197 Calories • 5 g Fat • 18 g Protein • 20 g Carbohydrate • 212 mg Sodium • 19 mg Calcium • 2 g Fiber

DIABETIC: 2 Meat • 1 Starch • ½ Vegetable

L.A. Burgers

Many people say that the most original (or even off-the-wall) food ideas come from the West Coast, and it could be true. This seemed to me like a recipe that would win hearts out in La-La Land. It's hearty, healthy, and a little bit wild . . . just like some of our favorite movie stars! ◑ Serves 6

16 ounces extra-lean ground sirloin beef or turkey breast
¾ cup peeled and chopped fresh tomatoes
¾ cup chopped onion
½ cup cold cooked rice
6 tablespoons dried fine bread crumbs
2 tablespoons reduced-sodium ketchup
1 teaspoon dried basil
6 lettuce leaves
6 small hamburger buns
3 (¾-ounce) slices Kraft reduced-fat mozzarella cheese

Plug in and generously spray both sides of double-sided electric contact grill with butter-flavored cooking spray and preheat for 5 minutes. Meanwhile, in a large bowl, combine meat, tomatoes, onion, rice, bread crumbs, ketchup, and basil. Using a ½ cup measuring cup as a guide, form into 6 burgers. Evenly arrange burgers on prepared grill. Close lid and grill for 6 to 8 minutes. Cut mozzarella cheese slices in half. For each sandwich, place a lettuce leaf on a hamburger bun bottom, arrange burger over lettuce leaf, place a half slice mozzarella cheese over burger, and place bun top over all.

HINT: Usually ⅓ cup uncooked instant rice cooks to about ½ cup.

Each serving equals:

HE: 2½ Protein • 1½ Bread • ½ Vegetable • 5 Optional Calories

255 Calories • 7 g Fat • 21 g Protein • 27 g Carbohydrate • 338 mg Sodium • 104 mg Calcium • 2 g Fiber

DIABETIC: 2½ Meat • 1½ Starch • ½ Vegetable

Fast-Food Lane Burgers

One of the reasons everyone seems to love the grill is that it gets food to the table FAST! Instead of lining up with the crowd in the drive-through, stir this up quickly and grill, grill, grill. You'll be rewarded with something special every time.   ☻   Serves 6

> 16 ounces extra-lean ground sirloin beef or turkey breast
> 1 teaspoon dried parsley flakes
> ⅛ teaspoon black pepper
> ⅓ cup Kraft fat-free mayonnaise
> 1 tablespoon reduced-sodium ketchup
> 1 tablespoon sweet pickle relish
> 6 lettuce leaves
> 6 (¼-inch) fresh tomato slices
> 6 small hamburger buns

Plug in and generously spray both sides of double-sided electric contact grill with butter-flavored cooking spray and preheat for 5 minutes. Meanwhile, in a large bowl, combine meat, parsley flakes, and black pepper. Using a ⅓ cup measuring cup as a guide, form into 6 burgers. Evenly arrange burgers on prepared grill. Close lid and grill for 5 to 7 minutes. Meanwhile, in a small bowl, combine mayonnaise, ketchup, and pickle relish. For each sandwich, place a lettuce leaf and tomato slice on a hamburger bun bottom, arrange burger on tomato, spoon about 1 tablespoon sauce over burger, and place hamburger bun top over all.

Each serving equals:

HE: 2 Protein • 1 Bread • ¼ Vegetable •
14 Optional Calories

---

185 Calories • 5 g Fat • 17 g Protein •
18 g Carbohydrate • 319 mg Sodium •
11 mg Calcium • 2 g Fiber

DIABETIC: 2 Meat • 1 Starch

Russian Borscht Burgers

While I was preparing this recipe, I thought that it would be fun to serve them as part of a festive Fourth of July red-white-and-blue menu, since beets do tend to turn whatever dish they're part of a rosy red. But whatever you're celebrating, this dish will deliver luscious, creamy flavor. ☻ Serves 6

2 tablespoons Land O Lakes no-fat sour cream
2 teaspoons prepared horseradish sauce
16 ounces extra-lean ground sirloin beef or turkey breast
⅔ cup instant potato flakes
1 (8-ounce) can diced beets, rinsed and well drained
½ cup chopped onion
1 cup shredded cabbage
⅛ teaspoon black pepper
6 small hamburger buns

Plug in and generously spray both sides of double-sided electric contact grill with butter-flavored cooking spray and preheat for 5 minutes. Meanwhile, in a large bowl, combine sour cream and horseradish sauce. Add meat, potato flakes, beets, onion, cabbage, and black pepper. Mix well to combine. Using a ½ cup measuring cup as a guide, form into 6 burgers. Evenly arrange burgers on prepared grill. Close lid and grill for 6 to 8 minutes. Serve on hamburger buns.

Each serving equals:

HE: 2 Protein • 1⅓ Bread • ⅔ Vegetable •
7 Optional Calories

221 Calories • 5 g Fat • 18 g Protein •
26 g Carbohydrate • 308 mg Sodium •
31 mg Calcium • 2 g Fiber

DIABETIC: 2 Meat • 1½ Starch • 1 Vegetable

Bavarian Burgers

We often get in a culinary rut, ordering the same few dishes on restaurant menus year after year after year. Are you a cheeseburger person who always has American cheese topping your burger? Why not break with tradition and try this Swiss cheese–inspired version that is also a little sweet and a touch tangy?   ☻   Serves 6

16 ounces extra-lean ground sirloin beef or turkey breast
1 (8-ounce) can sauerkraut, well drained
½ cup finely chopped onion
6 tablespoons dried fine bread crumbs
¼ cup reduced-sodium ketchup
½ teaspoon caraway seeds
1 tablespoon Splenda Granular
3 (¾-ounce) slices Kraft reduced-fat Swiss cheese
6 small hamburger buns

Plug in and generously spray both sides of double-sided electric contact grill with butter-flavored cooking spray and preheat for 5 minutes. Meanwhile, in a large bowl, combine meat, sauerkraut, onion, bread crumbs, ketchup, caraway seeds, and Splenda. Using a ¼ cup measuring cup as a guide, form into 12 thin burgers. Cut Swiss cheese slices in half. Arrange a half slice of Swiss cheese over 6 burgers and top each with another burger. Crimp edges to seal in cheese. Evenly arrange burgers on prepared grill. Close lid and grill for 5 to 6 minutes. Serve on hamburger buns.

Each serving equals:

HE: 2½ Protein • 1⅓ Bread • ½ Vegetable • 17 Optional Calories

247 Calories • 7 g Fat • 21 g Protein • 25 g Carbohydrate • 493 mg Sodium • 128 mg Calcium • 2 g Fiber

DIABETIC: 2½ Meat • 1 Starch • ½ Vegetable

Sweet 'n' Sour Burgers

When you mix the tomato sauce and vinegar into your meat, you'll know at a glance just why this recipe produces the moistest burgers you can imagine! And when you top them with more tangy sauce—well, who could blame anyone for wanting to lick the plate?

⊘ Serves 6

> 16 ounces extra-lean ground sirloin beef or turkey breast
> ½ cup finely chopped onion
> ½ cup finely chopped green bell pepper
> 14 small fat-free saltine crackers, made into crumbs
> 1 (8-ounce) can Hunt's Tomato Sauce ☆
> ¼ cup white distilled vinegar ☆
> ¼ cup Splenda Granular ☆
> 6 small hamburger buns

Plug in and generously spray both sides of double-sided electric contact grill with butter-flavored cooking spray and preheat for 5 minutes. Meanwhile, in a large bowl, combine meat, onion, green pepper, cracker crumbs, 2 tablespoons tomato sauce, 2 tablespoons vinegar, and 2 tablespoons Splenda. Using a ½ cup measuring cup as a guide, form into 6 burgers. Evenly arrange burgers on prepared grill. Close lid and grill for 5 to 7 minutes. Meanwhile, in a small saucepan, combine remaining tomato sauce, remaining 2 tablespoons vinegar, and remaining 2 tablespoons Splenda. Cook over medium-low heat while burgers are grilling, stirring occasionally. For each sandwich, place a burger on a hamburger bun bottom, drizzle about 2 tablespoons sauce over burger, and place bun top over all.

HINT: A self-seal sandwich bag works great for crushing crackers.

Each serving equals:

HE: 2 Protein • 1⅓ Bread • 1 Vegetable •
4 Optional Calories

254 Calories • 6 g Fat • 18 g Protein •
32 g Carbohydrate • 543 mg Sodium •
14 mg Calcium • 2 g Fiber

DIABETIC: 2 Meat • 1½ Starch • 1 Vegetable

German Pretzel Burgers

I bet most of you have never mixed crushed pretzels into your burger meat, and yes, I also suspect that the sauerkraut is a bit of a surprise as well. Why not launch Oktoberfest at your house with these fun and flavorful burgers—and a beer or root beer, if that's your pleasure? ◐ Serves 6

> 16 ounces extra-lean ground sirloin beef or turkey breast
> ¾ cup (2¼ ounces) crushed pretzels
> ½ cup finely chopped onion
> ¼ cup reduced-sodium ketchup
> 1½ teaspoons prepared yellow mustard
> 6 small hamburger buns
> 1 (8-ounce) can sauerkraut, well drained

Plug in and generously spray both sides of double-sided electric contact grill with butter-flavored cooking spray and preheat for 5 minutes. Meanwhile, in a large bowl, combine meat, pretzels, onion, ketchup, and mustard. Using a ⅓ cup measuring cup as a guide, form into 6 burgers. Evenly arrange burgers on prepared grill. Close lid and grill for 5 to 7 minutes. For each sandwich, place a burger on a hamburger bun bottom, spoon a full 1 tablespoon sauerkraut over burger, and place bun top over all.

HINT: A self-seal sandwich bag works great for crushing pretzels.

Each serving equals:

HE: 2 Protein • 1½ Bread • ½ Vegetable • 15 Optional Calories

238 Calories • 6 g Fat • 18 g Protein • 28 g Carbohydrate • 471 mg Sodium • 19 mg Calcium • 2 g Fiber

DIABETIC: 2 Meat • 1½ Starch • ½ Vegetable

Tex-Mex Burgers

I always say, why use ordinary bread crumbs in your burgers when you could be crumbling up corn chips? Mmm-mmm. This is such a fun recipe to serve, I bet you'll make it a regular on your table. I just hope the folks at your house can agree on the heat of the salsa. You might remember I live with a man who likes smoke coming out of his ears! ☻ Serves 6

16 ounces extra-lean ground
    sirloin beef or turkey
    breast
1 (1.5-ounce) package taco
    seasoning mix
½ cup (1⅓ ounces) crushed
    Dorito's Baked Corn Chips
    or WOW Tortilla Chips

¼ cup water
¾ cup chunky salsa (mild,
    medium, or hot)
6 tablespoons Land O Lakes
    no-fat sour cream
6 lettuce leaves
6 small hamburger buns

Plug in and generously spray both sides of double-sided electric contact grill with butter-flavored cooking spray and preheat for 5 minutes. Meanwhile, in a large bowl, combine meat, taco seasoning mix, crushed corn chips, and water. Using a ⅓ cup measuring cup as a guide, form into 6 burgers. Evenly arrange burgers on prepared grill. Close lid and grill for 5 to 7 minutes. Meanwhile, in a small bowl, combine salsa and sour cream. For each sandwich, place 1 lettuce leaf on a hamburger bun bottom, arrange a burger over lettuce, spoon 2 tablespoons salsa mixture over burger, and place bun top over all.

Each serving equals:

HE: 2 Protein • 1½ Bread • ¼ Vegetable •
15 Optional Calories

---

197 Calories • 5 g Fat • 18 g Protein •
20 g Carbohydrate • 466 mg Sodium •
29 mg Calcium • 2 g Fiber

DIABETIC: 2 Meat • 1½ Starch

San Francisco Open-Faced Burgers

Does it surprise you when a dish is both sweet and tangy? This recipe invites a varied crowd of flavors to work together, and their end product is something as unique as the Golden Gate Bridge!

○ Serves 6

16 ounces extra-lean ground sirloin beef or turkey breast

½ cup (2¼ ounces) wheat germ

1 teaspoon dried parsley flakes

¼ teaspoon dried minced garlic

¼ cup water

6 tablespoons grape spreadable fruit

6 tablespoons reduced-sodium ketchup

2 tablespoons slivered almonds

6 slices reduced-calorie sourdough bread, toasted

Plug in and generously spray both sides of double-sided electric contact grill with butter-flavored cooking spray and preheat for 5 minutes. Meanwhile, in a large bowl, combine meat, wheat germ, parsley flakes, garlic, and water. Using a ⅓ cup measuring cup as a guide, form into 6 burgers. Evenly arrange burgers on prepared grill. Close lid and grill for 5 to 7 minutes. Meanwhile, in a small saucepan, combine spreadable fruit, ketchup, and almonds. Simmer over low heat while burgers are grilling, stirring occasionally. For each sandwich, place 1 slice of toast on a plate, arrange a burger on toast, and spoon 1 tablespoon sauce over burger.

Each serving equals:

HE: 2 Protein • 1 Bread • 1 Fruit • ¼ Fat • ¼ Slider • 2 Optional Calories

250 Calories • 6 g Fat • 21 g Protein • 28 g Carbohydrate • 166 mg Sodium • 33 mg Calcium • 2 g Fiber

DIABETIC: 2 Meat • 1 Starch • 1 Fruit • ½ Fat

Open-Faced Stroganoff Burgers

Here's a recipe that reminds us just why we love the nonstick coating on our saucepans and grills—it makes for easy cleanup when the dish is this creamy-good! ☻ Serves 6

16 ounces extra-lean ground sirloin beef or turkey breast
1 (4-ounce) jar sliced mushrooms, drained ☆
½ cup + 1 tablespoon dried fine bread crumbs
2 teaspoons dried onion flakes
¼ cup Land O Lakes no-fat sour cream ☆
1 (10¾-ounce) can Healthy Request Cream of Mushroom Soup ☆
6 slices reduced-calorie white bread, toasted

Plug in and generously spray both sides of double-sided electric contact grill with butter-flavored cooking spray and preheat for 5 minutes. Meanwhile, in a large bowl, combine meat, ½ cup mushrooms, bread crumbs, onion flakes, 2 tablespoons sour cream, and 2 tablespoons mushroom soup. Using a ⅓ cup measuring cup as a guide, form into 6 burgers. Evenly arrange burgers on prepared grill. Close lid and grill for 5 to 7 minutes. Meanwhile, in a medium saucepan, combine remaining ½ cup mushrooms, remaining 2 tablespoons sour cream, and remaining mushroom soup. Cook over medium-low heat while burgers are grilling, stirring occasionally. For each sandwich, place 1 slice of toast on a plate, arrange a burger on toast, and spoon a full 2 tablespoons mushroom sauce over burger.

Each serving equals:

HE: 2 Protein • 1½ Bread • ⅓ Vegetable • ¼ Slider • 18 Optional Calories

226 Calories • 6 g Fat • 20 g Protein • 23 g Carbohydrate • 535 mg Sodium • 97 mg Calcium • 1 g Fiber

DIABETIC: 2 Meat • 1½ Starch/Carbohydrate

Salisbury Open-Faced Burgers

Cliff has always loved my many versions of Salisbury steak, so I expected him to gobble this one up with pleasure. I was right! The sauce is especially tasty, so make sure you spoon up every last little drop. 　　❤　　Serves 6

> 16 ounces extra-lean ground sirloin beef or turkey breast
> 6 tablespoons dried fine bread crumbs
> 1 cup finely chopped onion
> 1/4 cup reduced-sodium ketchup ☆
> 1 (10¾-ounce) can Healthy Request Cream of Mushroom Soup ☆
> 2 teaspoons prepared yellow mustard
> 6 slices reduced-calorie white bread, toasted

Plug in and generously spray both sides of double-sided electric contact grill with butter-flavored cooking spray and preheat for 5 minutes. Meanwhile, in a large bowl, combine meat, bread crumbs, onion, 2 tablespoons ketchup, and 2 tablespoons mushroom soup. Using a 1/2 cup measuring cup as a guide, form into 6 burgers. Evenly arrange burgers on prepared grill. Close lid and grill for 5 to 7 minutes. Meanwhile, in a medium saucepan, combine remaining 2 tablespoons ketchup, remaining mushroom soup, and mustard. Cook over medium-low heat while burgers are grilling, stirring occasionally. For each sandwich, place 1 slice of toast on a plate, arrange a burger on toast, and spoon about 2 tablespoons sauce mixture over burger.

Each serving equals:

> HE: 2 Protein • 1⅓ Bread • ⅓ Vegetable • ¼ Slider • 18 Optional Calories
>
> ---
>
> 222 Calories • 6 g Fat • 19 g Protein • 23 g Carbohydrate • 435 mg Sodium • 82 mg Calcium • 1 g Fiber
>
> ---
>
> DIABETIC: 2 Meat • 1½ Starch/Carbohydrate

Open-Faced Roman Burgers

Italian food is one of America's most popular ethnic cuisines, and this cheesy-tomato recipe is my idea of how burgers would be served in a family kitchen in Rome. (They might swap the Cheddar for mozzarella on occasion, but otherwise I bet they'd quickly ask for seconds!)   ☻   Serves 6

16 ounces extra-lean ground sirloin beef or turkey breast

½ cup + 1 tablespoon dried fine bread crumbs

½ cup finely chopped onion

⅓ cup (1½ ounces) shredded Kraft reduced-fat mozzarella cheese

1 (8-ounce) can Hunt's Tomato Sauce ☆

1 (8-ounce) can tomatoes, finely chopped and undrained

1 tablespoon Splenda Granular

1 teaspoon Italian seasoning

⅛ teaspoon black pepper

6 slices reduced-calorie Italian bread, toasted

Plug in and generously spray both sides of double-sided electric contact grill with olive oil–flavored cooking spray and preheat for 5 minutes. Meanwhile, in a large bowl, combine meat, bread crumbs, onion, mozzarella cheese, and ¼ cup tomato sauce. Using a ½ cup measuring cup as a guide, form into 6 burgers. Evenly arrange burgers on prepared grill. Close lid and grill for 5 to 7 minutes. Meanwhile, in a medium saucepan, combine remaining ¾ cup tomato sauce, undrained tomatoes, Splenda, Italian seasoning, and black pepper. Cook over medium-low heat while burgers are grilling, stirring occasionally. For each sandwich, place 1 piece of toast on a plate, arrange a burger on toast, and spoon about 3 tablespoons sauce mixture over burger.

Each serving equals:

HE: 2⅓ Protein • 1½ Bread • 1½ Vegetable •
1 Optional Calorie

222 Calories • 6 g Fat • 20 g Protein •
22 g Carbohydrate • 590 mg Sodium •
102 mg Calcium • 2 g Fiber

DIABETIC: 2 Meat • 1½ Starch • 1½ Vegetable

Marvelous Main Dishes

*M*ost of our most memorable meals center on rich and meaty entrées *that satisfy our taste buds and tummies at the same time they appeal to our eyes. I hope you'll agree that the recipes in this book are no exception. While most of us began using our grills to get the fat out of burgers and other meats, we soon learned that so much more was possible with this innovative appliance. I particularly like the way it worked for basics like chicken breasts and fish fillets, because grilling turns what could be ordinary into extraordinary in just a few minutes.*

Make every meal an occasion with these exciting main events, whatever cuisine you're in the mood for! If chicken is on the menu, you'll discover how fresh and fun poultry can taste with **Grilled Chicken with Sweet Cucumber Salsa, Grilled Sunshine Chicken Salad,** and **Tuscany Chicken and Pasta.** If your family is in the mood for fish, choose from **Mexican Fish Grill, Salmon Cakes with Cheese Sauce,** or **Batter Grilled Fish.** If they've got a hankering for pork or ham, you can opt for **Hawaiian Ham Grill, Maple-Glazed Pork Tenders, Creole Pork and Rice,** or **Tex-Mex Pork with Corn Salsa.** And if beef is the only thing that will satisfy, you can serve up **French Onion Meat Loaf Patties, Easy Beef and Broccoli, Horseradish Beef Hash,** or **Olive-Stuffed Steaks.**

Batter Grilled Fish

❄

This is so simple, you'll wonder why you haven't thought of doing it before now. You're getting all the pluses of deep-fried flavor with none of the negatives! (And children love it, too—just ask my granddaughter Ellie!)　●　Serves 4

6 tablespoons Bisquick Reduced Fat Baking Mix
⅓ cup fat-free milk
1 teaspoon lemon pepper
16 ounces white fish, cut into 4 pieces

Plug in and generously spray both sides of a double-sided electric contact grill with butter-flavored cooking spray and preheat for 5 minutes. Meanwhile, in a pie plate, combine baking mix, milk, and lemon pepper. Dip fish pieces into batter. Evenly arrange coated fish pieces on prepared grill. Drizzle any remaining batter evenly over fish pieces. Close lid and grill for 6 to 7 minutes or until fish flakes easily and batter is golden brown.

Each serving equals:

HE: 2¼ Protein • ½ Bread • 8 Optional Calories

173 Calories • 5 g Fat • 22 g Protein •
10 g Carbohydrate • 196 mg Sodium •
64 mg Calcium • 0 g Fiber

DIABETIC: 3 Meat • ½ Starch

Fiesta Fish

Salsa is best known to most of us as a dip for taco chips or something to spoon onto enchiladas. But it's also a great starting point for flavorful sauces and marinades that are sure to transform very plain ingredients like white fish and rice into the makings of a feast.

⭕ Serves 4

> ¼ cup thick, chunky salsa (mild, medium, or hot)
>
> ¾ cup chopped onion
>
> 1 teaspoon chili seasoning
>
> 16 ounces white fish, cut into 28 pieces
>
> 2 cups hot cooked rice

Plug in and generously spray both sides of double-sided electric contact grill with butter-flavored cooking spray and preheat for 5 minutes. Meanwhile, in a large bowl, combine salsa, onion, and chili seasoning. Gently stir in fish pieces. Evenly arrange fish mixture on prepared grill. Close lid and grill for 6 to 7 minutes or until fish flakes easily. For each serving, place ½ cup hot rice on a plate and spoon about ½ cup fish mixture over top.

HINT: Usually 1⅓ cups uncooked instant rice cooks to about 2 cups.

Each serving equals:

HE: 2¼ Protein • 1 Bread • ½ Vegetable

232 Calories • 4 g Fat • 27 g Protein •
22 g Carbohydrate • 306 mg Sodium •
54 mg Calcium • 2 g Fiber

DIABETIC: 3 Meat • 1 Starch • ½ Vegetable

Grande Fish Fillets

A cracker crust is an American country classic that goes back to the 1950s and even earlier, but it's a tradition that is still beloved today by many. It's perfect for holding in the moisture of tender, flaky fish.

● Serves 4

> ¼ cup Kraft Fat Free Catalina Dressing
> ½ teaspoon chili seasoning
> 1 teaspoon dried parsley flakes
> 10 Ritz Reduced Fat Crackers, made into fine crumbs
> 16 ounces white fish, cut into 4 pieces

Plug in and generously spray both sides of double-sided electric contact grill with butter-flavored cooking spray and preheat for 5 minutes. Meanwhile, in a shallow saucer, combine Catalina dressing, chili seasoning, and parsley flakes. Place cracker crumbs in another shallow saucer. Using a pastry brush, coat fish pieces on both sides with sauce mixture, then roll in cracker crumbs. Evenly arrange coated fish on prepared grill. Drizzle any remaining sauce mixture or cracker crumbs evenly over fish pieces. Lightly spray top of fish pieces with butter-flavored cooking spray. Close lid and grill for 6 to 7 minutes or until fish flakes easily.

HINT: A self-seal sandwich bag works great for crushing crackers.

Each serving equals:

HE: 2¼ Protein • ½ Bread • ¼ Slider •
5 Optional Calories

---

172 Calories • 4 g Fat • 24 g Protein •
10 g Carbohydrate • 328 mg Sodium •
51 mg Calcium • 0 g Fiber

DIABETIC: 3 Meat • ½ Starch/Carbohydrate

Mexican Fish Grill

Fish isn't the first thought most people have when they think of Mexican cooking, but the truth is that a lot of the country is coast-line, where seafood influences the local dishes. Here's a quick-and-easy way to enjoy a dip in the ocean, Mexican style.

◐ Serves 4

> ¼ cup Kraft Fat Free Catalina Dressing
>
> 1 teaspoon chili seasoning
>
> 16 ounces white fish, cut into 4 pieces
>
> 1 (10¾-ounce) can Healthy Request Tomato Soup
>
> ½ cup chunky salsa (mild, medium, or hot)
>
> ¼ cup (1 ounce) shredded Kraft reduced-fat Cheddar cheese

Plug in and generously spray both sides of double-sided electric contact grill with butter-flavored cooking spray and preheat for 5 minutes. Meanwhile, in a shallow saucer, combine Catalina dressing and chili seasoning. Using a pastry brush, coat fish pieces on both sides with sauce mixture. Evenly arrange coated fish pieces on prepared grill. Drizzle any remaining sauce mixture evenly over fish pieces. Close lid and grill for 6 to 7 minutes or until fish flakes easily. Meanwhile, in a medium saucepan, combine tomato soup and salsa. Cook over medium heat while fish is grilling, stirring often. For each serving, place 1 piece of fish on a plate, spoon ⅓ cup sauce over fish, and sprinkle 1 tablespoon Cheddar cheese over top.

Each serving equals:

HE: 2½ Protein • ¼ Vegetable • ¾ Slider • 12 Optional Calories

212 Calories • 4 g Fat • 25 g Protein • 19 g Carbohydrate • 766 mg Sodium • 43 mg Calcium • 2 g Fiber

DIABETIC: 3 Meat • 1 Starch/Carbohydrate

Scandinavian Grilled Fish ❄

Cliff's family originally came from a part of the world where fish is found in a place of honor at every festive meal. This luscious way to present plain fish fillets as something special would make them proud!   ☻   Serves 4

> 2 tablespoons Kraft Fat Free Ranch Dressing
> 1 tablespoon + 1 teaspoon I Can't Believe It's Not Butter! Light
>   Margarine, melted
> 16 ounces white fish, cut into 4 pieces
> 1 (10¾-ounce) can Healthy Request Cream of Mushroom Soup
> ¼ cup Land O Lakes no-fat sour cream
> 1 (2.5-ounce) can sliced mushrooms, drained
> ¼ teaspoon dried dill weed

Plug in and generously spray both sides of double-sided electric contact grill with butter-flavored cooking spray and preheat for 5 minutes. Meanwhile, in a shallow saucer, combine Ranch dressing and melted margarine. Using a pastry brush, coat fish pieces on both sides with sauce mixture. Evenly arrange coated fish pieces on prepared grill. Drizzle any remaining sauce mixture evenly over fish pieces. Close lid and grill for 6 to 7 minutes or until fish flakes easily. Meanwhile, in a medium saucepan, combine mushroom soup, sour cream, mushrooms, and dill weed. Cook over medium-low heat while fish is grilling, stirring often. For each serving, place 1 piece of fish on a plate and spoon about ⅓ cup mushroom sauce over top.

Each serving equals:

HE: 2¼ Protein • ½ Fat • ¼ Vegetable • ½ Slider •
14 Optional Calories

202 Calories • 6 g Fat • 25 g Protein •
12 g Carbohydrate • 590 mg Sodium •
128 mg Calcium • 1 g Fiber

DIABETIC: 3 Meat • 1 Starch/Carbohydrate • ½ Fat

Salmon Cakes with Cheese Sauce

Creamy, cheesy, scrumptious, and so good for you—can any dish live up to those expectations? The answer is in the eating and the applause that is sure to follow. ☯ Serves 6

> 1 cup instant potato flakes
> 1 (14¾-ounce) can skinless and boneless pink salmon, packed in
>   water, drained and flaked
> ¾ cup finely chopped onion
> 1 egg or equivalent in egg substitute
> 2 tablespoons hot water
> ¾ teaspoon dried dill weed ☆
> 1 (10¾-ounce) can Healthy Request Cream of Mushroom Soup
> ¾ cup (3 ounces) shredded Kraft reduced-fat Cheddar cheese

Plug in and generously spray both sides of double-sided electric contact grill with butter-flavored cooking spray and preheat for 5 minutes. Meanwhile, in a large bowl, combine dry potato flakes, salmon, onion, egg, water, and ½ teaspoon dill weed. Mix well to combine. Using a ⅓ cup measuring cup as a guide, form mixture into 6 cakes. Evenly arrange cakes on prepared grill. Lightly spray top of cakes with butter-flavored cooking spray. Close lid and grill for 5 to 6 minutes or until salmon cakes are golden brown. Meanwhile, in a medium saucepan, combine mushroom soup, Cheddar cheese, and remaining ¼ teaspoon dill weed. Cook over medium-low heat while salmon cakes are grilling, stirring occasionally. For each serving, place 1 salmon cake on a plate and drizzle a full 2 tablespoons cheese sauce over top.

Each serving equals:

HE: 3 Protein • ½ Bread • ¼ Vegetable • ¼ Slider •
8 Optional Calories

---

212 Calories • 8 g Fat • 20 g Protein •
15 g Carbohydrate • 735 mg Sodium •
291 mg Calcium • 1 g Fiber

DIABETIC: 3 Meat • 1 Starch/Carbohydrate

Pacific Tuna Cakes
with Cucumber Sauce

Many people who grew up on tuna fish sandwiches tend not to think any further when it comes to this canned staple found on nearly every pantry shelf. But I think it's time to view this healthy fish as a jewel to be surrounded with flavors that make it shimmer and shine.   ○   Serves 4

¾ cup Land O Lakes no-fat sour cream
½ cup finely chopped cucumber
¼ teaspoon dried dill weed
1 teaspoon dried onion flakes
2 (6-ounce) cans white tuna, packed in water, drained and flaked
6 tablespoons dried fine bread crumbs
½ cup chopped onion
½ cup finely chopped celery
1 egg, beaten, or equivalent in egg substitute
⅓ cup Kraft fat-free mayonnaise

Plug in and generously spray both sides of double-sided electric contact grill with butter-flavored cooking spray and preheat for 5 minutes. Meanwhile, in a medium bowl, combine sour cream, cucumber, dill weed, and onion flakes. Cover and refrigerate while preparing tuna cakes. In a large bowl, combine tuna, bread crumbs, onion, and celery. Add egg and mayonnaise. Mix well to combine. Using a ½ cup measuring cup as a guide, form into 4 cakes. Evenly arrange cakes on prepared grill. Lightly spray top of cakes with butter-flavored cooking spray. Close lid and grill for 6 to 7 minutes or until tuna cakes are golden brown. For each serving, place 1 tuna cake on a plate and spoon about ¼ cup cucumber sauce over top.

Each serving equals:

HE: 2½ Protein • ¾ Vegetable • ½ Bread •
½ Slider • 18 Optional Calories

213 Calories • 5 g Fat • 22 g Protein •
20 g Carbohydrate • 603 mg Sodium •
114 mg Calcium • 1 g Fiber

DIABETIC: 3 Meat • 1 Starch/Carboydrate • ½ Vegetable

New England Grilled Crab Cakes ❄

Crab cake recipes abound, but those that were born in New England may be the oldest tradition for crab in this country. Finding the perfect proportion between crabmeat and the rest of the ingredients is a fine art, but I hope you'll agree that these are lusciously moist and spiced just right. ☻ Serves 4 (2 cakes each)

> 2 (4.5-ounce drained weight) cans crabmeat, drained and flaked
> ¾ cup dried fine bread crumbs
> ½ cup finely chopped onion
> 1 (2-ounce) jar chopped pimiento, drained
> 1 egg or equivalent in egg substitute
> 2 tablespoons Land O Lakes no-fat sour cream
> 1 teaspoon dried parsley flakes
> ⅛ teaspoon black pepper

Plug in and generously spray both sides of double-sided electric contact grill with butter-flavored cooking spray and preheat for 5 minutes. Meanwhile, in a large bowl, combine crabmeat, bread crumbs, onion, and pimiento. Add egg, sour cream, parsley flakes, and black pepper. Mix well to combine. Using a ¼ cup measuring cup as a guide, form into 8 cakes. Evenly arrange crab cakes on prepared grill. Lightly spray top of cakes with butter-flavored cooking spray. Close lid and grill for 6 to 7 minutes or until crab cakes are golden brown.

Each serving equals:

HE: 2½ Protein • 1 Bread • ¼ Vegetable • 8 Optional Calories

180 Calories • 4 g Fat • 18 g Protein • 18 g Carbohydrate • 415 mg Sodium • 132 mg Calcium • 1 g Fiber

DIABETIC: 2½ Meat • 1 Starch

Sunshine Chicken Salad

If there's a "pure gold" salad recipe in this book, I'd say it was this one, because it's got the shimmering warmth of the sun in every single bite! It combines crunch and sweetness to deliver super-duper satisfaction. ◐ Serves 4

> ¼ cup orange marmalade spreadable fruit ☆
> 6 tablespoons Kraft Fat Free French Dressing ☆
> 1 teaspoon dried parsley flakes
> 1½ cups (8 ounces) diced cooked chicken breast
> ¼ cup (1 ounce) chopped walnuts
> 1 cup shredded carrots
> 4 cups shredded lettuce

Plug in and generously spray both sides of double-sided electric contact grill with butter-flavored cooking spray and preheat for 5 minutes. Meanwhile, in a large bowl, combine 2 tablespoons spreadable fruit, 2 tablespoons French dressing, and parsley flakes. Add chicken, walnuts, and carrots. Mix well to coat. Evenly arrange chicken mixture on prepared grill. Lightly spray top of chicken mixture with butter-flavored cooking spray. Close lid and grill for 6 to 7 minutes. Meanwhile, in same bowl, combine remaining 2 tablespoons spreadable fruit and remaining ¼ cup French dressing. Add lettuce. Toss well to coat. For each serving, place 1 cup lettuce mixture on a plate and spoon about ½ cup hot chicken mixture over top.

Each serving equals:

HE: 2¼ Protein • 1½ Vegetable • 1 Fruit • ½ Fat • ¼ Slider • 18 Optional Calories

243 Calories • 7 g Fat • 20 g Protein • 25 g Carbohydrate • 285 mg Sodium • 62 mg Calcium • 3 g Fiber

DIABETIC: 2 Meat • 1½ Vegetable • 1 Fruit • 1 Fat

Main Dish Chicken and Pear Salad

What a perfect summer salad this one is, with the kind of flavor combination you usually don't find on many menus. But this recipe proves that a little of this and a little of that makes for fireworks!

☻ Serves 4

> *3 tablespoons Kraft Fat Free Ranch Dressing*
> *1 tablespoon white distilled vinegar*
> *1 tablespoon Splenda Granular*
> *1½ cups (8 ounces) diced cooked chicken breast*
> *¼ cup (1 ounce) chopped walnuts*
> *1½ cups (3 small) sliced unpeeled Bartlett pears*
> *4 cups shredded lettuce*
> *¼ cup crumbled blue cheese*

Plug in and generously spray both sides of double-sided electric contact grill with butter-flavored cooking spray and preheat for 5 minutes. Meanwhile, in a large bowl, combine Ranch dressing, vinegar, and Splenda. Stir in chicken, walnuts, and pears. Evenly arrange chicken mixture on prepared grill. Lightly spray top of chicken mixture with butter-flavored cooking spray. Close lid and grill for 6 to 7 minutes. For each serving, place 1 cup lettuce on a plate, spoon about ¾ cup chicken mixture over lettuce, and sprinkle 1 tablespoon blue cheese over top.

Each serving equals:

HE: 2½ Protein • 1 Vegetable • ¾ Fruit • ½ Fat •
¼ Slider • 1 Optional Calorie

---

249 Calories • 9 g Fat • 22 g Protein •
20 g Carbohydrate • 302 mg Sodium •
106 mg Calcium • 3 g Fiber

DIABETIC: 2 Meat • 1 Vegetable • 1 Fruit • 1 Fat

Chicken and Orange Luncheon Salad

When you add heat to the fruity coating of plain chicken breast, you make magic! It's true—and it's terrific. If you just can't eat another bite of the usual grilled chicken salad, invite your fellow diners to whisper "abracadabra" and dine deliciously on the results.

○ Serves 4

¼ cup orange marmalade spreadable fruit

1 teaspoon dried onion flakes

1 teaspoon dried parsley flakes

16 ounces skinned and boned uncooked chicken breast,
*   cut into 36 pieces*

4 cups torn romaine lettuce

1 (11-ounce) can mandarin oranges, rinsed and drained

¼ cup Kraft Fat Free French Dressing

Plug in and generously spray both sides of double-sided electric contact grill with butter-flavored cooking spray and preheat for 5 minutes. Meanwhile, in a large bowl, combine spreadable fruit, onion flakes, and parsley flakes. Add chicken. Mix well to coat. Evenly arrange chicken mixture on prepared grill. Lightly spray top of chicken mixture with butter-flavored cooking spray. Close lid and grill for 7 to 8 minutes or until chicken is tender. Meanwhile, in another large bowl, combine romaine lettuce and mandarin oranges. Add French dressing. Toss gently to coat. For each serving, place a full cup lettuce mixture on a plate and spoon 9 chicken pieces over top.

Each serving equals:

HE: 3 Protein • 1½ Fruit • 1 Vegetable • ¼ Slider •
5 Optional Calories

231 Calories • 3 g Fat • 24 g Protein •
27 g Carbohydrate • 218 mg Sodium •
33 mg Calcium • 1 g Fiber

DIABETIC: 3 Meat • 1½ Fruit • 1 Vegetable

Chicken à la Grill with Noodles ❄

I've stirred up many versions of this old-fashioned delight, but making it on the grill seemed to be stretching it more than a little. But when I finally created the recipe, I discovered that everything old is new again—and tastier than ever!

☺ Serves 4

> ¼ cup Kraft fat-free mayonnaise
> 1 (2-ounce) jar chopped pimiento, undrained
> 1 teaspoon dried parsley flakes
> 1½ cups (8 ounces) diced cooked chicken breast
> 1 cup frozen peas, thawed
> 1 cup chopped fresh mushrooms
> 2 cups hot cooked noodles, rinsed and drained
> ¼ cup Land O Lakes no-fat sour cream

Plug in and generously spray both sides of double-sided electric contact grill with butter-flavored cooking spray and preheat for 5 minutes. Meanwhile, in a large bowl, combine mayonnaise, undrained pimiento, and parsley flakes. Add chicken, peas, and mushrooms. Mix well to combine. Evenly arrange chicken mixture on prepared grill. Lightly spray top of chicken mixture with butter-flavored cooking spray. Close lid and grill for 10 minutes. For each serving, place ½ cup noodles on a plate, spoon about ½ cup chicken mixture over noodles, and top with 1 tablespoon sour cream.

HINTS: 1. Thaw peas by placing in a colander and rinsing under hot water for 1 minute.
2. Usually 1¾ cups uncooked noodles cooks to about 2 cups.

Each serving equals:

HE: 2 Protein • 1½ Bread • ½ Vegetable • ¼ Slider •
5 Optional Calories

---

252 Calories • 4 g Fat • 24 g Protein •
30 g Carbohydrate • 230 mg Sodium •
48 mg Calcium • 3 g Fiber

DIABETIC: 2 Meat • 1½ Starch • ½ Vegetable

Chicken and Carrots in Orange Glaze

❋

When heat meets sweet, *wheeeeee*—amazing flavors emerge! This dish turns a couple of unlikely ingredients (the marmalade and Diet Mountain Dew) into the stuff of sweet dreams.   ◑   Serves 4

> 6 tablespoons orange marmalade spreadable fruit
> ¼ cup Diet Mountain Dew
> 1 teaspoon dried parsley flakes
> 16 ounces skinned and boned uncooked chicken breast, cut into 32
>   pieces
> 2 cups frozen sliced carrots, thawed
> ½ cup chopped onion
> 2 cups hot cooked rice

Plug in and generously spray both sides of double-sided electric contact grill with butter-flavored cooking spray and preheat for 5 minutes. Meanwhile, in a large bowl, combine spreadable fruit, Diet Mountain Dew, and parsley flakes. Add chicken, carrots, and onion. Mix well to coat. Evenly arrange chicken mixture on prepared grill. Lightly spray top of chicken mixture with butter-flavored cooking spray. Close lid and grill for 7 to 8 minutes or until chicken is tender. For each serving, place ½ cup rice on a plate and spoon about 1 cup chicken mixture over top.

HINT: Usually 1⅓ cups uncooked instant rice cooks to about 2
    cups.

Each serving equals:

HE: 3 Protein • 1½ Fruit • 1¼ Vegetable • 1 Bread

275 Calories • 3 g Fat • 26 g Protein •
36 g Carbohydrate • 100 mg Sodium •
43 mg Calcium • 3 g Fiber

DIABETIC: 3 Meat • 1½ Fruit • 1 Vegetable • 1 Starch

Chicken with Sweet Cucumber Salsa

I've heard it said that there are as many kinds of salsa as there are days in the year, but certainly all kinds of fresh veggies can be combined into a fantastic salsa blend like this one! If you've got a garden like mine that by summer's end seems to be bursting with produce, start chopping—and eating well! ☻ Serves 4

1 tablespoon white distilled vinegar

2 tablespoons Splenda Granular

1 cup unpeeled and chopped cucumber

¼ cup finely chopped red onion

¼ cup chopped red bell pepper

¼ cup sliced ripe olives

¼ cup Kraft Fat Free Catalina Dressing

16 ounces skinned and boned uncooked chicken breast,
*   cut into 4 pieces*

Plug in and generously spray both sides of double-sided electric contact grill with butter-flavored cooking spray and preheat for 5 minutes. Meanwhile, in a medium bowl, combine vinegar and Splenda. Add cucumber, red onion, red pepper, and olives. Mix well to combine. Refrigerate while preparing chicken. Using a pastry brush, coat each chicken piece with 1 tablespoon Catalina dressing. Evenly arrange coated chicken pieces on prepared grill. Lightly spray top of chicken pieces with butter-flavored cooking spray. Close lid and grill for 5 to 7 minutes or until chicken is tender. For each serving, place 1 piece of chicken on a plate and spoon about ⅓ cup cucumber salsa over top.

Each serving equals:

HE: 3 Protein • ¾ Vegetable • ¼ Fat • ¼ Slider •
8 Optional Calories

---

167 Calories • 3 g Fat • 23 g Protein •
12 g Carbohydrate • 312 mg Sodium •
26 mg Calcium • 1 g Fiber

DIABETIC: 3 Meat • ½ Vegetable •
1½ Starch/Carbohydrate

Italian Sweet 'n' Sour Chicken ❄

Do I have a row of jars of spreadable fruit in my fridge? You bet I do! Each kind supplies a remarkable intensity of flavor without added sugar or artificial ingredients. Don't feel you have to invest in a dozen jars right off, of course. This recipe would work with peach as well. ☉   Serves 4

> ¼ cup apricot spreadable fruit
> ¼ cup Kraft Fat Free Italian Dressing
> 16 ounces skinned and boned uncooked chicken breast, cut into 4
>   pieces

Plug in and generously spray both sides of double-sided electric contact grill with olive oil–flavored cooking spray and preheat for 5 minutes. Meanwhile, in a shallow saucer, combine spreadable fruit and Italian dressing. Reserve ¼ cup sauce mixture. Using a pastry brush, coat chicken pieces on both sides with remaining sauce mixture. Evenly arrange coated chicken pieces on prepared grill. Lightly spray top of chicken pieces with olive oil–flavored cooking spray. Close lid and grill for 4 to 5 minutes. Evenly spread about 1 tablespoon of reserved sauce mixture over top of each chicken piece. Close lid and continue grilling for 2 to 3 minutes longer or until chicken is tender.

Each serving equals:

HE: 3 Protein • 1 Fruit • 8 Optional Calories

167 Calories • 3 g Fat • 23 g Protein •
12 g Carbohydrate • 225 mg Sodium •
11 mg Calcium • 0 g Fiber

DIABETIC: 3 Meat • 1 Fruit

Grilled Raspberry
Chicken Breasts

When you're planning a romantic meal, there's no prettier dish than this one, with its rosy color and sweet flavors. I'd serve it for a ladies' luncheon, too, because every woman feels pretty in pink!

● Serves 4

> 16 ounces skinned and boned uncooked chicken breast,
>   cut into 4 pieces
> ¼ cup raspberry spreadable fruit
> 2 tablespoons Diet Mountain Dew
> 1 teaspoon dried onion flakes
> 1 teaspoon dried parsley flakes

Plug in and generously spray both sides of double-sided electric contact grill with butter-flavored cooking spray and preheat for 5 minutes. Evenly arrange chicken pieces on prepared grill. Lightly spray tops of chicken with butter-flavored cooking spray. Close lid and grill for 5 minutes. Meanwhile, in a small bowl, combine spreadable fruit, Diet Mountain Dew, onion flakes, and parsley flakes. Using a pastry brush, evenly coat tops of partially grilled chicken pieces with raspberry sauce. Drizzle any remaining sauce mixture evenly over chicken. Close lid and grill for 2 to 3 minutes longer or until chicken is tender.

Each serving equals:

HE: 3 Protein • 1 Fruit

159 Calories • 3 g Fat • 23 g Protein •
10 g Carbohydrate • 59 mg Sodium •
12 mg Calcium • 0 g Fiber

DIABETIC: 3 Meat • 1 Fruit

Crunchy Grilled Garlic Chicken ❄

I have never apologized for using scrumptious prepared food products to make my recipes taste as delicious as possible. One of this clever cook's favorites is great fat-free dressings, which make good food remarkably better! ☻ Serves 4

¼ cup Kraft Fat Free Ranch Dressing

1½ teaspoons dried minced garlic

1 teaspoon dried parsley flakes

½ cup (¾ ounce) crushed cornflakes

16 ounces skinned and boned uncooked chicken breast, cut into 4
  pieces

Plug in and generously spray both sides of double-sided electric contact grill with butter-flavored cooking spray and preheat for 5 minutes. Meanwhile, in a shallow saucer, combine Ranch dressing, garlic, and parsley flakes. Place cornflake crumbs in another shallow saucer. Dip chicken pieces first in dressing mixture, then into cornflake crumbs. Evenly arrange chicken pieces on prepared grill. Drizzle any remaining dressing mixture or cornflake crumbs evenly over chicken pieces. Lightly spray top of chicken pieces with butter-flavored cooking spray. Close lid and grill for 7 to 8 minutes or until chicken is tender.

Each serving equals:

HE: 3 Protein • ¼ Bread • ¼ Slider •
5 Optional Calories

159 Calories • 3 g Fat • 23 g Protein •
10 g Carbohydrate • 291 mg Sodium •
13 mg Calcium • 1 g Fiber

DIABETIC: 3 Meat • ½ Starch

Crunchy Buttermilk Chicken Breasts

Every Southern lady has at least one great recipe for truly crunchy fried chicken, and now all of us can add this healthy version to our repertoires! The secret really is in the buttermilk, a dairy product that sounds decadent but isn't.　　　●　　Serves 4

> 16 ounces skinned and boned uncooked chicken breast, cut into 4 pieces
> ⅓ cup Carnation Nonfat Dry Milk Powder
> ½ cup water
> 1 teaspoon white distilled vinegar
> ½ cup (¾ ounce) cornflake crumbs

Plug in and generously spray both sides of double-sided electric contact grill with butter-flavored cooking spray and preheat for 5 minutes. Meanwhile, in a shallow saucer, combine dry milk powder, water, and vinegar. Place cornflake crumbs in another shallow saucer. Dip chicken pieces first in milk mixture, then into cornflake crumbs. Evenly arrange coated chicken pieces on prepared grill. Drizzle any remaining milk or cornflake crumbs evenly over chicken pieces. Lightly spray top of chicken pieces with butter-flavored cooking spray. Close lid and grill for 7 to 8 minutes or until chicken is tender.

Each serving equals:

HE: 3 Protein • ¼ Fat Free Milk • ¼ Bread

163 Calories • 3 g Fat • 25 g Protein •
9 g Carbohydrate • 143 mg Sodium •
86 mg Calcium • 0 g Fiber

DIABETIC: 3 Meat • ½ Starch

Sweet and Sour Grilled Chicken ❄

Most of us first tried "sweet and sour" at a local Chinese restaurant, but now it's easy to enjoy that tangy taste without dialing up for it. I like apricot spreadable fruit for this, but it's also good with peach if that's all you have on hand.　　●　Serves 4

1/4 cup apricot spreadable fruit
1/4 cup Kraft Fat Free Catalina Dressing
16 ounces skinned and boned uncooked chicken breast, cut into 32
　　pieces
1 cup coarsely chopped onion
1 cup coarsely chopped green bell pepper
2 cups hot cooked rice

Plug in and generously spray both sides of double-sided electric contact grill with butter-flavored cooking spray and preheat for 5 minutes. Meanwhile, in a large bowl, combine spreadable fruit and Catalina dressing. Add chicken pieces, onion, and green pepper. Mix well to coat. Evenly arrange chicken mixture on prepared grill. Lightly spray top of chicken mixture with butter-flavored cooking spray. Close lid and grill for 5 to 6 minutes or until chicken is tender. For each serving, place 1/2 cup hot rice on a plate and spoon about 3/4 cup chicken mixture over top.

HINT: Usually 1 1/3 cups uncooked instant rice cooks to about 2
　　cups.

Each serving equals:

HE: 3 Protein • 1 Bread • 1 Fruit • 1 Vegetable •
1/4 Slider • 5 Optional Calories

275 Calories • 3 g Fat • 26 g Protein •
36 g Carbohydrate • 242 mg Sodium •
29 mg Calcium • 2 g Fiber

DIABETIC: 3 Meat • 1 Starch • 1 Fruit • 1 Vegetable

Grilled Chicken Hash

Some dishes are never as good as when they're made on the grill, and I think hash is one of those. Just think of the times you've enjoyed it in a down-home-style restaurant and you'll know what I mean. Now that special flavor can be yours at home—and fast.

○ Serves 4 (1 cup)

> ¼ cup Kraft fat-free mayonnaise
> 1 (2-ounce) jar chopped pimiento, drained
> 1 teaspoon dried parsley flakes
> ⅛ teaspoon black pepper
> 1½ cups (8 ounces) diced cooked chicken breast
> 1½ cups (8 ounces) diced cooked potatoes
> ½ cup finely chopped celery
> ½ cup finely chopped onion

Plug in and generously spray both sides of double-sided electric contact grill with butter-flavored cooking spray and preheat for 5 minutes. Meanwhile, in a large bowl, combine mayonnaise, pimiento, parsley flakes, and black pepper. Add chicken, potatoes, celery, and onion. Mix well to coat. Evenly arrange chicken mixture on prepared grill. Lightly spray top of chicken mixture with butter-flavored cooking spray. Close lid and grill for 6 minutes.

Each serving equals:

HE: 2 Protein • ½ Bread • ½ Vegetable •
10 Optional Calories

187 Calories • 3 g Fat • 20 g Protein •
20 g Carbohydrate • 191 mg Sodium •
29 mg Calcium • 4 g Fiber

DIABETIC: 2 Meat • ½ Starch • ½ Vegetable

Tuscany Chicken with Pasta ❄

What makes food so fantastic in Tuscan kitchens is the freshness of the ingredients—the tomatoes picked hours earlier, the pasta prepared moments before the meal is served. You can bring that kind of flavor home with a dish that joins so much "good stuff"!

○ Serves 4

> ¼ cup Kraft Fat Free Italian Dressing
> ¼ cup reduced-sodium ketchup
> 16 ounces skinned and boned uncooked chicken breast, cut into 32 pieces
> 1 cup chopped red onion
> 1½ cups chopped fresh mushrooms
> 1½ cups peeled and chopped fresh tomatoes
> 2 cups hot cooked rotini pasta or any pasta

Plug in and generously spray both sides of double-sided electric contact grill with olive oil–flavored cooking spray and preheat for 5 minutes. Meanwhile, in a large bowl, combine Italian dressing and ketchup. Add chicken, red onion, and mushrooms. Mix well to combine. Stir in tomatoes. Evenly arrange chicken mixture on prepared grill. Lightly spray top of chicken mixture with olive oil–flavored cooking spray. Close lid and grill for 8 to 10 minutes or until chicken is tender. For each serving, place ½ cup pasta on a plate and spoon about 1 cup chicken mixture over top.

HINT: Usually 1½ cups uncooked rotini pasta cooks to about 2 cups.

Each serving equals:

HE: 3 Protein • 2 Vegetable • 1 Bread • ¼ Slider • 4 Optional Calories

---

259 Calories • 3 g Fat • 28 g Protein •
30 g Carbohydrate • 290 mg Sodium •
27 mg Calcium • 2 g Fiber

DIABETIC: 3 Meat • 1½ Vegetable • 1 Starch

Chicken and Asparagus Grill ❄

I've had people visit with me at a cooking demonstration or write to me care of my newsletter and ask what to do with asparagus. This luxurious seasonal vegetable makes any meal special, and it responds beautifully to the double-sided heat of your grill.

◐ Serves 4 (¾ cup)

¼ cup Kraft Fat Free French Dressing
2 teaspoons Grey Poupon Country Dijon Mustard
⅛ teaspoon black pepper
2 cups chopped fresh asparagus
½ cup chopped onion
16 ounces skinned and boned uncooked chicken breast, cut into 32 pieces

Plug in and generously spray both sides of double-sided electric contact grill with butter-flavored cooking spray and preheat for 5 minutes. Meanwhile, in a large bowl, combine French dressing, mustard, and black pepper. Add asparagus and onion. Mix well to combine. Stir in chicken. Evenly arrange chicken mixture on prepared grill. Lightly spray top of chicken mixture with butter-flavored cooking spray. Close lid and grill for 7 to 8 minutes or until asparagus and chicken are tender.

Each serving equals:

HE: 3 Protein • 1¼ Vegetable • ¼ Slider • 5 Optional Calories

171 Calories • 3 g Fat • 25 g Protein • 11 g Carbohydrate • 236 mg Sodium • 29 mg Calcium • 2 g Fiber

DIABETIC: 3 Meat • 1 Vegetable • ½ Starch/Carbohydrate

Cliff's Chicken and Steak Fajita Grill

I created this recipe for my favorite meat-lovin' man, who believes (as so many husbands do) that the more meat, the better! Cliff also loves Mexican food, so these tangy homemade fajitas easily won his heart. 😊 Serves 4 (¾ cup)

¼ cup Kraft Fat Free Catalina Dressing
1 teaspoon chili seasoning
½ teaspoon dried minced garlic
8 ounces skinned and boned uncooked chicken breast, cut into 24 pieces
8 ounces lean round steak, cut into 24 pieces
1 cup chopped onion
1 cup chopped green bell pepper
½ cup chopped red bell pepper

Plug in and generously spray both sides of double-sided electric contact grill with butter-flavored cooking spray and preheat for 5 minutes. Meanwhile, in a large bowl, combine Catalina dressing, chili seasoning, and garlic. Add chicken, steak, onion, green pepper, and red pepper. Mix well to coat. Evenly arrange meat mixture on prepared grill. Lightly spray top of meat mixture with butter-flavored cooking spray. Close lid and grill for 8 to 10 minutes.

HINT: Serve as is, over rice, or as filling for fajitas.

Each serving equals:

HE: 3 Protein • 1¼ Vegetable • ¼ Slider • 5 Optional Calories

197 Calories • 5 g Fat • 26 g Protein • 12 g Carbohydrate • 241 mg Sodium • 23 mg Calcium • 2 g Fiber

DIABETIC: 3 Meat • 1 Vegetable

Old-Fashioned "Sausage" Patties with Mushroom Gravy ❄

Don't give up the pleasure that sausage provides if you're determined to eat healthy—just make a little change in ingredients! Grilling perfectly spiced meat patties intensifies the flavors beautifully. ◐ Serves 4

16 ounces extra-lean ground
    sirloin beef or turkey
    breast
1 teaspoon ground sage
½ teaspoon garlic powder
1 teaspoon poultry seasoning
1 (10¾-ounce) can Healthy
    Request Cream of
    Mushroom Soup

¼ cup Land O' Lakes no-fat
    sour cream
1 teaspoon dried onion flakes
1 teaspoon dried parsley flakes
⅛ teaspoon black pepper

Plug in and generously spray both sides of double-sided electric contact grill with butter-flavored cooking spray and preheat for 5 minutes. Meanwhile, in a large bowl, combine meat, sage, garlic powder, and poultry seasoning. Using a ⅓ cup measuring cup as a guide, form into 4 patties. Evenly arrange patties on prepared grill. Close lid and grill for 5 to 6 minutes. Meanwhile, in a small saucepan, combine mushroom soup, sour cream, onion flakes, parsley flakes, and black pepper. Cook over medium-low heat while patties are grilling, stirring occasionally. For each serving, place 1 patty on a plate and spoon a full ¼ cup mushroom gravy over top.

Each serving equals:

HE: 3 Protein • ½ Slider • 16 Optional Calories

---

178 Calories • 6 g Fat • 22 g Protein •
9 g Carbohydrate • 379 mg Sodium • 85 mg Calcium •
0 g Fiber

DIABETIC: 3 Meat • ½ Starch/Carbohydrate

Meat Lovers' Mushrooms and Onions

Many Americans eat large servings of meat, far more than nutritionists usually recommend—but it's often because they want to feel FULL. Well, a great way to extend the taste satisfaction of a meaty dish is with vegetables like mushrooms and onions that take on all the rich flavor—and also to cook with a hearty splash of Worcestershire sauce. ◗ Serves 4 (¾ cup)

2 cups sliced fresh mushrooms
2 cups sliced onion
8 ounces extra-lean ground sirloin beef or turkey breast
2 tablespoons Worcestershire sauce

Plug in and generously spray both sides of double-sided electric contact grill with butter-flavored cooking spray and preheat for 5 minutes. Meanwhile, in a large bowl, combine mushrooms and onion. Evenly arrange on prepared grill. Sprinkle meat evenly over vegetables. Drizzle Worcestershire sauce evenly over top. Close lid and grill for 10 to 12 minutes.

HINT: Great as is or served over rice, baked potatoes, pasta, or scrambled eggs.

Each serving equals:

HE: 2 Vegetable • 1½ Protein

115 Calories • 3 g Fat • 13 g Protein •
9 g Carbohydrate • 78 mg Sodium • 22 mg Calcium •
2 g Fiber

DIABETIC: 1½ Vegetable • 1½ Meat

Cabbage Patch Meat Loaf Patties ❄

Because I know just how long it takes to make old-fashioned stuffed cabbage, I wanted to find a delicious and speedy way to get the taste I longed for but with much less trouble and time spent. I think you'll agree I've done it with these patties that weave cabbage into a recipe that would be plenty good on its own. ☻ Serves 6

    16 ounces extra-lean ground sirloin beef or turkey breast
    2 cups grated cabbage
    ½ cup finely chopped onion
    ¼ cup fat-free milk
    ⅛ teaspoon black pepper
    1 (12-ounce) jar Heinz Fat Free Beef Gravy
    1 teaspoon dried parsley flakes

Plug in and generously spray both sides of double-sided electric contact grill with butter-flavored cooking spray and preheat for 5 minutes. Meanwhile, in a large bowl, combine meat, cabbage, onion, milk, and black pepper. Using a ½ cup measuring cup as a guide, form into 6 patties. Evenly arrange patties on prepared grill. Close lid and grill for 7 to 8 minutes. Meanwhile, in a small saucepan, combine gravy and parsley flakes. Cook over medium-low heat while patties are grilling, stirring occasionally. For each serving, place 1 patty on a plate and drizzle about ¼ cup gravy mixture over top.

Each serving equals:

    HE: 2 Protein • ½ Vegetable • ¼ Slider •
    9 Optional Calories

    115 Calories • 3 g Fat • 16 g Protein •
    6 g Carbohydrate • 404 mg Sodium •
    30 mg Calcium • 1 g Fiber

    DIABETIC: 2 Meat • ½ Vegetable

Shepherd's Pie Patties in Potato Mounds

All the delectable flavors of a classic shepherd's pie are woven into this dish, a superb choice to please the meat-and-potatoes lovers in your life! It's so creamy and rich, you'll feel satisfied in every way.

○ Serves 6

16 ounces extra-lean ground sirloin beef or turkey breast
1 cup frozen peas and carrots blend, thawed
½ cup + 1 tablespoon Land O Lakes no-fat sour cream ☆
⅛ teaspoon black pepper
1 (10¾-ounce) can Healthy Request Cream of Mushroom Soup
2 teaspoons dried parsley flakes
2 cups instant potato flakes
2¼ cups boiling water
2 teaspoons dried onion flakes

Plug in and generously spray both sides of double-sided electric contact grill with butter-flavored cooking spray and preheat for 5 minutes. Meanwhile, in a large bowl, combine meat, peas and carrots, ¼ cup sour cream, and black pepper. Using a ⅓ cup measuring cup as a guide, form into 6 patties. Evenly arrange patties on prepared grill. Close lid and grill for 6 minutes. Meanwhile, in a medium saucepan, combine mushroom soup, ¼ cup sour cream, and parsley flakes. Cook over medium-low heat while patties are grilling, stirring occasionally. In a large bowl, combine dry potato flakes, boiling water, and onion flakes, mixing with a fork until fluffy. Stir in remaining 1 tablespoon sour cream. For each serving, place ½ cup potato mixture on a plate, make an indentation in center, arrange a patty in indentation, and spoon about 3 tablespoons mushroom sauce over top.

HINT: Thaw peas and carrots by placing in a colander and rinsing under hot water for 1 minute.

Each serving equals:

HE: 2 Protein • 1 Bread • ½ Slider •
19 Optional Calories

---

193 Calories • 5 g Fat • 17 g Protein •
20 g Carbohydrate • 298 mg Sodium • 78 mg Calcium
• 1 g Fiber

DIABETIC: 2 Meat • 1½ Starch/Carbohydrate

Oktoberfest Meat Loaf Patties ❄

There's a heartiness to the dishes inspired by the famous fall festival celebrating the treasures of the season, and this one remains true to that inspiration. But applesauce in meat loaf, you may inquire? Oh yes, absolutely! And grilling just deepens the rich flavors.

Serves 6

16 ounces extra-lean ground sirloin beef or turkey breast
¾ cup (1½ ounces) crushed cornflakes
¾ cup chopped onion
¾ cup Musselman's No Sugar Added Applesauce ☆
1 (10¾-ounce) can Healthy Request Tomato Soup
½ teaspoon prepared yellow mustard
1 teaspoon dried parsley flakes

Plug in and generously spray both sides of double-sided electric contact grill with butter-flavored cooking spray and preheat for 5 minutes. Meanwhile, in a large bowl, combine meat, cornflakes, onion, and ¼ cup applesauce. Using a ½ cup measuring cup as a guide, form into 6 patties. Evenly arrange patties on prepared grill. Close lid and grill for 5 to 6 minutes. Meanwhile, in a medium saucepan, combine tomato soup, remaining ½ cup applesauce, mustard, and parsley flakes. Cook over medium-low heat while patties are grilling, stirring occasionally. For each serving, place 1 patty on a plate and spoon a full 2 tablespoons sauce mixture over top.

Each serving equals:

HE: 2 Protein • ⅓ Bread • ¼ Fruit • ¼ Vegetable •
¼ Slider • 10 Optional Calories

---

172 Calories • 4 g Fat • 16 g Protein •
18 g Carbohydrate • 338 mg Sodium •
5 mg Calcium • 2 g Fiber

DIABETIC: 2 Meat • 1 Starch/Carbohydrate

Apple Harvest Meat Loaf Patties ❄

If you've never even thought about folding diced apples into your meat loaf, let alone applesauce and sour cream, all I can say is, "Believe!" This unusual combination of ingredients that sing out the glories of fall harvest time will delight you and your family.

☻ Serves 6

> 16 ounces extra-lean ground sirloin beef or turkey breast
> ½ cup + 1 tablespoon dried fine bread crumbs
> 1 cup (2 small) cored, peeled, and finely diced cooking apples
> ½ cup Musselman's No Sugar Added Applesauce
> 1 teaspoon dried onion flakes
> 1 teaspoon dried parsley flakes
> 6 tablespoons Land O Lakes no-fat sour cream

Plug in and generously spray both sides of double-sided electric contact grill with butter-flavored cooking spray and preheat for 5 minutes. Meanwhile, in a large bowl, combine meat, bread crumbs, apples, applesauce, onion flakes, and parsley flakes. Using a ½ cup measuring cup as a guide, form into 6 patties. Evenly arrange patties on prepared grill. Close lid and grill for 7 to 8 minutes. When serving, top each with 1 tablespoon sour cream.

Each serving equals:

> HE: 2 Protein • ½ Bread • ½ Fruit •
> 15 Optional Calories
>
> ---
>
> 160 Calories • 4 g Fat • 16 g Protein •
> 15 g Carbohydrate • 167 mg Sodium •
> 45 mg Calcium • 1 g Fiber
>
> ---
>
> DIABETIC: 2 Meat • ½ Starch • ½ Fruit

Reuben Meat Loaf Patties ❄

If it works for deli sandwiches, why couldn't it work for meat loaf patties, I wondered. So I set out to prove to myself and others that the special combo of culinary magic that is celebrated as the Reuben would be wonderful on the grill. Here's the proof!

◐ Serves 6

> 2 tablespoons Kraft Fat Free Thousand Island Dressing
> 2 tablespoons Land O Lakes no-fat sour cream
> 16 ounces extra-lean ground sirloin beef or turkey breast
> 6 slices reduced-calorie rye bread, made into small crumbs
> 1 (8-ounce) can sauerkraut, well drained
> ½ cup finely chopped onion
> 3 (¾-ounce) slices Kraft reduced-fat Swiss cheese, shredded

Plug in and generously spray both sides of double-sided electric contact grill with butter-flavored cooking spray and preheat for 5 minutes. Meanwhile, in a large bowl, combine Thousand Island dressing and sour cream. Add meat, bread crumbs, sauerkraut, onion, and Swiss cheese. Mix well to combine. Using a ¾ cup measuring cup as a guide, form into 6 large patties. Evenly arrange patties on prepared grill. Close lid and grill for 7 to 8 minutes.

Each serving equals:

HE: 2½ Protein • ½ Bread • ½ Vegetable • 13 Optional Calories

207 Calories • 7 g Fat • 21 g Protein • 15 g Carbohydrate • 461 mg Sodium • 164 mg Calcium • 4 g Fiber

DIABETIC: 2½ Meat • ½ Starch • ½ Vegetable

French Onion Meat Loaf Patties ❄

Here's the scenario—imagine, if you will, some French onion soup tumbling into the bowl where you're mixing up your meat loaf. Suddenly, onions are everywhere, and so is the rich taste of Swiss cheese. From a culinary "accident" comes a scrumptious celebration of friendship between nations. ○ Serves 6

16 ounces extra-lean ground sirloin beef or turkey breast
1½ cups chopped onion
6 tablespoons dried fine bread crumbs
3 (¾-ounce) slices Kraft reduced-fat Swiss cheese, shredded
¼ cup Kraft Fat Free French Dressing
2 teaspoons dried parsley flakes

Plug in and generously spray both sides of double-sided electric contact grill with butter-flavored cooking spray and preheat for 5 minutes. Meanwhile, in a large bowl, combine meat, onion, bread crumbs, Swiss cheese, French dressing, and parsley flakes. Using a ½ cup measuring cup as a guide, form into 6 patties. Evenly arrange patties on prepared grill. Close lid and grill for 6 to 7 minutes.

Each serving equals:

HE: 2½ Protein • ½ Vegetable • ⅓ Bread • 17 Optional Calories

195 Calories • 7 g Fat • 20 g Protein •
13 g Carbohydrate • 354 mg Sodium •
151 mg Calcium • 1 g Fiber

DIABETIC: 2½ Meat • ½ Vegetable •
½ Starch/Carbohydrate

Zesty Onion Meat Loaf Patties ❄

The dictionary defines *zest* as "enthusiasm, excitement, and energy," which describes the special nature of this meaty dish. If you love onions as much as I do, you'll make this often. ☺ Serves 6

16 ounces extra-lean ground sirloin beef or turkey breast
1½ cups finely chopped onion
10 Ritz Reduced Fat Crackers, made into crumbs
1 (10¾-ounce) can Healthy Request Tomato Soup
2 tablespoons fat-free milk
1 teaspoon dried parsley flakes
⅛ teaspoon black pepper

Plug in and generously spray both sides of double-sided electric contact grill with butter-flavored cooking spray and preheat for 5 minutes. Meanwhile, in a large bowl, combine meat, onion, cracker crumbs, and ¼ cup tomato soup. Using a ½ cup measuring cup as a guide, form into 6 patties. Evenly arrange patties on prepared grill. Close lid and grill for 7 to 8 minutes. Meanwhile, in a medium saucepan, combine remaining tomato soup, milk, parsley flakes, and black pepper. Cook over medium-low heat while patties are grilling, stirring occasionally. For each serving, place 1 patty on a plate and spoon about 2 tablespoons sauce mixture over top.

Each serving equals:

HE: 2 Protein • ½ Vegetable • ⅓ Bread • ¼ Slider • 12 Optional Calories

165 Calories • 5 g Fat • 16 g Protein • 14 g Carbohydrate • 278 mg Sodium • 26 mg Calcium • 1 g Fiber

DIABETIC: 2 Meat • ½ Vegetable • ½ Starch/Carbohydrate

Mom's Meat Loaf Patties

Plain old burgers on the grill taste good, but for a little taste of greatness, stir in just a few more fixings to make an anytime-at-all dinner seem special!   ☕   Serves 6

> 16 ounces extra-lean ground sirloin beef or turkey breast
> ¾ cup finely chopped onion
> ¼ cup finely chopped green bell pepper
> 6 tablespoons dried fine bread crumbs
> ¼ cup reduced-sodium ketchup
> ⅛ teaspoon black pepper

Plug in and generously spray both sides of double-sided electric contact grill with butter-flavored cooking spray and preheat for 5 minutes. Meanwhile, in a large bowl, combine meat, onion, green pepper, bread crumbs, ketchup, and black pepper. Using a ½ cup measuring cup as a guide, form into 6 patties. Evenly arrange patties on prepared grill. Close lid and grill for 6 to 7 minutes.

Each serving equals:

HE: 2 Protein • ⅓ Bread • ⅓ Vegetable •
10 Optional Calories

---

140 Calories • 4 g Fat • 16 g Protein •
10 g Carbohydrate • 104 mg Sodium • 22 mg Calcium •
1 g Fiber

DIABETIC: 2 Meat • ½ Starch/Carbohydrate

Pizza Lovers' Meat Loaf Patties ❄

Pizza in the morning, pizza in the evening, pizza at suppertime? But if your home houses some pizza "maniacs," here's a fun way to win them away from their crusty passion. ◐ Serves 6

> 16 ounces extra-lean ground sirloin beef or turkey breast
> 1/3 cup (1 1/2 ounces) shredded Kraft reduced-fat Cheddar cheese
> 1/3 cup (1 1/2 ounces) shredded Kraft reduced-fat mozzarella cheese
> 6 tablespoons dried fine bread crumbs
> 1/3 cup sliced ripe olives
> 1/2 cup chopped onion
> 1 (2.5-ounce) jar sliced mushrooms, drained
> 1 (8-ounce) can Hunt's Tomato Sauce ☆
> 1 tablespoon Splenda Granular
> 1 1/2 teaspoons pizza or Italian seasoning

Plug in and generously spray both sides of double-sided electric contact grill with olive oil–flavored cooking spray and preheat for 5 minutes. Meanwhile, in a large bowl, combine meat, Cheddar cheese, mozzarella cheese, bread crumbs, olives, onion, mushrooms, and 1/4 cup tomato sauce. Using a 1/2 cup measuring cup as a guide, form into 6 patties. Evenly arrange patties on prepared grill. Close lid and grill for 6 to 7 minutes. Meanwhile, in a medium saucepan, combine remaining 3/4 cup tomato sauce, Splenda, and pizza seasoning. Cook over medium-low heat while patties are grilling, stirring occasionally. For each serving, place 1 meat loaf patty on a plate and drizzle about 2 tablespoons tomato sauce over top.

Each serving equals:

HE: 2 2/3 Protein • 1 Vegetable • 1 1/3 Bread • 1/4 Fat • 1 Optional Calorie

---

183 Calories • 7 g Fat • 20 g Protein • 10 g Carbohydrate • 556 mg Sodium • 124 mg Calcium • 1 g Fiber

---

DIABETIC: 2 1/2 Meat • 1 Vegetable • 1/2 Starch

Creole Meat Loaf Patties

Creole food is savory, with heat sharing the stage with sweetness. These meat patties will surprise you with their rich flavors.

● Serves 6

16 ounces extra-lean ground sirloin beef or turkey breast	1 teaspoon Worcestershire sauce
6 tablespoons dried fine bread crumbs	1 (8-ounce) can Hunt's Tomato Sauce
½ cup chopped onion	1 (8-ounce) can tomatoes, finely chopped and undrained
½ cup chopped green bell pepper	2 tablespoons Splenda Granular
¼ cup reduced-sodium ketchup	1 teaspoon dried parsley flakes

Plug in and generously spray both sides of double-sided electric contact grill with butter-flavored cooking spray and preheat for 5 minutes. Meanwhile, in a large bowl, combine meat, bread crumbs, onion, green pepper, ketchup, and Worcestershire sauce. Using a ⅓ cup measuring cup as a guide, form into 6 patties. Evenly arrange patties on prepared grill. Close lid and grill for 6 to 8 minutes. Meanwhile, in a medium saucepan, combine tomato sauce, undrained tomatoes, Splenda, and parsley flakes. Cook over medium-low heat while patties are grilling, stirring occasionally. For each serving, place 1 patty on a plate and spoon about ¼ cup tomato sauce over top.

Each serving equals:

HE: 2 Protein • 1⅓ Vegetable • ⅓ Bread • 12 Optional Calories

160 Calories • 4 g Fat • 17 g Protein • 14 g Carbohydrate • 411 mg Sodium • 34 mg Calcium • 1 g Fiber

DIABETIC: 2 Meat • 1½ Vegetable • ½ Starch/Carbohydrate

Sauerbraten Patties in Tomato Sauce ❄

The right combination of spices to makes all the difference. Here the dash of pumpkin pie spice that turned "pretty good" into "wow, that's tasty!" ☻ Serves 6

> 16 ounces extra-lean ground sirloin beef or turkey breast
> ½ cup + 1 tablespoon purchased graham cracker crumbs or 9
>   (2½-inch) graham cracker squares, made into crumbs
> 1 (10¾-ounce) can Healthy Request Tomato Soup
> 1 teaspoon pumpkin pie spice
> 1 teaspoon dried onion flakes
> 1 (8-ounce) can tomatoes, finely diced and undrained
> 1 teaspoon dried parsley flakes

Plug in and generously spray both sides of double-sided electric contact grill with butter-flavored cooking spray and preheat for 5 minutes. Meanwhile, in a large bowl, combine meat, graham cracker crumbs, ⅓ cup tomato soup, pumpkin pie spice, and onion flakes. Using a ⅓ cup measuring cup as a guide, form into 6 patties. Evenly arrange patties on prepared grill. Close lid and grill for 6 to 7 minutes. Meanwhile, in a medium saucepan, combine remaining tomato soup, undrained tomatoes, and parsley flakes. Cook over medium-low heat while patties are grilling, stirring often. For each serving, place a patty on a plate and spoon about ¼ cup tomato sauce over top.

HINT: A self-seal sandwich bag works great for crushing crackers.

Each serving equals:

> HE: 2 Protein • ½ Bread • ¼ Slider •
> 10 Optional Calories
> _____
> 177 Calories • 5 g Fat • 16 g Protein •
> 17 g Carbohydrate • 369 mg Sodium •
> 12 mg Calcium • 1 g Fiber
> _____
> DIABETIC: 2 Meat • 1 Starch/Carbohydrate

Broccoli Meat Loaf Patties with Mushroom Sauce

If you're looking for ways to eat more veggies without ignoring your family's appetite for hearty meat dishes, here's a winner of a way to incorporate broccoli into a meat patty—and it's downright delectable! ☻ Serves 6

16 ounces extra-lean ground sirloin beef or turkey breast
1 cup finely chopped fresh broccoli
½ cup finely chopped onion
½ cup quick oats

1 teaspoon lemon pepper ☆
½ cup fat-free milk ☆
1 (10¾-ounce) can Healthy Request Cream of Mushroom Soup
1 teaspoon dried parsley flakes

Plug in and generously spray both sides of double-sided electric contact grill with butter-flavored cooking spray and preheat for 5 minutes. Meanwhile, in a large bowl, combine meat, broccoli, onion, oats, ½ teaspoon lemon pepper, and ¼ cup milk. Using a ½ cup measuring cup as a guide, form into 6 patties. Evenly arrange patties on prepared grill. Close lid and grill for 7 to 8 minutes. Meanwhile, in a medium saucepan, combine mushroom soup, remaining remaining ½ teaspoon lemon pepper, ¼ cup milk, and parsley flakes. Cook over medium-low heat while patties are grilling, stirring occasionally. For each serving, place 1 patty on a plate and spoon a full 3 tablespoons mushroom sauce over top.

Each serving equals:

HE: 2 Protein • ½ Vegetable • ⅓ Bread • ¼ Slider • 15 Optional Calories

157 Calories • 5 g Fat • 17 g Protein • 11 g Carbohydrate • 293 mg Sodium • 80 mg Calcium • 1g Fiber

DIABETIC: 2 Meat • ½ Vegetable • ½ Starch/Carbohydrate

Chili "Steaks" with Salsa Sauce ❄

Grilling locks in the seasonings you choose, so that only a little bit goes a long way toward magnificent flavor. These South-of-the-Border treats are both hot and hearty, a perfect combo for a cool November night!   ◑   Serves 6

> 16 ounces extra-lean ground sirloin beef or turkey breast
> 1 (8-ounce) can kidney beans, rinsed, drained, and mashed
> 6 tablespoons dried fine bread crumbs
> ½ cup finely chopped onion
> ¼ cup reduced-sodium tomato juice
> 1 teaspoon chili seasoning
> 1 (10¾-ounce) can Healthy Request Tomato Soup
> ¾ cup chunky salsa (mild, medium, or hot)

Plug in and generously spray both sides of double-sided electric contact grill with olive oil–flavored cooking spray and preheat for 5 minutes. Meanwhile, in a large bowl, combine meat, kidney beans, bread crumbs, onion, tomato juice, and chili seasoning. Using a ½ cup measuring cup as a guide, form into 6 patties. Evenly arrange patties on prepared grill. Close lid and grill for 6 to 7 minutes. Meanwhile, in a medium saucepan, combine tomato soup and salsa. Cook over medium-low heat while patties are grilling, stirring occasionally. For each serving, place 1 "steak" on a plate and spoon about ¼ cup salsa sauce over top.

Each serving equals:

HE: 2½ Protein • ½ Vegetable • ⅓ Bread • ¼ Slider • 10 Optional Calories

217 Calories • 5 g Fat • 20 g Protein • 23 g Carbohydrate • 535 mg Sodium • 28 mg Calcium • 4 g Fiber

DIABETIC: 2½ Meat • 1 Starch • ½ Vegetable

Cheese-Stuffed "Steaks" with Pizza Sauce ❄

This is a kind of smart chef's "trick"—slipping the savory surprise of cheese into the middle of a sirloin or turkey burger. ☯   Serves 4

16 ounces extra-lean ground sirloin beef or turkey breast
6 tablespoons dried fine bread crumbs
1 tablespoon dried onion flakes
1/4 cup fat-free milk
4 (3/4-ounce) slices Kraft reduced-fat mozzarella cheese
1 (8-ounce) can Hunt's Tomato Sauce
1 (8-ounce) can tomatoes, finely chopped and undrained
1 tablespoon Splenda Granular
1 1/2 teaspoons pizza or Italian seasoning

Plug in and generously spray both sides of double-sided electric contact grill with olive oil–flavored cooking spray and preheat for 5 minutes. Meanwhile, in a medium bowl, combine meat, bread crumbs, onion flakes, and milk. Using a 1/4 cup measuring cup as a guide, form into 8 patties. For each steak, place 1 slice mozzarella cheese between 2 patties, crimping edges to seal cheese in. Evenly arrange "steaks" on prepared grill. Close lid and grill for 6 to 7 minutes. Meanwhile, in a medium saucepan, combine tomato sauce, undrained tomatoes, Splenda, and pizza seasoning. Cook over medium-low heat while burgers are grilling, stirring occasionally. For each serving, place 1 "steak" on a plate and spoon a full 1/3 cup pizza sauce over top.

Each serving equals:

HE: 4 Protein • 1 1/2 Vegetable • 1/2 Bread •
7 Optional Calories

265 Calories • 9 g Fat • 31 g Protein •
15 g Carbohydrate • 746 mg Sodium •
199 mg Calcium • 2 g Fiber

DIABETIC: 4 Meat • 1 1/2 Vegetable • 1/2 Starch

Salsa "Steaks"

Never forget that ground sirloin began life as a STEAK, and treat yourself to the best you can find when it comes to flavor and health. This recipe celebrates all that a meat patty can be when it's viewed with just the right point of view. ☻ Serves 6

> *16 ounces extra-lean ground sirloin beef or turkey breast*
> *15 Ritz Reduced Fat Crackers, made into crumbs*
> *1 (10¾-ounce) can Healthy Request Tomato Soup ☆*
> *1 teaspoon Worcestershire sauce*
> *1 teaspoon dried onion flakes*
> *1 teaspoon dried parsley flakes*
> *¾ cup chunky salsa (mild, medium, or hot)*

Plug in and generously spray both sides of double-sided electric contact grill with butter-flavored cooking spray and preheat for 5 minutes. Meanwhile, in a large bowl, combine meat, cracker crumbs, ⅓ cup tomato soup, Worcestershire sauce, onion flakes, and parsley flakes. Using a ⅓ cup measuring cup as a guide, form into 6 patties. Evenly arrange patties on prepared grill. Close lid and grill for 6 to 7 minutes. Meanwhile, in a medium saucepan, combine remaining tomato soup and salsa. Cook over medium-low heat while patties are grilling, stirring often. For each serving, place 1 "steak" on a plate and spoon about 3 tablespoons sauce over top.

HINT: A self-seal sandwich bag works great for crushing crackers.

Each serving equals:

HE: 2 Protein • ½ Bread • ¼ Vegetable • ¼ Slider • 10 Optional Calories

173 Calories • 5 g Fat • 16 g Protein •
16 g Carbohydrate • 529 mg Sodium •
10 mg Calcium • 1 g Fiber

DIABETIC: 2 Meat • 1 Starch/Carbohydrate

Swedish "Steaks" and Gravy ❄

The explorers who sailed the oceans weren't only searching for new lands to conquer; they also wanted a quick and easy way to bring home the exotic spices of the East Indies. Nutmeg is one of those spices, something worth risking life and limb for. Nowadays, of course, we can add it to our recipes without nearly that much trouble—but it's still worth a detour!   ☻   Serves 4

> 16 ounces extra-lean ground sirloin beef or turkey breast
> 6 tablespoons dried fine bread crumbs
> ¼ cup Land O Lakes no-fat sour cream
> 2 teaspoons dried onion flakes
> ¾ teaspoon ground nutmeg
> 1 (10¾-ounce) can Healthy Request Cream of Mushroom Soup
> 1 (2.5-ounce) jar chopped mushrooms, drained
> 1 teaspoon dried parsley flakes

Plug in and generously spray both sides of double-sided electric contact grill with butter-flavored cooking spray and preheat for 5 minutes. Meanwhile, in a large bowl, combine meat, bread crumbs, sour cream, onion flakes, and nutmeg. Using a ½ cup measuring cup as a guide, form into 4 large patties. Evenly arrange "steaks" on prepared grill. Close lid and grill for 6 to 7 minutes. Meanwhile, in a medium saucepan, combine mushroom soup, mushrooms, and parsley flakes. Cook over medium-low heat while "steaks" are grilling, stirring occasionally. For each serving, place 1 "steak" on a plate and spoon a full ¼ cup gravy over top.

Each serving equals:

HE: 3 Protein • ½ Bread • ¼ Vegetable • ½ Slider •
16 Optional Calories

---

223 Calories • 7 g Fat • 23 g Protein •
17 g Carbohydrate • 550 mg Sodium •
109 mg Calcium • 1 g Fiber

DIABETIC: 3 Meat • 1 Starch/Carbohydrate

Horseradish Beef Hash

It's fiercely flavorful, but horseradish is also an ingredient that makes roast beef sizzle with unforgettable taste! Just a little goes a long way, though, so measure carefully.

◑ Serves 4 (¾ cup)

> ¼ cup Kraft Fat Free Ranch Dressing
> 2 teaspoons prepared horseradish sauce
> 1 teaspoon dried parsley flakes
> 1½ cups (8 ounces) diced cooked lean roast beef
> 1½ cups (8 ounces) diced cooked potatoes
> ½ cup chopped onion

Plug in and generously spray both sides of double-sided electric contact grill with butter-flavored cooking spray and preheat for 5 minutes. Meanwhile, in a large bowl, combine Ranch dressing, horseradish sauce, and parsley flakes. Add roast beef, potatoes, and onion. Mix well to coat. Evenly arrange coated hash mixture on prepared grill. Lightly spray top of hash mixture with butter-flavored cooking spray. Close lid and grill for 6 to 7 minutes.

Each serving equals:

HE: 2 Protein • ½ Bread • ¼ Vegetable • ¼ Slider • 5 Optional Calories

193 Calories • 5 g Fat • 18 g Protein • 19 g Carbohydrate • 222 mg Sodium • 12 mg Calcium • 2 g Fiber

DIABETIC: 2 Meat • 1 Starch

Beef and Broccoli Combo ❄

Sure, you could call the local Chinese restaurant every time you have a hankering for the irresistible flavor of beef and broccoli, but why not try this home-grilled version that cooks up faster than the deliveryman can ring your bell? You'll save money *and* time!

○ Serves 4 (1 cup)

½ cup Kraft Fat Free Catalina Dressing
2 tablespoons reduced-sodium soy sauce
¼ teaspoon dried minced garlic
2 full cups (12 ounces) diced cooked lean roast beef
3 cups chopped fresh broccoli
1 cup chopped onion
1 cup shredded carrots

Plug in and generously spray both sides of double-sided electric contact grill with butter-flavored cooking spray and preheat for 5 minutes. Meanwhile, in a large bowl, combine Catalina dressing, soy sauce, and garlic. Add roast beef, broccoli, onion, and carrots. Mix well to coat. Evenly arrange coated beef mixture on prepared grill. Lightly spray top of beef mixture with butter-flavored cooking spray. Close lid and grill for 7 to 8 minutes.

Each serving equals:

HE: 3 Protein • 2½ Vegetable • ½ Slider •
10 Optional Calories

251 Calories • 7 g Fat • 25 g Protein •
22 g Carbohydrate • 714 mg Sodium •
54 mg Calcium • 3 g Fiber

DIABETIC: 3 Meat • 2 Vegetable •
½ Starch/Carbohydrate

Olive-Stuffed Steak Rolls ❄

Are you an olive lover, just like so many of my family and friends? The world seems to be divided into those who adore olives and those who don't. If you're in this culinary club, here's a perfect party recipe that is bound to win your heart. ♥ Serves 4

4 slices reduced-calorie white
    bread, toasted and cut
    into small cubes
¼ cup sliced ripe olives
¼ cup finely chopped celery
¼ cup finely chopped onion
1 (12-ounce) jar Heinz Fat
    Free Beef Gravy ☆

¼ cup water
⅛ teaspoon black pepper
4 (4-ounce) lean tenderized
    minute or cube steaks
1 teaspoon parsley flakes

Plug in and generously spray both sides of double-sided electric contact grill with olive oil–flavored cooking spray and preheat for 5 minutes. Meanwhile, in a large bowl, combine bread cubes, olives, celery, and onion. Add ¼ cup beef gravy, water, and black pepper. Mix well to combine. Spread about ½ cup stuffing mixture in center of each minute steak. Roll meat over stuffing and secure with toothpicks. Evenly arrange steak rolls on prepared grill. Close lid and grill for 8 to 9 minutes or until meat is cooked through. Meanwhile, in a small saucepan, combine remaining gravy and parsley flakes. Cook over medium-low heat while steaks are grilling, stirring occasionally. For each serving, place a stuffed steak on a plate, carefully remove toothpicks, and spoon ¼ cup gravy over top.

Each serving equals:

HE: 3 Protein • ½ Bread • ¼ Fat • ¼ Vegetable •
¼ Slider • 18 Optional Calories

254 Calories • 6 g Fat • 32 g Protein •
18 g Carbohydrate • 771 mg Sodium •
36 mg Calcium • 1 g Fiber

DIABETIC: 3 Meat • 1 Starch

Maple-Glazed Pork Tenders

It may astonish you that something as simple as sugar-free maple syrup can transform your meat from good to spectacular, but it's the truth! I've tried this dish with fancier mustards, but good old yellow tasted just right to Cliff and me. ☺ Serves 4

½ cup Log Cabin Sugar Free Maple Syrup
1 teaspoon prepared yellow mustard
1 teaspoon dried parsley flakes
4 (4-ounce) lean tenderized pork tenderloins

Plug in and generously spray both sides of double-sided electric contact grill with butter-flavored cooking spray and preheat for 5 minutes. Meanwhile, in a small bowl, combine maple syrup, mustard, and parsley flakes. Reserve ¼ cup sauce mixture. Using a pastry brush, coat tenderloins on both sides with remaining sauce. Evenly arrange coated tenderloins on prepared grill. Close lid and grill for 6 minutes. Evenly spread about 1 tablespoon of reserved sauce mixture over top of each tenderloin. Close lid and continue grilling for 2 minutes longer or until pork is cooked through.

Each serving equals:

HE: 3 Protein • ¼ Slider

152 Calories • 4 g Fat • 24 g Protein •
5 g Carbohydrate • 112 g Sodium • 7 mg Calcium •
0 g Fiber

DIABETIC: 3 Meat

Just Plain Good Tenderloins

You'll find that lean and tender meat usually needs added moisture to make it cook up perfectly, and these pork tenders are no exception. Just as mint jelly celebrates the glories of fresh lamb, a little bit of grape essence brings pork to a higher realm.

◑ Serves 4

4 (4-ounce) lean pork tenderloins
¼ cup grape spreadable fruit
1 tablespoon cider vinegar
2 tablespoons reduced-sodium ketchup
1 teaspoon dried onion flakes

Plug in and generously spray both sides of double-sided electric contact grill with butter-flavored cooking spray and preheat for 5 minutes. Evenly arrange pork tenderloins on prepared grill. Lightly spray top of tenderloins with butter-flavored cooking spray. Close lid and grill for 5 minutes. Meanwhile, in a small bowl, combine spreadable fruit, vinegar, ketchup, and onion flakes. Using a pastry brush, coat tops of partially grilled tenderloins with sauce mixture. Drizzle any remaining sauce mixture evenly over tenderloins. Close lid and continue to grill for 3 or 4 minutes longer or until tenderloins are cooked through.

Each serving equals:

HE: 3 Protein • 1 Fruit • 8 Optional Calories

176 Calories • 4 g Fat • 24 g Protein •
11 g Carbohydrate • 56 mg Sodium • 6 mg Calcium •
0 g Fiber

DIABETIC: 3 Meat • 1 Fruit

Pork Tenders with Orange Pecan Sauce

My taste testers smiled when I announced the title of this recipe, because just about anyone who knows me knows I like pecans with nearly everything! But with pork, some of them wondered? I convinced them with just one bite, as I hope to convince you, too!

● Serves 4

> ¼ cup Kraft Fat Free French Dressing
> 1 teaspoon dried onion flakes
> 4 (4-ounce) lean tenderized pork tenderloins
> ¼ cup orange marmalade spreadable fruit
> 1 teaspoon dried parsley flakes
> 2 tablespoons chopped pecans

Plug in and generously spray both sides of double-sided electric contact grill with butter-flavored cooking spray and preheat for 5 minutes. Meanwhile, in a shallow saucer, combine French dressing and onion flakes. Using a pastry brush, coat tenderloins on both sides. Evenly arrange coated tenderloins on prepared grill. Lightly spray top of tenderloins with butter-flavored cooking spray. Close lid and grill for 6 to 7 minutes. Meanwhile, in a medium saucepan, combine spreadable fruit and parsley flakes. Stir in pecans. Cook over medium-low heat while tenderloins are grilling, stirring often. For each serving, place 1 tenderloin on a plate and drizzle 1 tablespoon hot sauce over top.

Each serving equals:

HE: 3 Protein • 1 Fruit • ½ Fat • ¼ Slider •
5 Optional Calories

---

199 Calories • 7 g Fat • 24 g Protein •
10 g Carbohydrate • 198 mg Sodium •
12 mg Calcium • 1 g Fiber

DIABETIC: 3 Meat • 1 Fruit • ½ Fat

Creole Pork and Rice

Creamy, rich, and luscious—and lowfat, too? Your family will cheer the pleasures of this pork dish with every bite!   ☻   Serves 4

1 (8-ounce) can Hunt's Tomato Sauce ☆
1 (8-ounce) can tomatoes, finely chopped and undrained
1 cup fat-free milk
2 tablespoons Splenda Granular
1 cup uncooked Minute Rice
16 ounces lean pork steak or cutlets, cut into 28 pieces
1 cup chopped celery
1 cup chopped green bell pepper
½ cup chopped onion
1 teaspoon dried parsley flakes

Plug in and generously spray both sides of double-sided electric contact grill with butter-flavored cooking spray and preheat for 5 minutes. Reserve ⅓ cup tomato sauce. In a medium saucepan, combine remaining tomato sauce, undrained tomatoes, milk, and Splenda. Stir in uncooked instant rice. Cook over medium-low heat until rice is tender, stirring occasionally. Meanwhile, in a large bowl, combine pork, celery, green pepper, onion, parsley flakes, and reserved ⅓ cup tomato sauce. Evenly arrange pork mixture on prepared grill. Close lid and grill for 9 to 10 minutes or until pork is cooked through. For each serving, place a full ½ cup rice mixture on a plate and spoon about ¾ cup pork mixture evenly over top.

Each serving equals:

HE: 3 Protein • 2¾ Vegetable • ¾ Bread •
¼ Fat Free Milk • 3 Optional Calories

293 Calories • 5 g Fat • 30 g Protein •
32 g Carbohydrate • 590 mg Sodium •
126 mg Calcium • 3 g Fiber

DIABETIC: 3 Meat • 2½ Vegetable • 1 Starch

French Pork Tenders with Noodles

Now that lean pork cutlets are available in just about every super-market, we've got so many more luscious ways to enjoy this healthy, hearty meat! Served over noodles, this dish is perfect for a quiet dinner with friends or can easily be doubled or tripled if a noisy family gathering is planned.   ☻   Serves 4

> 4 (4-ounce) lean tenderized pork tenderloins or cutlets
> ½ cup Kraft Fat Free French Dressing
> 2 teaspoons dried onion flakes
> 2 teaspoons I Can't Believe It's Not Butter! Light Margarine
> 1 teaspoon dried parsley flakes
> 2 cups hot cooked noodles

Plug in and generously spray both sides of double-sided electric contact grill with butter-flavored cooking spray and preheat for 5 minutes. Evenly arrange pork pieces on prepared grill. Lightly spray top of pork pieces with butter-flavored cooking spray. Close lid and grill for 5 minutes. Meanwhile, in a small bowl, combine French dressing and onion flakes. Using a pastry brush, evenly coat tops of partially grilled tenderloins. Close lid and grill for 2 to 3 minutes longer or until pork is cooked through. Just before serving, stir margarine and parsley flakes into hot noodles. For each serving, place ½ cup hot noodles on a plate and arrange 1 tenderloin over top.

HINT: Usually 1¾ cups uncooked noodles cooks to about 2 cups.

Each serving equals:

> HE: 3 Protein • 1 Bread • ¼ Fat • ½ Slider •
> 13 Optional Calories
> _____
> 286 Calories • 6 g Fat • 28 g Protein •
> 30 g Carbohydrate • 373 mg Sodium •
> 17 mg Calcium • 1 g Fiber
> _____
> DIABETIC: 3 Meat • 1½ Starch/Carbohydrate

Tex-Mex Pork with Corn Salsa

Corn is a wonderful accompaniment to the tender pleasures of pork, and as long as you've got a can or two on the shelf, you can stir up this tasty dish. Don't try to substitute plain white vinegar for the cider vinegar, as you won't get the right "tang" in the dressing.

🔄 Serves 4

1 (8-ounce) can whole-kernel corn, rinsed and drained
¼ cup chopped green onion
¼ cup chopped green bell pepper
2 tablespoons cider vinegar
1 tablespoon Splenda Granular
2 teaspoons olive oil
2 tablespoons chopped fresh parsley or cilantro
½ cup peeled and chopped fresh tomato
4 (4-ounce) lean pork tenderloins or cutlets
¼ cup Kraft Fat Free Catalina Dressing
½ teaspoon chili seasoning

Plug in and generously spray both sides of double-sided electric contact grill with olive oil–flavored cooking spray and preheat for 5 minutes. Meanwhile, in a medium bowl, combine corn, green onion, and green pepper. Add vinegar, Splenda, olive oil, and parsley. Mix well to combine. Stir in tomato. Refrigerate while preparing pork. In a shallow saucer, combine Catalina dressing and chili seasoning. Using a pastry brush, coat both sides of meat with dressing mixture. Evenly arrange coated pork on prepared grill. Close lid and grill for 6 to 8 minutes or until pork is cooked through. For each serving, place 1 piece of meat on a plate and spoon about ½ cup corn salsa mixture over top.

Each serving equals:

HE: 3 Protein • ½ Bread • ½ Fat • ½ Vegetable •
¼ Slider • 4 Optional Calories

---

227 Calories • 7 g Fat • 25 g Protein •
16 g Carbohydrate • 323 mg Sodium •
13 mg Calcium • 2 g Fiber

DIABETIC: 3 Meat • 1 Starch/Carbohydrate • ½ Fat •
½ Vegetable

Pork and Sweet Potato Grill   ❄

Did you know that sweet potatoes deliver loads of nutrition, much more than the white potatoes that turn up on supper plates nearly every night? I wanted to find more ways to serve this super-veggie this year, and this is one of my newest favorites.

☉ Serves 4 (¾ cup)

¼ cup Kraft Fat Free Catalina Dressing
1 teaspoon prepared yellow mustard
1 teaspoon dried parsley flakes
1½ cups (8 ounces) diced cooked lean roast pork
1½ cups (8 ounces) peeled and diced cooked sweet potatoes
1 cup chopped celery
½ cup chopped onion

Plug in and generously spray both sides of double-sided electric contact grill with butter-flavored cooking spray and preheat for 5 minutes. Meanwhile, in a large bowl, combine Catalina dressing, mustard, and parsley flakes. Add pork, sweet potatoes, celery, and onion. Mix well to coat. Evenly arrange pork mixture on prepared grill. Lightly spray top of pork mixture with butter-flavored cooking spray. Close lid and grill for 7 to 8 minutes.

Each serving equals:

HE: 2 Protein • ¾ Vegetable • ½ Bread • ¼ Slider • 5 Optional Calories

193 Calories • 5 g Fat • 17 g Protein • 20 g Carbohydrate • 284 mg Sodium • 40 mg Calcium • 2 g Fiber

DIABETIC: 2 Meat • 1 Starch • ½ Vegetable

Chinese Pork Stew

Sometimes the busy working mom's best friend is a recipe that calls for combining ready-made ingredients in a quick and tasty dish that doesn't taste last-minute. This Asian-inspired stew comes together quickly and cooks up super-fast. Enjoy!

● Serves 4

> 2 tablespoons reduced-sodium soy sauce
> 1 (8-ounce) can pineapple chunks, packed in fruit juice, drained and ¼ cup liquid reserved
> ½ teaspoon ground ginger
> 1½ cups (8 ounces) diced cooked lean roast pork
> ½ cup chopped onion
> 1 cup chopped green bell pepper
> 2 cups shredded cabbage
> 2 cups hot cooked rice

Plug in and generously spray both sides of double-sided electric contact grill with butter-flavored cooking spray and preheat for 5 minutes. Meanwhile, in a large bowl, combine soy sauce, reserved pineapple liquid, and ginger. Add pork, pineapple chunks, onion, and green pepper. Mix well to combine. Stir in cabbage. Evenly arrange pork mixture on prepared grill. Lightly spray top of pork mixture with butter-flavored cooking spray. Close lid and grill for 10 minutes. For each serving, place ½ cup hot rice on a plate and spoon about ¾ cup pork mixture over top.

HINT: Usually 1⅓ cups uncooked instant rice cooks to about 2 cups.

Each serving equals:

HE: 2 Protein • 1¼ Vegetable • 1 Bread • ½ Fruit

---

262 Calories • 6 g Fat • 19 g Protein •
33 g Carbohydrate • 175 mg Sodium •
45 mg Calcium • 3 g Fiber

DIABETIC: 2 Meat • 1 Vegetable • 1 Starch • ½ Fruit

Heavenly Grilled Ham

When I was touring the American South looking for great regional recipes, I learned that some cooks guard their family's ham-baking secrets with their lives! But I'm happy to share one of mine, which combines an unusual mélange of flavors to produce truly splendid results. ❂ Serves 2

> 1 tablespoon Diet 7-UP
> 2 tablespoons apricot spreadable fruit
> ½ teaspoon prepared yellow mustard
> 1 teaspoon dried parsley flakes
> 2 (3-ounce) slices Dubuque 97% fat-free ham or any extra-lean ham

Plug in and generously spray both sides of double-sided electric contact grill with butter-flavored cooking spray and preheat for 5 minutes. Meanwhile, in a shallow saucer, combine Diet 7-UP, spreadable fruit, mustard, and parsley flakes. Using a pastry brush, evenly coat both sides of ham slices. Evenly arrange coated ham slices on prepared grill. Drizzle any remaining mixture evenly over ham slices. Lightly spray top of ham slices with butter-flavored cooking spray. Close lid and grill for 4 to 5 minutes.

HINT: A ⅓-inch thick slice of ham usually weighs 3 ounces.

Each serving equals:

HE: 2 Protein • 1 Fruit

122 Calories • 2 g Fat • 14 g Protein •
12 g Carbohydrate • 689 mg Sodium •
3 mg Calcium • 0 g Fiber

DIABETIC: 2 Meat • 1 Fruit

Hawaiian Ham Grill

When I first tasted a dish that combined sweet potatoes and pineapple, I was quickly convinced these two foods were made for each other! And since ham and pineapple are another lovin' couple, this recipe provides a trio with a sweet song that everyone will adore! ☻   Serves 4 (¾ cup)

2 tablespoons Kraft Fat Free Catalina Dressing
1 (8-ounce) can pineapple chunks, packed in fruit juice, drained
    and 2 tablespoons liquid reserved
1 teaspoon dried onion flakes
1 teaspoon dried parsley flakes
1½ cups (9 ounces) diced Dubuque 97% fat-free ham or any
    extra-lean ham
1½ cups (8 ounces) peeled and diced sweet potatoes
½ cup chopped green bell pepper

Plug in and generously spray both sides of double-sided electric contact grill with butter-flavored cooking spray and preheat for 5 minutes. Meanwhile, in a large bowl, combine Catalina dressing, reserved pineapple liquid, onion flakes, and parsley flakes. Add ham, pineapple chunks, sweet potatoes, and green pepper. Mix well to coat. Evenly arrange ham mixture on prepared grill. Lightly spray top of ham mixture with butter-flavored cooking spray. Close lid and grill for 8 to 9 minutes.

Each serving equals:

HE: 1½ Protein • ½ Bread • ½ Fruit • ¼ Vegetable •
12 Optional Calories

158 Calories • 2 g Fat • 12 g Protein •
23 g Carbohydrate • 623 mg Sodium •
25 mg Calcium • 2 g Fiber

DIABETIC: 1½ Meat • 1 Starch • ½ Fruit

Ham Loaf Patties

If rich and meaty is your favorite flavor, then this dish has your name on it! Ham is one of those meats that makes people feel they're celebrating, so I wanted my ham patties to be worthy of that emotion, too. After one taste, I think you'll agree!

☻ Serves 6

> 1½ cups (16 ounces) ground Dubuque 97% fat-free ham or any extra-lean ham
> 4 ounces extra-lean ground sirloin beef or turkey breast
> ¾ cup purchased graham cracker crumbs or 12 (2½-inch) graham cracker squares, made into crumbs
> 2 tablespoons fat-free milk
> ½ cup reduced-sodium ketchup ☆
> 2 tablespoons Splenda Granular
> ½ teaspoon dried onion flakes
> 1 teaspoon dried parsley flakes

Plug in and generously spray both sides of double-sided electric contact grill with butter-flavored cooking spray and preheat for 5 minutes. Meanwhile, in a large bowl, combine ham, beef, graham cracker crumbs, and milk. Add ¼ cup ketchup. Mix well to combine. Using a ½ cup measuring cup as a guide, form into 6 patties. Evenly arrange patties on prepared grill. Close lid and grill for 7 to 8 minutes. Meanwhile, in a 2-cup glass measuring cup, combine remaining ¼ cup ketchup, Splenda, onion flakes, and parsley flakes. Microwave on HIGH (100% power) for 30 seconds or until warm. When serving, top each patty with about 1 tablespoon sauce mixture.

HINTS: 1. A self-seal sandwich bag works great for crushing crackers.
2. If you don't have a grinder, ask your butcher to grind ham.

Each serving equals:

HE: 2 Protein • ⅔ Bread • ¼ Slider •
4 Optional Calories

189 Calories • 5 g Fat • 17 g Protein •
19 g Carbohydrate • 703 mg Sodium •
14 mg Calcium • 1 g Fiber

DIABETIC: 2 Meat • 1 Starch/Carbohydrate

Ham Patties in Tomato-Pea Sauce

If your family loves ham patties as much as mine does, you might decide to buy a quantity of ground ham from the butcher to package and freeze. Stocking your freezer with healthy foods you love is a good way to ensure that you'll choose good-for-you when you're wondering, "What's for dinner?" ☻ Serves 4

⅓ cup Carnation Nonfat Dry Milk Powder

½ cup water

1 cup (9 ounces) ground Dubuque 97% fat-free ham or any extra-lean ham

6 tablespoons purchased graham cracker crumbs or 6 (2½-inch) graham crackers, made into crumbs

2 teaspoons dried onion flakes

1 teaspoon dried parsley flakes

1 (10¾-ounce) can Healthy Request Tomato Soup

1 teaspoon Worcestershire sauce

1 teaspoon prepared yellow mustard

1 cup frozen peas, thawed

Plug in and generously spray both sides of double-sided electric contact grill with butter-flavored cooking spray and preheat for 5 minutes. Meanwhile, in a small bowl, combine dry milk powder and water. In a large bowl, combine ham, graham cracker crumbs, onion flakes, parsley flakes, and 2 tablespoons milk mixture. Using a ¼ cup measuring cup as a guide, form into 4 patties. Evenly arrange patties on prepared grill. Close lid and grill for 5 minutes. Meanwhile, in a medium saucepan, combine tomato soup, remaining milk mixture, Worcestershire sauce, mustard, and peas. Cook over medium-low heat while patties are grilling, stirring occasionally. For each serving, place 1 patty on a plate and spoon a full ⅓ cup sauce over top.

HINTS: 1. If you don't have a grinder or food processor, grind ham in a blender or ask your butcher to grind entire ham. Freeze unused portions for future use. Don't forget to date and mark packages.
2. A self-seal sandwich bag works great for crushing graham crackers.
3. Thaw peas by placing in a colander and rinsing under hot water for 1 minute.

Each serving equals:

HE: 1½ Protein • 1 Bread • ¼ Fat Free Milk • ½ Slider • 5 Optional Calories

216 Calories • 4 g Fat • 16 g Protein • 29 g Carbohydrate • 953 mg Sodium • 90 mg Calcium • 3 g Fiber

DIABETIC: 1½ Meat • 1½ Starch/Carbohydrate

Frankfurter Salad Bowl

I don't believe in rules when it comes to what's right or wrong in a salad—do you? When I found myself imagining a bowl of lettuce joining hands with some tangy hot dog chunks, I knew from the start that it would be a winner. Taste it and see!

◐ Serves 6

> 1 (16 ounce) package Oscar Mayer or Healthy Choice reduced-fat
>   frankfurters, cut into ½-inch chunks
> 1½ cups chopped onion
> ½ cup Kraft Fat Free French Dressing ☆
> 2 tablespoons sweet pickle relish
> 6 cups shredded lettuce

Plug in and generously spray both sides of double-sided electric contact grill with butter-flavored cooking spray and preheat for 5 minutes. Meanwhile, in a large bowl, combine frankfurter chunks, onion, and ¼ cup French dressing. Mix well to coat. Evenly arrange frankfurter mixture on prepared grill. Close lid and grill for 5 to 6 minutes. Meanwhile, in same bowl, combine remaining ¼ cup French dressing and pickle relish. Add lettuce. Toss well to coat. For each serving, place about 1 cup lettuce mixture on a plate and spoon about ½ cup hot frankfurter mixture over top. Serve at once.

Each serving equals:

HE: 1¾ Protein • 1½ Vegetable • ¼ Slider •
5 Optional Calories

150 Calories • 2 g Fat • 11 g Protein •
22 g Carbohydrate • 822 mg Sodium •
23 mg Calcium • 2 g Fiber

DIABETIC: 2 Meat • 1½ Vegetable •
½ Starch/Carbohydrate

Grilled Hot Dog Supper

On one of those nights when no one wants to do the dishes, this "one-pot" meal is a great solution. Just combine all the ingredients, turn up the heat, and enjoy!   ☻   Serves 4 (1 cup)

> ¼ cup Kraft Fat Free French Dressing
> 2 tablespoons reduced-sodium ketchup
> 1 teaspoon dried parsley flakes
> 8 ounces Oscar Mayer or Healthy Choice reduced-fat
>   frankfurters, cut into ½-inch pieces
> 1½ cups (8 ounces) diced cooked potatoes
> 1½ cups frozen cut green beans, thawed
> ½ cup chopped onion

Plug in and generously spray both sides of double-sided electric contact grill with butter-flavored cooking spray and preheat for 5 minutes. Meanwhile, in a large bowl, combine French dressing, ketchup, and parsley flakes. Add frankfurter pieces, potatoes, green beans, and onion. Mix well to coat. Evenly arrange frankfurter mixture on prepared grill. Lightly spray top of frankfurter mixture with butter-flavored cooking spray. Close lid and grill for 6 to 7 minutes.

HINT: Thaw green beans by placing in a colander and rinsing under hot water for 1 minute.

Each serving equals:

HE: 1⅓ Protein • 1 Vegetable • ½ Bread • ¼ Slider •
12 Optional Calories

183 Calories • 3 g Fat • 10 g Protein •
29 g Carbohydrate • 731 mg Sodium •
28 mg Calcium • 3 g Fiber

DIABETIC: 1 Meat • 1 Vegetable •
1 Starch/Carbohydrate

Frankfurter Kabobs

If you've got teenagers who think family meals are so-o-o-o boring, here's a fun recipe sure to make them sit up and smile! Chunky foods on skewers just seem to be part of a celebration without even trying hard. ☻ Serves 4

> 1 (8-ounce) can pineapple chunks, packed in fruit juice, drained
>   and ¼ cup liquid reserved
> 2 tablespoons reduced-sodium soy sauce
> 1 tablespoon prepared yellow mustard
> 8 ounces Oscar Mayer or Healthy Choice reduced-fat
>   frankfurters, cut into 1-inch chunks
> 1 cup coarsely chopped green bell pepper

Plug in and generously spray both sides of double-sided electric contact grill with butter-flavored cooking spray and preheat for 5 minutes. Meanwhile, in a large bowl, combine reserved pineapple liquid, soy sauce, and mustard. Add frankfurter chunks. Mix well to combine. Using 4 skewers, alternately string frankfurter pieces, pineapple chunks, and green peppers. Evenly arrange kabobs on prepared grill. Drizzle any remaining liquid mixture evenly over kabobs. Close lid and grill for 5 to 6 minutes. Serve at once.

Each serving equals:

HE: 1⅓ Protein • ½ Fruit • ½ Vegetable

127 Calories • 3 g Fat • 8 g Protein •
17 g Carbohydrate • 874 mg Sodium •
6 mg Calcium • 1 g Fiber

DIABETIC: 1½ Meat • ½ Fruit • ½ Vegetable

Kielbasa Supper

What a tasty meal you can make with some ready-made foods! When you prepare and cook potatoes for one dish, be sure to make some extra to have on hand for recipes just like this one. ❂

Serves 4 (¾ cup)

> 2 tablespoons white distilled vinegar
> 2 tablespoons Splenda Granular
> ⅛ teaspoon black pepper
> 1½ cups (8 ounces) diced cooked potatoes
> ½ cup chopped onion
> 1 (8-ounce) can sauerkraut, well drained
> 8 ounces Healthy Choice 97% lean kielbasa sausage, sliced into
>   ¼-inch pieces

Plug in and generously spray both sides of double-sided electric contact grill with butter-flavored cooking spray and preheat for 5 minutes. Meanwhile, in a large bowl, combine vinegar, Splenda, and black pepper. Add potatoes, onion, and sauerkraut. Mix well to combine. Stir in sausage. Evenly arrange sausage mixture on prepared grill. Lightly spray top of sausage mixture with butter-flavored cooking spray. Close lid and grill for 6 to 7 minutes.

Each serving equals:

HE: 2 Protein • ¾ Vegetable • ½ Bread •
3 Optional Calories

171 Calories • 3 g Fat • 9 g Protein •
27 g Carbohydrate • 604 mg Sodium •
40 mg Calcium • 2 g Fiber

DIABETIC: 2 Meat • 1 Vegetable • ½ Starch

Splendid Snacks,

Desserts, and More

*I*made an important decision when I decided to begin eating the Healthy Exchanges Way all those years ago. I told myself that living well meant enjoying desserts every day; I committed to eating healthy snacks; and I insisted it was possible to find tasty alternatives to the kinds of high-fat, high-sugar dishes I used to serve at parties and family gatherings. I believed then (and still do now) that creating delicious desserts, tasty snacks, and delectable party foods was the key to sticking with my new lifestyle. Maybe that's why I particularly love this section—a selection of breakfast treats, festive dishes, and sweets of all kinds that are perfect for preparing on the grill!

If you'd describe yourself as a snacker who prefers small meals five or six times a day, you're likely to find pleasure in the sweet goodness of my **Fried Apple Rings** or my **Blueberry Thrill Snacks**; if your favorite part of every meal is dessert, then you've simply got to try my **Pears Perfection Shortcakes** and **Ellie's Fruit Cocktail "Pies"**; and if your idea of heaven is eating breakfast all day long, you've got some terrific choices here: **Zach's Bird in the Nest, Grilled Cornmeal Mush**, and **Aaron's Grilled French Toast**, just to name three.

Broccoli Frittata

This savory specialty makes a terrific choice for brunch on weekends . . . though I still can't persuade Cliff that broccoli is oh-so-tasty! This dish is a handy last-minute supper, since you're likely to have eggs and frozen veggies on hand.   ◐   Serves 2

3 eggs or equivalent in egg substitute

1 teaspoon Italian seasoning

1 (2-ounce) jar chopped pimiento, drained

*¼ cup (¾ ounce) Kraft Reduced Fat Parmesan Style Grated
     Topping*

1 cup frozen chopped broccoli, thawed, and finely chopped

Plug in and generously spray both sides of double-sided electric contact grill with olive oil–flavored cooking spray and preheat for 5 minutes. Meanwhile, in a medium bowl, combine eggs, Italian seasoning, pimiento, and Parmesan cheese. Add broccoli. Mix well to combine. Carefully pour mixture onto prepared grill, being certain not to pour too close to bottom. Close lid and grill for 6 to 7 minutes or until eggs are set. Divide into 2 servings.

HINT: Thaw broccoli by placing in a colander and rinsing under
     hot water for 1 minute.

Each serving equals:

HE: 2 Protein • 1 Vegetable

182 Calories • 10 g Fat • 13 g Protein •
10 g Carbohydrate • 277 mg Sodium •
150 mg Calcium • 3 g Fiber

DIABETIC: 2 Meat • 1 Vegetable

Grilled Breakfast Sausage Patties

Ever since my first Healthy Exchanges cookbook, I've worked a little culinary magic to turn a few good-for-you ingredients into my version of sausage. Now even if the "real thing" is off-limits, my special sausage patties will make you a believer! ☻   Serves 6

16 ounces extra-lean ground sirloin beef or turkey breast
1 teaspoon ground sage
½ teaspoon garlic powder
1 teaspoon poultry seasoning

Plug in and generously spray both sides of double-sided electric contact grill with butter-flavored cooking spray and preheat for 5 minutes. Meanwhile, in a large bowl, combine meat, sage, garlic powder, and poultry seasoning. Using a ⅓ cup measuring cup as a guide, form into 6 patties. Evenly arrange patties on prepared grill. Close lid and grill for 5 to 6 minutes.

Each serving equals:

HE: 2 Protein

87 Calories • 3 g Fat • 15 g Protein •
0 g Carbohydrate • 43 mg Sodium • 4 mg Calcium •
0 g Fiber

DIABETIC: 2 Meat

Zach's Bird in the Nest

The people I love best have always inspired my recipes, and this one is a special favorite of my grandson Zach. He likes his eggs served just perfectly nestled in a piece of toast, with a little bread "hat" on top—and I bet your kids will too!   ☻   Serves 2

2 slices reduced-calorie white bread
2 eggs or equivalent in egg substitute
⅛ teaspoon table salt
⅛ teaspoon black pepper

Plug in and generously spray both sides of double-sided electric contact grill with butter-flavored cooking spray and preheat for 5 minutes. Meanwhile, using a 2½-inch biscuit or cookie cutter, cut a round hole in center of bread slices. Evenly arrange both bread slices and holes on prepared grill. Break eggs, one at a time, into a saucer. Carefully slide each egg into a hole in bread. Evenly sprinkle salt and pepper over eggs. Lightly spray tops with butter-flavored cooking spray. Close lid and grill for 5 to 6 minutes. When serving, place bread and egg on a plate and top with bread circle.

Each serving equals:

HE: 1 Protein • ½ Bread

117 Calories • 5 g Fat • 9 g Protein •
9 g Carbohydrate • 323 mg Sodium •
42 mg Calcium • 0 g Fiber

DIABETIC: 1 Meat • ½ Starch

Aaron's Grilled French Toast ❄

It's a classic made even more scrumptious on the grill! If you're used to making French toast on weekends only, this quick-and-easy version may encourage you to make everyday breakfasts more special! My grandson Aaron says this is his favorite, so I had to name it after him! ☻ Serves 4

1 egg, beaten, or equivalent in egg substitute
1 cup fat-free milk
¼ teaspoon ground cinnamon
2 teaspoons Splenda Granular
8 slices reduced-calorie white bread

Plug in and generously spray both sides of double-sided electric contact grill with butter-flavored cooking spray and preheat for 5 minutes. Meanwhile, in a medium saucer, combine egg and milk. Stir in cinnamon and Splenda. Soak bread slices in mixture, turning to coat both sides. Evenly arrange coated bread on prepared grill. Evenly drizzle any remaining milk mixture over top of bread. Lightly spray top of bread pieces with butter-flavored cooking spray. Close lid and grill for 7 to 8 minutes or until bread is golden brown. Serve at once.

HINT: If necessary, grill toast in 2 batches.

Each serving equals:

HE: 1 Bread • ¼ Fat Free Milk • ¼ Protein •
1 Optional Calorie

138 Calories • 2 g Fat • 9 g Protein •
21 g Carbohydrate • 277 mg Sodium •
118 mg Calcium • 1 g Fiber

DIABETIC: 1½ Starch

Grilled Cornmeal Mush

They know how to make breakfast really special in the South, and cornmeal patties like these are part of a beloved hearty tradition. These are great on the grill, and both kids and adults will clamor for seconds! ☻ Serves 2

> 6 tablespoons yellow cornmeal
> ¼ teaspoon table salt
> ¼ cup cold water
> 1 cup boiling water
> ½ cup Log Cabin Sugar Free Maple Syrup

Spray a 9-by-5-inch loaf pan with butter-flavored cooking spray. In a medium saucepan, combine cornmeal, salt, and cold water. Add boiling water, stirring rapidly. Bring mixture to a boil, stirring constantly. Lower heat, cover, and simmer for 10 minutes, stirring occasionally. Pour cornmeal into prepared loaf pan. Cover and refrigerate for several hours or overnight. When ready to prepare, plug in and generously spray both sides of double-sided electric contact grill with butter-flavored cooking spray and preheat for 5 minutes. Cut set mush mixture into 6 slices. Evenly arrange mush slices on prepared grill. Lightly spray tops with butter-flavored cooking spray. Close lid and grill for 5 to 6 minutes. Meanwhile, place maple syrup in a microwave-safe container and microwave on HIGH (100% power) for 20 seconds or until hot. For each serving, place 3 slices of grilled mush on a plate and drizzle ¼ cup hot maple syrup over top.

Each serving equals:

HE: 1 Bread • ½ Slider

120 Calories • 0 g Fat • 2 g Protein •
28 g Carbohydrate • 379 mg Sodium •
1 mg Calcium • 2 g Fiber

DIABETIC: 1½ Starch/Carbohydrate

Blueberry Thrill Snacks

Here's a perfect after-school "pocket" delight that will win cheers from kids and adults alike. My taste-testers voted for blueberry, but if you prefer strawberry or apricot, go for it!

◐ Serves 2 (2 each)

1 pita bread round
2 tablespoons (1 ounce) Philadelphia fat-free soft cream cheese
3 tablespoons blueberry spreadable fruit
2 tablespoons coarsely chopped walnuts

Plug in and generously spray both sides of double-sided electric contact grill with butter-flavored cooking spray and preheat for 5 minutes. Meanwhile, cut pita bread in half and then cut each half in half again to form 4 wedges. In a small bowl, stir cream cheese and spreadable fruit until blended. Stir in walnuts. Spread about 1 full tablespoon blueberry mixture between each wedge. Evenly arrange wedges on prepared grill. Lightly spray tops with butter-flavored cooking spray. Close lid and grill for 4 to 5 minutes. Serve at once.

Each serving equals:

HE: 1 Bread • 1 Fruit • ¾ Protein • ½ Fat

205 Calories • 5 g Fat • 6 g Protein •
34 g Carbohydrate • 234 mg Sodium •
74 mg Calcium • 1 g Fiber

DIABETIC: 1 Starch • 1 Fruit • 1 Fat • ½ Meat

Cheyanne's Peanut Butter and Carrot Pita Snacks

If you're searching for the perfect after-school snack or something healthy to handle the famous four o'clock munchies, this should fill the bill! It couldn't be quicker or tastier, and it delivers a lot of good nutrition too! My granddaughter Cheyanne gives me the sweetest smile when she's gobbling these. ☻ Serves 2 (2 each)

> 1 pita bread round
> 2 tablespoons Peter Pan reduced-fat peanut butter
> 1 tablespoon orange marmalade spreadable fruit
> ½ cup grated carrots
> 2 tablespoons raisins

Plug in and generously spray both sides of double-sided electric contact grill with butter-flavored cooking spray and preheat for 5 minutes. Meanwhile, cut pita in half and then cut each half in half again to form 4 wedges. In a small bowl, combine peanut butter and spreadable fruit. Add carrots and raisins. Mix well to combine. Evenly spread about 2 tablespoons carrot mixture between each wedge. Evenly arrange wedges on prepared grill. Lightly spray tops with butter-flavored cooking spray. Close lid and grill for 4 to 5 minutes. Serve at once.

Each serving equals:

HE: 1 Bread • 1 Fruit • 1 Protein • 1 Fat • ½ Vegetable

226 Calories • 6 g Fat • 7 g Protein • 36 g Carbohydrate • 248 mg Sodium • 37 mg Calcium • 3 g Fiber

DIABETIC: 1½ Starch/Carbohydrate • 1 Fruit • ½ Meat • ½ Fat • ½ Vegetable

Gringo Cheese Snacks

Here's my version of a tangy quesadillalike snack using just enough heat to please your tastebuds. *Gracias* to the clever folks who found a way to make that old favorite Cheez Whiz so light and still so good. ☻ Serves 2 (2 each)

> 1 pita bread round
> ¼ cup Cheez Whiz Light
> ¼ cup thick, chunky salsa (mild, medium, or hot)

Plug in and generously spray both sides of double-sided electric contact grill with butter-flavored cooking spray and preheat for 5 minutes. Meanwhile, cut pita bread in half and then cut each half in half again to form 4 wedges. In a small bowl, combine Cheez Whiz Light and salsa. Spread about 2 tablespoons cheese mixture between each wedge. Evenly arrange wedges on prepared grill. Lightly spray tops with butter-flavored cooking spray. Close lid and grill for 4 to 5 minutes. Serve at once.

Each serving equals:

HE: 1 Bread • ½ Protein • ¼ Vegetable

163 Calories • 3 g Fat • 9 g Protein •
25 g Carbohydrate • 977 mg Sodium •
172 mg Calcium • 2 g Fiber

DIABETIC: 1½ Starch/Carbohydrate • ½ Meat

Spencer's Stuffed Cheese Pizza Snacks

It couldn't be simpler or tastier, but this quick-fix lunch is an ideal way to use your grill. It brings out the best in the pita bread, and melts the cheese so thoroughly, you'll be munching away in moments. My grandson Spencer gave me a big hug after munching one of these!   ☉   Serves 2

1 pita bread round
¼ cup reduced-sodium ketchup
½ teaspoon pizza or Italian seasoning
3 tablespoons shredded Kraft reduced-fat Cheddar cheese
3 tablespoons shredded Kraft reduced-fat mozzarella cheese

Plug in and generously spray both sides of double-sided electric contact grill with olive oil–flavored cooking spray and preheat for 5 minutes. Meanwhile, cut pita bread in half and then cut each half in half again to form 4 wedges. In a small bowl, combine ketchup, pizza seasoning, Cheddar cheese, and mozzarella cheese. Evenly spread about 1½ tablespoons sauce mixture between each wedge. Evenly arrange wedges on prepared grill. Lightly spray top with olive oil–flavored cooking spray. Close lid and grill for 4 to 5 minutes. Serve at once.

Each serving equals:

HE: 1 Bread • 1 Protein • ¼ Slider •
10 Optional Calories

176 Calories • 4 g Fat • 10 g Protein •
25 g Carbohydrate • 343 mg Sodium •
185 mg Calcium • 1 g Fiber

DIABETIC: 1½ Starch/Carbohydrate • 1 Meat

East Indies Chicken Cocktail Appetizers

After just one bite, it's not that difficult to imagine yourself standing in the shadows of the glorious Taj Mahal! You don't have to know anything about exotic dishes of Asia to enjoy the special sizzle of this dish. ❂ Serves 4 (2 each)

1 cup (5 ounces) finely chopped cooked chicken breast
2 teaspoons dried onion flakes
1 egg or equivalent in egg substitute
6 tablespoons dried fine bread crumbs
2 tablespoons Kraft fat-free mayonnaise
½ teaspoon prepared yellow mustard
1 teaspoon chili seasoning

Plug in and generously spray both sides of double-sided electric contact grill with butter-flavored cooking spray and preheat for 5 minutes. Meanwhile, in a medium bowl, combine chicken and onion flakes. Add egg, bread crumbs, mayonnaise, mustard, and chili seasoning. Mix well to combine. Using a full tablespoon as a guide, form into 8 patties. Evenly arrange patties on prepared grill. Lightly spray tops with butter-flavored cooking spray. Close lid and grill for 5 to 7 minutes or until appetizers are golden brown. Serve at once.

Each serving equals:

HE: 1½ Protein • ½ Bread • 5 Optional Calories

119 Calories • 3 g Fat • 14 g Protein •
9 g Carbohydrate • 203 mg Sodium •
38 mg Calcium • 1 g Fiber

DIABETIC: 1½ Meat • ½ Starch

Corned Beef Potato Appetizers

Are you one of those corned beef lovers who could gobble it every day for lunch? Well, there are lots of you out there, and this savory snack—ideal for party food—will please every last one!

● Serves 4 (2 each)

> ¾ cup boiling water
>
> 1 cup instant potato flakes
>
> ⅓ cup Kraft fat-free mayonnaise
>
> 1 tablespoon prepared horseradish sauce
>
> 2 teaspoons dried onion flakes
>
> 1 teaspoon dried parsley flakes
>
> ⅛ teaspoon black pepper
>
> 2 (2.5-ounce) packages Carl Buddig lean corned beef, finely shredded

Plug in and generously spray both sides of double-sided electric contact grill with butter-flavored cooking spray and preheat for 5 minutes. Meanwhile, in a medium bowl, combine boiling water, dry potato flakes, and mayonnaise. Add horseradish sauce, onion flakes, parsley flakes, and black pepper. Mix well to combine. Stir in shredded corned beef. Using a full tablespoon as a guide, form into 8 patties. Evenly arrange patties on prepared grill. Lightly spray tops with butter-flavored cooking spray. Close lid and grill for 8 to 10 minutes or until appetizers are golden brown. Serve at once.

Each serving equals:

HE: 1¼ Protein • ¾ Bread • 15 Optional Calories

---

140 Calories • 4 g Fat • 9 g Protein •
17 g Carbohydrate • 670 mg Sodium •
13 mg Calcium • 1 g Fiber

DIABETIC: 1 Meat • 1 Starch

Cocktail Meatballs

This is one of those classic cocktail party offerings, but if you've never had a cocktail party, don't skip this sweet-and-tangy party food—just celebrate with family anytime!   ☻   Serves 4

8 ounces extra-lean ground sirloin beef or turkey breast

6 tablespoons dried fine bread crumbs

1 tablespoon dried onion flakes

⅛ teaspoon black pepper

2 tablespoons water

½ cup chili sauce

¼ cup grape spreadable fruit

Plug in and generously spray both sides of a double-sided electric contact grill with butter-flavored cooking spray and preheat for 5 minutes. Meanwhile, in a medium bowl, combine meat, bread crumbs, onion flakes, black pepper, and water. Form into 16 (1-inch) balls. Evenly arrange balls on prepared grill. Close lid and grill for 4 to 5 minutes. Meanwhile, in a small saucepan, combine chili sauce and spreadable fruit. Cook over medium-low heat, while meatballs are grilling, stirring occasionally. For each serving, place 4 meatballs on a plate and drizzle about 2 tablespoons sauce over top.

Each serving equals:

HE: 1½ Protein • 1 Fruit • ½ Bread • ½ Slider

187 Calories • 3 g Fat • 12 g Protein •
28 g Carbohydrate • 983 mg Sodium •
25 mg Calcium • 0 g Fiber

DIABETIC: 1½ Meat • 1 Fruit • 1 Starch/Carbohydrate

Pickle and Ham Canapes

When you're picking out the party food for your next festive occasion, why not please your guests and yourself with these flavorful "best bites"? They're great for last-minute guests because the ingredients are likely to be poised for action in your pantry and fridge.

◐ Serves 5 (2 each)

> 1 (7.5-ounce) can Pillsbury refrigerated buttermilk biscuits
> ¼ cup (2 ounces) Philadelphia fat-free cream cheese
> 1 (2.5-ounce) package lean Carl Buddig ham, finely shredded
> 10 dill pickle chips

Plug in and generously spray both sides of double-sided electric contact grill with butter-flavored cooking spray and preheat for 5 minutes. Meanwhile, separate biscuits and then separate again so there are 20 biscuit halves. In a medium bowl, stir cream cheese with a sturdy spoon until soft. Add shredded ham. Mix well to combine. Spread about 1½ teaspoons ham mixture on 10 biscuit halves. Arrange pickle chip in center of each. Top each with another biscuit half. Seal edges with tines of a fork. Evenly arrange biscuits on prepared grill. Close lid and grill for 4 to 5 minutes.

HINTS: 1. Biscuits work best when chilled
2. Pat pickles dry using a paper towel, before using.
3. Spray the tines of a fork with butter-flavored cooking spray before sealing edges of biscuit.

Each serving equals:

HE: 1½ Bread • ¾ Protein

---

134 Calories • 2 g Fat • 8 g Protein •
21 g Carbohydrate • 608 mg Sodium •
40 mg Calcium • 0 g Fiber

DIABETIC: 1½ Starch • 1 Meat

Josh's Grilled Corn Dog Snacks

A down-home, Heartland original, corn dogs bring back all those wonderful memories of childhood, including visits to the state fair, when you couldn't wait to gobble one of these down! I've truly enjoying "making memories" for my grandson Josh, who dearly loves these. ☽ Serves 5 (4 each)

6 tablespoons yellow cornmeal

¾ cup Bisquick Reduced Fat Baking Mix

2 eggs, beaten, or equivalent in egg substitute

⅓ cup fat-free milk

1 (16-ounce) package Oscar Mayer or Healthy Choice reduced-fat
    frankfurters, cut in half crosswise

Plug in and generously spray both sides of double-sided electric contact grill with butter-flavored cooking spray and preheat for 5 minutes. Meanwhile, in a pie plate, combine cornmeal and baking mix. Add eggs and milk. Mix well to combine. Slowly roll frankfurter pieces in cornmeal mixture to coat. Evenly arrange coated frankfurter pieces on prepared grill. Lightly spray tops with butter-flavored cooking spray. Close lid and grill for 4 to 5 minutes or until coating is golden brown. Serve at once.

Each serving equals:

HE: 2½ Protein • 1 Bread • 19 Optional Calories

225 Calories • 5 g Fat • 17 g Protein •
28 g Carbohydrate • 978 mg Sodium •
48 mg Calcium • 1 g Fiber

DIABETIC: 2½ Meat • 1 Starch

"Fried" Apple Rings

I've always thought "an apple a day" was good advice, though I suspect that any healthy fruit will help keep the doctor away. Here's a delectable way to include yummy-tasting fruit in your daily menus—enjoy the flavor and the health benefits, too!

♥ Serves 2

> 1 (large-sized) Macintosh apple
> 2 tablespoons lemon juice
> ¼ cup + 2 teaspoons Splenda Granular ☆
> ⅛ teaspoon ground cinnamon

Plug in and generously spray both sides of double-sided electric contact grill with butter-flavored cooking spray and preheat for 5 minutes. Meanwhile, core apple, then cut in half and cut each half into 4 (¼-inch) rings. In a large flat bowl, combine lemon juice and ¼ cup Splenda. Stir apple rings into lemon juice mixture. Evenly arrange coated apple rings on prepared grill. Close lid and grill for 4 to 5 minutes. In a small bowl, combine remaining 2 teaspoons Splenda and cinnamon. For each serving, place 4 rings on a dessert plate and sprinkle ½ teaspoon cinnamon mixture over top.

Each serving equals:

HE: 1 Fruit • 18 Optional Calories

80 Calories • 0 g Fat • 0 g Protein •
20 g Carbohydrate • 0 mg Sodium • 11 mg Calcium •
3 g Fiber

DIABETIC: 1 Fruit

Maple Apple Grill

Some flavors just go hand-in-hand forever, and tops among those are apples and maple syrup. I spooned a serving of this on top of hot cereal one chilly morning and smiled all day long! This is one of my grandchildren's favorites, and one taste will persuade you to join our "club"!   ☻   Serves 4 (½ cup)

¼ cup Log Cabin Sugar Free Maple Syrup

1 tablespoon Splenda Granular

¼ teaspoon apple pie spice

2 cups (4 small) cored, peeled, and sliced cooking apples

¼ cup chopped walnuts

2 tablespoons raisins

Plug in and generously spray both sides of double-sided electric contact grill with butter-flavored cooking spray and preheat for 5 minutes. Meanwhile, in a large bowl, combine maple syrup, Splenda, and apple pie spice. Add apples, walnuts, and raisins. Mix well to coat. Evenly arrange apple mixture on prepared grill. Close lid and grill for 6 minutes. Serve at once.

HINT: Good served "as is" or spooned over sugar- and fat-free vanilla ice cream, but if using, don't forget to count calories accordingly.

Each serving equals:

HE: 1¼ Fruit • ½ Fat • ¼ Protein •
11 Optional Calories

109 Calories • 5 g Fat • 1 g Protein •
15 g Carbohydrate • 25 mg Sodium •
15 mg Calcium • 2 g Fiber

DIABETIC: 1 Fruit • 1 Fat

Abram's Grilled Banana Slices

If the only way you eat bananas is sliced on top of your morning cereal, it's time to break out of your rut and "go bananas!" My grandson Abram prefers his serving ladled over ice cream; I bet you will, too! ☉   Serves 2

> 1 (medium-sized) firm banana
> ⅛ teaspoon ground cinnamon
> 2 tablespoons Splenda Granular

Plug in and generously spray both sides of double-sided electric contact grill with butter-flavored cooking spray and preheat for 5 minutes. Meanwhile, in a medium saucer, combine cinnamon and Splenda. Peel banana and slice into ¼-inch slices. Coat banana slices in cinnamon mixture. Evenly arrange coated banana slices on prepared grill. Close lid and grill for 1½ minutes. Divide evenly into 2 servings and serve at once.

HINT: Good "as is" or served warm over sugar- and fat-free vanilla ice cream, but if using, don't forget to count calories accordingly.

Each serving equals:

HE: 1 Fruit • 6 Optional Calories

76 Calories • 0 g Fat • 1 g Protein •
18 g Carbohydrate • 1 mg Sodium • 6 mg Calcium •
2 g Fiber

DIABETIC: 1 Fruit

Apple "Pie" à la Mode Sundaes

The irresistible aroma of apples baking will perfume your entire home, and this easy-to-fix ice cream topping will be a treat your family requests regularly!   ☻   Serves 4

> 2 tablespoons Diet Mountain Dew
> 2 tablespoons Musselman's No Sugar Added Applesauce
> 1 teaspoon apple pie spice
> 3 cups (6 small) cored, peeled, and chopped cooking apples
> 2 cups Wells' Blue Bunny sugar- and fat-free vanilla ice cream
>   or any sugar- and fat-free ice cream

Plug in and generously spray both sides of double-sided electric contact grill with butter-flavored cooking spray and preheat for 5 minutes. Meanwhile, in a large bowl, combine Diet Mountain Dew, applesauce, and apple pie spice. Stir in chopped apples. Mix well to coat. Evenly arrange apple mixture on prepared grill. Close lid and grill for 6 minutes. For each serving, place ½ cup ice cream in a dessert dish and spoon about ½ cup warm apple mixture over top. Serve at once.

Each serving equals:

HE: 1½ Fruit • 1 Slider • 2 Optional Calories

136 Calories • 0 g Fat • 4 g Protein •
30 g Carbohydrate • 51 mg Sodium •
131 mg Calcium • 2 g Fiber

DIABETIC: 1½ Fruit • 1 Starch/Carbohydrate

Peach Becky Sundaes

Ever since she was a little girl, my daughter, Becky, loved peaches, and so many of my peachy recipes are dedicated to her. Now that she (and her brothers) have made me the happiest of grandmas, she's still first in line for any dessert that stars peaches!

◗ Serves 4

> ¼ cup peach spreadable fruit
> 2 cups (4 medium) peeled and sliced fresh peaches
> ¼ cup chopped pecans
> 2 cups Wells' Blue Bunny sugar- and fat-free vanilla ice cream
>   or any sugar- and fat-free ice cream

Plug in and generously spray both sides of double-sided electric contact grill with butter-flavored cooking spray and preheat for 5 minutes. Meanwhile, in a large bowl, stir spreadable fruit until soft. Add peaches and pecans. Mix well to coat. Evenly arrange peach mixture on prepared grill. Close lid and grill for 3 to 4 minutes until peaches are warm, but not too soft. For each serving, place ½ cup ice cream in a dessert dish and spoon about ⅓ cup warm fruit mixture over ice cream. Serve at once.

Each serving equals:

HE: 2 Fruit • 1 Fat • 1 Slider • 2 Optional Calories

204 Calories • 4 g Fat • 5 g Protein •
37 g Carbohydrate • 53 mg Sodium •
129 mg Calcium • 2 g Fiber

DIABETIC: 2 Fruit • 1 Fat • 1 Starch/Carbohydrate

Hawaiian Hash Sundaes

Your kids won't be begging for a trip to the local ice cream parlor once they see and savor this sweet-and-crunchy dessert topping that is like a quick trip to the islands of Paradise! You don't need to wait for a party; simply celebrate that you're sharing today with the people you love.   ☻   Serves 6

3 tablespoons orange marmalade spreadable fruit

¼ teaspoon coconut extract

1 cup (1 medium) diced banana

1 (8-ounce) can pineapple tidbits, packed in fruit juice, drained

1 (11-ounce) can mandarin oranges, rinsed and drained

2 tablespoons chopped macadamia nuts

¼ cup flaked coconut

2 cups Wells' Blue Bunny sugar- and fat-free vanilla ice cream
     or any sugar- and fat-free ice cream

¼ cup Cool Whip Lite

Plug in and spray both sides of double-sided electric contact grill with butter-flavored cooking spray and preheat for 5 minutes. Meanwhile, in a large bowl, combine spreadable fruit and coconut extract. Add banana, pineapple, mandarin oranges, macadamia nuts, and coconut. Mix well to coat. Evenly arrange fruit mixture on prepared grill. Lightly spray top of fruit mixture with butter-flavored cooking spray. Close lid and grill for 5 to 6 minutes or until fruit is warm, but not too soft. For each serving, place ⅓ cup ice cream in a dessert dish, spoon about ⅓ cup fruit mixture over ice cream, and top with 1 tablespoon Cool Whip Lite. Serve at once.

Each serving equals:

HE: 1½ Fruit • ⅓ Fat • ¾ Slider •
13 Optional Calories

183 Calories • 3 g Fat • 3 g Protein •
36 g Carbohydrate • 49 mg Sodium •
84 mg Calcium • 1 g Fiber

DIABETIC: 1½ Fruit • ½ Starch/Carbohydrate • ½ Fat

Muddy Bottom Strawberry Sundaes

Mmmm, doesn't the name of this recipe just get your taste buds tingling? I'm a fan of anything strawberry, but adding nuts and chocolate shoots off some real culinary fireworks! ☽ Serves 4

2 tablespoons strawberry spreadable fruit

2 tablespoons Diet Mountain Dew

3 cups sliced fresh strawberries

2 cups Wells' Blue Bunny sugar- and fat-free chocolate ice cream
        or any sugar- and fat-free ice cream

6 (2½-inch) chocolate graham cracker squares, made into crumbs

2 tablespoons dry-roasted peanuts

¼ cup Cool Whip Lite

Plug in and generously spray both sides of double-sided electric contact grill with butter-flavored cooking spray and preheat for 5 minutes. Meanwhile, in a large bowl, combine spreadable fruit and Diet Mountain Dew. Stir in sliced strawberries. Mix well to coat. Evenly arrange strawberry mixture on prepared grill. Close lid and grill for 3 minutes or just until strawberries are warm but not too soft. For each serving, sprinkle 2 tablespoons chocolate graham cracker crumbs in a sundae or dessert dish, spoon ½ cup ice cream over crumbs, drizzle about ⅓ cup warm strawberry mixture over ice cream, sprinkle 1½ teaspoons peanuts over strawberry mixture, and garnish with 1 tablespoon Cool Whip Lite. Serve at once.

HINT: A self-seal sandwich bag works great for crushing graham
        crackers.

Each serving equals:

HE: 1¼ Fruit • ½ Bread • ¼ Fat • 1 Slider •
16 Optional Calories

204 Calories • 4 g Fat • 6 g Protein •
36 g Carbohydrate • 88 mg Sodium •
140 mg Calcium • 3 g Fiber

DIABETIC: 1½ Starch/Carbohydrate • 1 Fruit

Tropicana Sundaes

Imagine arriving at a glamorous resort under the steamiest possible sun—and you've got an idea of what this citrusy-sweet taste treat feels like as it tumbles toward your tummy! Ice cream will seem undressed without this fabulous blend on top.   ☯   Serves 4

¼ cup apricot spreadable fruit
1 (8-ounce) can pineapple chunks, packed in fruit juice, drained and 1 tablespoon liquid reserved
1 (11-ounce) can mandarin oranges, rinsed and drained
2 cups Wells' Blue Bunny sugar- and fat-free vanilla ice cream or any sugar- and fat-free ice cream
1 tablespoon + 1 teaspoon chopped pecans

Plug in and generously spray both sides of double-sided electric contact grill with butter-flavored cooking spray and preheat for 5 minutes. Meanwhile, in a large bowl, combine spreadable fruit and reserved pineapple liquid. Add mandarin oranges and pineapple chunks. Mix well to coat. Evenly arrange fruit mixture on prepared grill. Close lid and grill for 4 to 5 minutes. For each serving, place ½ cup ice cream in a dessert dish, spoon about ¼ cup warm fruit mixture over ice cream, and garnish with 1 teaspoon pecans. Serve at once.

Each serving equals:

HE: 2 Fruit • 1 Slider • 7 Optional Calories

203 Calories • 3 g Fat • 5 g Protein •
39 g Carbohydrate • 67 mg Sodium •
120 mg Calcium • 1 g Fiber

DIABETIC: 2 Fruit • 1 Starch/Carbohydrate

Ellie's Fruit Cocktail "Pies"

A grill is the perfect appliance to turn store-bought bread into a wonderful sweet dessert! If you've loved fruit cocktail since you were a kid, give this old-fashioned treat a try. (I named this recipe after a real kid—my granddaughter Ellie, who adores these!)

○ Serves 4

> 2 tablespoons orange marmalade spreadable fruit
> 8 slices raisin-cinnamon bread
> 1 (8-ounce) can fruit cocktail, packed in fruit juice, well drained

Plug in and generously spray both sides of double-sided electric contact grill with butter-flavored cooking spray and preheat for 5 minutes. Meanwhile, spread 1½ teaspoons spreadable fruit on 4 slices of bread. Evenly spoon a full 2 tablespoons fruit cocktail over top of each slice. Arrange another slice of bread on each. Evenly arrange "pies" on prepared grill. Lightly spray tops with butter-flavored cooking spray. Close lid and grill for 4 to 5 minutes or until bread is toasted and filling is hot. Serve at once.

Each serving equals:

HE: 2 Bread • 1 Fruit

---

191 Calories • 3 g Fat • 6 g Protein •
38 g Carbohydrate • 214 mg Sodium •
5 mg Calcium • 2 g Fiber

DIABETIC: 2 Starch • 1 Fruit

Pita Dessert Wedges

Does it surprise you that I "hired" the handy pita bread for dessert duty? It's a wonderful option because it takes on the sweet or savory flavor of whatever you stuff inside. This time, it's fruity, nutty, and fun fun fun! ☻ Serves 4

1 pita bread round
¼ cup raspberry spreadable fruit
¼ cup chopped walnuts
¼ cup mini chocolate chips
1 cup Wells' Blue Bunny sugar-and fat-free vanilla ice cream or
* any sugar-and fat-free ice cream*

Plug in and generously spray both sides of double-sided electric contact grill with butter-flavored cooking spray and preheat for 5 minutes. Meanwhile, cut pita in half and cut each half in half again to form 4 wedges. In a small bowl, combine spreadable fruit, walnuts, and chocolate chips. Evenly spread about 2 tablespoons filling mixture between each wedge. Evenly arrange wedges on prepared grill. Lightly spray tops with butter-flavored cooking spray. Close lid and grill for 4 minutes. For each serving, place 1 warm wedge on dessert plate and spoon ¼ cup ice cream over top. Serve at once.

Each serving equals:

HE: 1 Fruit • ½ Bread • ½ Fat • ¼ Protein •
¾ Slider • 17 Optional Calories

207 Calories • 7 g Fat • 5 g Protein •
31 g Carbohydrate • 110 mg Sodium •
82 mg Calcium • 1 g Fiber

DIABETIC: 1 Fruit • 1 Starch/Carbohydrate • 1 Fruit

Grilled Peach Melba Shortcakes

Even your fanciest restaurants may not have thought of serving this dessert delight in just this fun way! Choose the freshest peaches you can find, and you're bound to win "Bravos" from the crowd at your table. ☻ Serves 4

¼ cup raspberry spreadable fruit
2 cups (4 medium) peeled and sliced fresh ripe peaches
1 cup Wells' Blue Bunny sugar-and fat-free vanilla ice cream or
  any sugar-and fat-free ice cream
4 individual sponge cake dessert cups

Plug in and generously spray both sides of double-sided electric contact grill with butter-flavored cooking spray and preheat for 5 minutes. Meanwhile, in a large bowl, stir spreadable fruit until soft. Add sliced peaches. Mix well to coat. Evenly arrange peach mixture on prepared grill. Close lid and grill for 3 minutes or until peaches are warm, but not too soft. For each serving, place 1 sponge cake dessert cup in a dessert dish, arrange ¼ cup ice cream over dessert cup, and spoon about ½ cup warm peach mixture over top. Serve at once.

Each serving equals:

HE: 2 Fruit • 1 Bread • ½ Slider • 5 Optional Calories

222 Calories • 2 g Fat • 5 g Protein •
46 g Carbohydrate • 158 mg Sodium •
84 mg Calcium • 3 g Fiber

DIABETIC: 2 Fruit • 1½ Starch/Carbohydrate

Pears Perfection Shortcakes

I've had readers tell me they've got a zillion recipes for apples but not nearly enough for those ripe pears piled high in their supermarkets and fruit stands! Pear-lovers, it's your lucky day, because this great grilled dessert celebrates what is most perfect about your favorite fruit.   ☻   Serves 4

> 2 tablespoons raspberry spreadable fruit
> 2 tablespoons Diet Mountain Dew
> 3 cups (6 medium) peeled and chopped Bartlett pears
> 1/4 cup chopped walnuts
> 4 individual sponge cake dessert cups
> 1/4 cup Cool Whip Lite
> 1 tablespoon + 1 teaspoon mini chocolate chips

Plug in and generously spray both sides of double-sided electric contact grill with butter-flavored cooking spray and preheat for 5 minutes. Meanwhile, in a large bowl, combine spreadable fruit and Diet Mountain Dew. Add chopped pears and walnuts. Mix well to coat. Evenly arrange pear mixture on prepared grill. Close lid and grill for 7 minutes. For each serving, place 1 sponge cake dessert cup in a dessert dish, spoon about 1/2 cup warm pear mixture over dessert cup, top with 1 tablespoon Cool Whip Lite, and sprinkle 1 teaspoon chocolate chips over top. Serve at once.

Each serving equals:

HE: 2 Fruit • 1 Bread • 1/2 Fat • 1/4 Protein •
1/2 Slider • 18 Optional Calories

272 Calories • 8 g Fat • 4 g Protein •
46 g Carbohydrate • 133 mg Sodium •
43 mg Calcium • 5 g Fiber

DIABETIC: 2 Fruit • 1 1/2 Starch • 1 Fat

Big Island Shortcakes

If your budget doesn't allow for weekends in Hawaii (ours sure doesn't!), you can still enjoy the pleasures of paradise with this fast and fabulous dessert that says "Aloha" with every bite.

☕ Serves 4

> 2 tablespoons strawberry spreadable fruit
> 1 (8-ounce) can pineapple chunks, packed in fruit juice, drained and 2 tablespoons liquid reserved
> 1/4 teaspoon coconut extract
> 4 cups sliced fresh strawberries
> 2 tablespoons chopped pecans
> 4 individual sponge cake dessert cups
> 1/2 cup Cool Whip Lite
> 1 tablespoon + 1 teaspoon flaked coconut

Plug in and generously spray both sides of double-sided electric contact grill with butter-flavored cooking spray and preheat for 5 minutes. Meanwhile, in a large bowl, combine spreadable fruit, reserved pineapple liquid, and coconut extract. Stir in strawberries, pineapple chunks, and pecans. Mix well to coat. Evenly arrange fruit mixture on prepared grill. Close lid and grill for 3 to 4 minutes, or just until strawberries are warm but not too soft. For each serving, place 1 sponge cake dessert cup in a dessert dish, spoon about 1/2 cup hot fruit mixture over dessert cup, and top with 2 tablespoons Cool Whip Lite and 1 teaspoon flaked coconut. Serve at once.

Each serving equals:

HE: 2 Fruit • 1 Bread • 1/2 Fat • 1/4 Slider • 5 Optional Calories

234 Calories • 6 g Fat • 3 g Protein • 42 g Carbohydrate • 141 mg Sodium • 34 mg Calcium • 4 g Fiber

DIABETIC: 2 Fruit • 1 Starch • 1 Fat

Stuffed Shortcakes

If you love surprises as much as I do (and who doesn't?), these are a terrific way to tickle the taste buds of your family and friends. Someone once suggested that "it's what's inside that counts," and this recipe makes that truer than true. You could make these with a different flavor of fruit for every day of the week if you wanted to!

◑ Serves 5 (2 each)

1 (7.5-ounce) can Pillsbury refrigerated buttermilk biscuits
5 tablespoons spreadable fruit, any flavor ☆
1 tablespoon + 2 teaspoons Splenda Granular
1¼ cups Wells' Blue Bunny sugar-and fat-free ice cream or any sugar-and fat-free ice cream

Plug in and generously spray both sides of double-sided electric contact grill with butter-flavored cooking spray and preheat for 5 minutes. Meanwhile, separate biscuits and then separate again so there are 20 biscuit halves. Evenly spread 1 teaspoon spreadable fruit over 10 biscuit halves. Top each with another biscuit. Seal edges using the tines of a fork. Evenly arrange biscuits on prepared grill. Lightly spray top of biscuits with butter-flavored cooking spray, then sprinkle ½ teaspoon Splenda over top of each. Close lid and grill for 4 to 5 minutes. Meanwhile, place remaining spreadable fruit in a microwave-safe container and microwave on HIGH (100% power) for 15 to 20 seconds or until melted. For each serving, place 2 warm stuffed biscuits in a dessert dish, spoon ¼ cup ice cream over biscuits, and drizzle 2 teaspoons warm fruit spread over top. Serve at once.

HINTS: 1. Biscuits work best when chilled.
2. Spray the tines of a fork with butter-flavored cooking spray before sealing edges of biscuits.

Each serving equals:

HE: 1½ Bread • 1 Fruit • ½ Slider •
2 Optional Calories

---

185 Calories • 1 g Fat • 8 g Protein •
36 g Carbohydrate • 417 mg Sodium •
120 mg Calcium • 1 g Fiber

DIABETIC: 2 Starch/Carbohydrate • 1 Fruit

Peanut Butter Cup Shortcakes with Hot Chocolate Sauce

Want a winning team to please the "sweet teeth" of the entire family? Couple chocolate and peanut butter, then cover your ears so the cheers don't send you out of the room! What a delectable way to enjoy two favorites in one nearly perfect dish! ☻ Serves 5

> 1 (7.5-ounce) can Pillsbury refrigerated buttermilk biscuits
> ¼ cup + 1 tablespoon Peter Pan reduced-fat peanut butter ☆
> 5 tablespoons mini chocolate chips
> 1 (4-serving) package JELL-O sugar-free chocolate cook-and-serve pudding mix
> ⅔ cup Carnation Nonfat Dry Milk Powder
> 1¾ cups water
> 1 teaspoon vanilla extract

Plug in and generously spray both sides of double-sided electric contact grill with butter-flavored cooking spray and preheat for 5 minutes. Meanwhile, separate biscuits and then separate again so there are 20 biscuit halves. Evenly spread 1 teaspoon peanut butter on all 20 biscuit halves. Sprinkle 1½ teaspoons mini chocolate chips on 10 halves. Top each with remaining biscuit halves, peanut butter side down. Seal edges with tines of a fork. Evenly arrange biscuits on prepared grill. Lightly spray tops with butter-flavored cooking spray. Close lid and grill for 6 to 7 minutes. Meanwhile, in a medium saucepan, combine dry pudding mix, dry milk powder, and water. Cook over medium heat, until mixture thickens, stirring constantly using a wire whisk. Remove from heat. Stir in remaining 5 teaspoons peanut butter and vanilla extract. For each serving, place 2 shortcakes on a dessert plate and spoon a full ⅓ cup hot chocolate sauce over top. Serve at once.

HINTS: 1. Biscuits work best when chilled.
2. Spray the tines of a fork with butter-flavored cooking spray, before sealing edges of biscuits.

3. Also good with sugar-and fat-free ice cream, but don't forget to count calories accordingly.

Each serving equals:

HE: 1½ Bread • 1 Protein • 1 Fat • ⅓ Fat Free Milk • ¼ Slider • 15 Optional Calories

297 Calories • 9 g Fat • 12 g Protein • 42 g Carbohydrate • 578 mg Sodium • 123 mg Calcium • 2 g Fiber

DIABETIC: 2 Starch/Carbohydrate • 1 Meat • 1 Fat

Great Grilling Menus

If your double-sided grill has been sitting on your kitchen counter because you're not sure how to construct satisfying and delicious family meals using it, here are my suggestions for festive menus that you will enjoy preparing and that everyone else will devour with pleasure! While you may not choose to use your grill for all the parts of a particular meal, isn't it great to know that you can?

Warm-Up Winter Brunch

Broccoli Frittata
Aaron's Grilled French Toast
Maple Apple Grill
Grilled Breakfast Sausage Patties

"Hot Hot Hot" Valentine's Day Dinner

Cocktail Meatballs
Grilled Raspberry Chicken Breasts
Daddy's Potato Patties
Muddy Bottom Strawberry Sundaes

Sizzling Spring Supper

East Indies Chicken Cocktail Appetizers
Grilled Asparagus in Mustard Butter
Crunchy Grilled Garlic Chicken
Apple "Pie" à la Mode Sundaes

"God Bless the USA" Fireworks Party

New England Grilled Crab Cakes
Tex-Mex Veggie Grill
L.A. Burgers
Hawaiian Hash Sundaes

Rainy Day Indoor "Barbecue"

Gringo Cheese Snacks
Mexican Grilled Hash Browns
Chili "Steaks" with Salsa Sauce
Tropicana Sundaes

Family Fun Fall Luncheon

Sweet Potato Cakes
Cajun Grilled Mixed Vegetables
Josh's Grilled Corn Dog Snacks
Peanut Butter Cup Shortcakes with Hot Chocolate Sauce

Making

Healthy Exchanges

Work for You

You're ready now to begin a wonderful journey to better health. In the preceding pages, you've discovered the remarkable variety of good food available to you when you begin eating the Healthy Exchanges way. You've stocked your pantry and learned many of my food preparation "secrets" that will point you on the way to delicious success.

But before I let you go, I'd like to share a few tips that I've learned while traveling toward healthier eating habits. It took me a long time to learn how to eat *smarter*. In fact, I'm still working on it. But I am getting better. For years, I could *inhale* a five-course meal in five minutes flat—and still make room for a second helping of dessert!

Now I follow certain signposts on the road that help me stay on the right path. I hope these ideas will help point you in the right direction as well.

1. **Eat slowly** so your brain has time to catch up with your tummy. Cut and chew each bite slowly. Try putting your fork down between bites. Stop eating as soon as you feel full. Crumple your napkin and throw it on top of your plate so you don't continue to eat when you are no longer hungry.

2. **Smaller plates** may help you feel more satisfied by your food portions *and* limit the amount you can put on the plate.

3. **Watch portion size.** If you are *truly* hungry, you can always add more food to your plate once you've finished your initial serving. But remember to count the additional food accordingly.

4. **Always eat at your dining-room or kitchen table.** You deserve better than nibbling from an open refrigerator or over the sink. Make an attractive place setting, even if you're eating alone. Feed your eyes as well as your stomach. By always eating at a table, you will become much more aware of your true food intake. For some reason, many of us conveniently "forget" the food we swallow while standing over the stove or munching in the car or on the run.

5. **Avoid doing anything else while you are eating.** If you read the paper or watch television while you eat, it's easy to consume too much food without realizing it, because you are concentrating on something else besides what you're eating. Then, when you look down at your plate and see that it's empty, you wonder where all the food went and why you still feel hungry.

Day by day, as you travel the path to good health, it will become easier to make the right choices, to eat *smarter*. But don't ever fool yourself into thinking that you'll be able to put your eating habits on cruise control and forget about them. Making a commitment to eat good healthy food and sticking to it takes some effort. But with all the good-tasting recipes in this Healthy Exchanges cookbook, just think how well you're going to eat—and enjoy it—from now on!

Healthy Lean Bon Appétit!

Index

Page numbers in **bold** indicate tables.

I want to hear from you . . .

Besides my family, the love of my life is creating "common folk" healthy recipes and solving everyday cooking questions in *The Healthy Exchanges Way*. Everyone who uses my recipes is considered part of the Healthy Exchanges Family, so please write to me if you have any questions, comments, or suggestions. I will do my best to answer. With your support, I'll continue to stir up even more recipes and cooking tips for the Family in the years to come.

Write to: JoAnna M. Lund
            c/o Healthy Exchanges, Inc.
            P.O. Box 80
            DeWitt, IA 52742-0080

If you prefer, you can fax me at (563) 659-2126 or contact me via e-mail by writing to HealthyJo@aol.com. Or visit my Healthy Exchanges website at: www.healthyexchanges.com.

Ever since I began stirring up Healthy Exchanges recipes, I wanted every dish to be rich in flavor and lively in taste. As part of my pursuit of satisfying eating and healthy living for a lifetime, I decided to create my own line of spices.

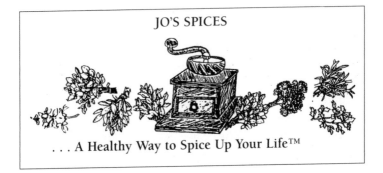

JO'S SPICES

. . . A Healthy Way to Spice Up Your Life™

JO's Spices are salt-, sugar-, wheat-, and MSG-free, and you can substitute them in any of the recipes calling for traditional spice mixes. If you're interested in hearing more about my special blends, please call Healthy Exchanges at (563) 659-8234 for more information or to order. If you prefer, write to JO's Spices, c/o Healthy Exchanges, P.O. Box 80, DeWitt, IA 52742.

Now That You've Seen
Hot Off the Grill:
The Electric Grilling Cookbook,
Why Not Order
The Healthy Exchanges Food Newsletter?

If you enjoyed the recipes in this cookbook and would like to cook up even more of these "common folk" healthy dishes, you may want to subscribe to *The Healthy Exchanges Food Newsletter*.

This monthly 12-page newsletter contains 30-plus new recipes *every month* in such columns as:

- Reader Exchange
- Reader Requests
- Recipe Makeover
- Micro Corner
- Dinner for Two

- Crock Pot Luck
- Meatless Main Dishes
- Rise & Shine
- Our Small World

- Brown Bagging It
- Snack Attack
- Side Dishes
- Main Dishes
- Desserts

In addition to all the recipes, other regular features include:

- The Editor's Motivational Corner
- Dining Out Question & Answer
- Cooking Question & Answer
- New Product Alert
- Success Profiles of Winners in the Losing Game
- Exercise Advice from a Cardiac Rehab Specialist
- Nutrition Advice from a Registered Dietitian
- Positive Thought for the Month

Just as in this cookbook, all *Healthy Exchanges Food Newsletter* recipes are calculated in three distinct ways: 1) Weight Loss Choices, 2) Calories with Fat and Fiber Grams, and 3) Diabetic Exchanges.

The cost for a one-year (12-issue) subscription is $25.00. To order, simply complete the form and mail to us *or* call our toll-free number. We accept all major credit cards.

_____ Yes, I want to subscribe to *The Healthy Exchanges Food Newsletter.* $25.00 Yearly Subscription Cost with Storage Binder $_____

_____ $22.50 Yearly Subscription Cost without Binder . . . . $_____

_____ Foreign orders please add $6.00 for money exchange and extra postage . . . . $_____

_____ I'm not sure, so please send me a sample copy at $3.50 . . . . $_____

Please make check payable to HEALTHY EXCHANGES or pay by VISA, MasterCard, Discover, or American Express

CARD NUMBER: _____ EXPIRATION DATE: _____

SIGNATURE: _____
Signature required for all credit card orders.

Or order toll-tree, using your credit card, at 1-800-766-8961

NAME: _____

ADDRESS: _____

CITY: _____ STATE: _____ ZIP: _____

TELEPHONE:( ) _____

If additional orders for the newsletter are to be sent to an address other than the one listed above, please use a separate sheet and attach to this form.

MAIL TO: **HEALTHY EXCHANGES**
P.O. BOX 80
DeWitt, IA 52742-0124

1-800-766-8961 for Customer Orders
1-563-659-8234 for Customer Service

Thank you for your order and for choosing to become a part of the Healthy Exchanges Family!

About the Author

JoAnna M. Lund, a graduate of the University of Western Illinois, worked as a commercial insurance underwriter for eighteen years before starting her own business, Healthy Exchanges, Inc., which publishes cookbooks, a monthly newsletter, motivational booklets, and inspirational audiotapes. Healthy Exchanges Cookbooks have more than 1 million copies in print. A popular speaker with hospitals, support groups for heart patients and diabetics, and service and volunteer organizations, she has appeared on QVC and on hundreds of regional television and radio shows, and has been featured in newspapers and magazines across the country.

The recipient of numerous business awards, JoAnna was an Iowa delegate to the national White House Conference on Small Business. She is a member of the International Association of Culinary Professionals, the Society for Nutritional Education, and other professional publishing and marketing associations. She lives with her husband, Clifford, in DeWitt, Iowa.